Global Lynching and Collective Violence
VOLUME 1

Global Lynching and Collective Violence

Asia, Africa, and the Middle East
VOLUME 1

EDITED BY MICHAEL J. PFEIFER

UNIVERSITY OF ILLINOIS PRESS
Urbana, Chicago, and Springfield

© 2017 by the Board of Trustees
of the University of Illinois
All rights reserved
Manufactured in the United States of America
1 2 3 4 5 C P 5 4 3 2 1
♾ This book is printed on acid-free paper.

Library of Congress Cataloging-in-Publication Data
Names: Pfeifer, Michael J. (Michael James), 1968– editor.
Title: Global lynching and collective violence : volume 1: Asia, Africa,
    and the Middle East / edited by Michael J. Pfeifer.
Description: Urbana, Chicago, and Springfield : University of Illinois
    Press, 2017. | Includes bibliographical references and index.
Identifiers: LCCN 2016031719 (print) | LCCN 2017000754 (ebook) |
    ISBN 9780252040801 (hardback) | ISBN 9780252082313 (paper) |
    ISBN 9780252099304 (ebook)
Subjects: LCSH: Lynching. | Race discrimination. | BISAC: SOCIAL
    SCIENCE / Violence in Society. | SOCIAL SCIENCE / Discrimination
    & Race Relations. | HISTORY / World.
Classification: LCC HV6455 .G56 2017 (print) | LCC HV6455 (ebook) |
    DDC 364.1/34—dc23
LC record available at https://lccn.loc.gov/2016031719

Contents

Acknowledgments   vii

Introduction   1
   Michael J. Pfeifer

1 Lynching, Public Violence, and the Internet in Indonesia   10
   Laurens Bakker

2 A Different Kind of War: Summary Execution and the Politics of Men of Force in Late-Qing China, 1864–1911   34
   Weiting Guo

3 Banzai! And the Others Die—Collective Violence in the Rape of Nanking   78
   Frank Jacob

4 Making Sense of Lynching in Medieval Nepal   103
   Yogesh Raj

5 Public Anger, Violence, and the Legacy of Decolonization in India   126
   Nandana Dutta

6 New Situations Demand Old Magic: Necklacing in South Africa, Past and Present   156
   Nicholas Rush Smith

7 Sitting on the Volcano: Mob Violence and Lynching
   in the Zionist-Palestinian Conflict   185
   Shaiel Ben-Ephraim and Or Honig

Contributors   223

Index   227

Acknowledgments

Numerous people helped to make this book possible. Laurie Matheson once again was a model editor, offering exemplary encouragement and support to the project; Amanda Wicks, Brigette M. Brown, Julie R. Laut, and Jennifer Clark also provided splendid editorial assistance. It was a pleasure to work again with Nancy Albright, who is a superb copy editor. Others supported the research, writing, and editing in a variety of ways, including Hyunhee Park, Fumihiko Kobayashi, Sara McDougall, Jürgen Martschukat, David Enos, Ginger and Matti Vehaskari, George Dansker, Jack Belsom, Daniel Golebiewski, and several anonymous readers.

Global Lynching and Collective Violence

VOLUME 1

Introduction

MICHAEL J. PFEIFER

The word *lynching* is most likely American in origin, but the practice of lynching, defined by scholars as extralegal group assault and/or murder motivated by social control concerns,[1] can be found in many global cultures and eras. This collection of essays looks at lynching and related varieties of collective violence, such as vigilantism and rioting, across world cultures. Analyzing lynching and collective violence in Asia, Africa, and the Middle East, the chapters highlight both the presence of mob violence in a number of cultures and eras and the particularity of its occurrence in certain cultural and historical contexts.

Scholars have argued that lynching—summary group attack and/or homicide seeking to punish behavior defined as deviant—against individuals often deemed socially distant, typically occurs in conditions of social flux, for example in transitions from homogeneous tribal societies to plural, heterogeneous social orders; in locales where patterns of racial or ethnic dominance have been challenged or collapsed; in settings shifting rapidly from rural to urban social arrangements; in polities where authority has effectively lost legitimacy or where multiple, contradictory legal regimes contend for popular support; amid perceptions of a crisis of legal order brought on by rampant criminality; and in contested or fragile states as opposed to settings where the state is able to, in Weberian terms, successfully claim a monopoly of violence. But while lynching violence may occur in many global cultures and eras, it is hardly a universal phenomenon and it does not occur in other temporal and social landscapes. To state perhaps the obvious, lynching does not occur where the conditions stated above are not present, that is, where social, legal, and political arrangements are by comparison fairly stable and where, at least in recent times, the state enjoys a monopoly over the use of force and the respect of the populace at large.[2] By contrast, the essays in this volume examine the conditions in which extralegal collective violence has in fact occurred in an array of settings in Asia, Africa, and the Middle East. Each of the essays offers ideas for how such acts of summary group violence may be interpreted in their particular cultural contexts; several of the essays also address how such practices of summary group punishment can be viewed in a comparative, cross-cultural fashion.

I have argued at length elsewhere that the origins of American lynching can best be understood as a national, indeed a transnational, process of cultural and legal formation. Diverging significantly from England and western Europe, the U.S. transition to a capitalist economy was not accompanied by the emergence of a strong, centralized national state that claimed and enforced an exclusive monopoly over violence and the administration of criminal justice to secure the rule of law. Rather, American criminal justice developed along a distinctive path that emphasized local authority and opinion, self-help and ad hoc law enforcement practices, and the toleration of extralegal violence. Lynching was an important aspect of this distinctive American trajectory from the late eighteenth through the early twentieth centuries, evolving from traditions of popular violence with roots in the early modern British Isles but registering many Americans' rejection of due process and the exclusive claims of state authority in criminal law. The formation of American criminal justice was a highly contested process, as lawyers, judges, and middle-class reformers fought for due process and the rule of law against rural elites and working-class people who sought to retain "rough justice," that is, criminal justice grounded in local prerogatives of race, ethnicity, class, honor, gender, and crime control. Because of factors of demography, economics, and historical development that included slavery, westward migration, urbanization, and industrialization, the due process forces were at their strongest in the Northeast but weakest in the South, with the West and Midwest lying in between. American mobs acting out the punitive rough justice vision would lynch thousands of persons over the long nineteenth century, including several thousand African Americans, as well as hundreds of Mexicans, Native Americans, and whites, and dozens of Chinese and Sicilians.[3]

The conflict between rough justice and due process sentiments persisted for decades after Reconstruction in the American regions beyond the Alleghenies. Vividly recalling the emancipation of the slaves and Reconstruction in the 1860s and '70s as an era in which they had lost control of the social order, criminal courts, and political offices, many white southerners turned again to collective murder outside the law amid racial and political conflict shaped by the depressed cotton economy of the 1890s. In a contagion of collective murder that was less overtly political and less systematically organized but even more racial than the collective violence of Reconstruction, lynching became a prime means of punishing black resistance and criminality for white southerners skeptical of the efficacy of law and legal processes in the perpetuation of white supremacy in the New South. Southern urbanization and industrialization at the turn of the twentieth century catalyzed anxieties over racial mixing and, in some cases, evoked large-scale spectacle lynchings, but eventually a southern white middle class coalesced against mob violence. Embarrassed by the increasing spotlight African American activists and a nationalizing culture shone upon lynching and fearing the loss of investment that might promote economic growth and prosperity in the region, middle-class white southerners in the early twentieth century pressed instead for "legal lynchings," expedited trials and executions that merged legal forms with the popular clamor for rough justice. As the frequency of lynchings in the American South plummeted in the middle decades of the twentieth century, the practice went underground as lynchers no longer acted in large public mobs but instead in small, secretive groups that murdered in an expression of racial intimidation that, by the late twentieth century, was more often called a "hate crime" than a "lynching."[4]

The American Midwest and the American West were not as directly burdened by the legacy of antebellum racial slavery, and the trajectory of rough justice and lynching took different forms in those regions. North and west of Dixie, lynching also persisted into the middle decades of the twentieth century, surfacing after allegations of particularly heinous crimes and under the influence of events such as African American in-migration and the heightened racism of the Jim Crow era, the Mexican Revolution (precipitating the lynching of persons of Mexican descent), World War I (the migrations and racial leveling of the war inspired whites to lynch African Americans in northern locales, while nativist and antiradical sentiment informed acts of collective murder in the West and the Midwest), and the social tensions of the Great Depression. In the Midwest and West, as in the South, legislators reshaped the death penalty in the early twentieth century to make capital punishment more efficient and even more racial, achieving a compromise between the observation of legal forms long emphasized by due process advocates and the lethal, ritualized retribution long sought by rough justice supporters.[5]

Sometimes, group assault and killing across global cultures has, like American lynching in the late nineteenth and early twentieth centuries, reflected ambivalence about alterations in law and social values and rejection of seemingly ineffectual legal regimes that ostensibly do not offer sufficient protections for the property or security of communities. Collective assault and killing across global cultures in recent centuries has often flowed from local dynamics contesting the anxieties and ambiguities of legal change and authority in the context of decentralized, weak, fragmented, or transitional states. The emergence of informal group assault and killing in situations of legal ambiguity, contestation of state legitimacy, or even communal support and legitimation of imperiled authority, can be seen in the cases of Indonesia, China, Nepal, India, South Africa, and Palestine/Israel analyzed in this volume. Sometimes collective violence bears a nebulous relation to state authority, as seen in the brutal attacks Japanese soldiers—agents of the Japanese state—made on Chinese civilians during the Second Sino-Japanese War, the subject of Frank Jacob's chapter. The particular pattern of group violence, however, invariably reflects the local culture from which it stems, eliding easy generalizations or casual efforts at taxonomizing lynching and collective violence across broad spans of time and culture.

Keeping this in mind, the book begins with a substantial consideration of lynching and collective violence across a variety of Asian societies. In his chapter, Laurens Bakker argues that brutal, extralegal violence against individuals or small groups considered as a threat to local society has a long and varied history in Indonesia. Its usage includes extrajudicial killings and mutilations of thieves and other wrongdoers by local communities as well as a more sophisticated application of such violence by local power holders aimed at inspiring fear and obeisance in the population. Bakker argues that Indonesia's recent transition from a nation ruled by a dictatorial central regime, which made ample use of violence to maintain its grip, to a democracy, in which the role of government power is considerably more regulated, has seen the "regime of fear" strategy also successfully make this transition. Broadly recognized as a proof of power and of the social cohesion of those committing the violent acts, its application signifies communities' capacity and willingness to defend themselves and their interests, even if this means going against national law. Such acts are met with assent and respect by at least part of the population. By whom, and why, depends on individual cases but, as the chapter shows, can include the nation's president as well. By referring to two recent high-profile cases—the killing of Ahmadis by local Muslims and the revenge killings of local gangsters by the military—and their aftermaths, Bakker argues that such violence in Indonesia continues to bear popular connotations of justice, sincerity, and even patriotism, while the official legal apparatus is perceived to be corrupt and deficient. Such sentiments sustain the potential for brutal violence in society and, as Bakker discusses in the final part of his chapter, the internet is a popular medium for local militias and other potentially violent groups to spread the message of their own capabilities as well as of the threat posed by others.

In his chapter, Weiting Guo examines the history of extralegal executions in modern China. From the mid-nineteenth century to the mid-twentieth century, China witnessed the largest number of summary executions annually in its history. The extensive use of this extraordinary procedure in conjunction with the regular public executions by political regimes, local officials, and militia had considerable influence on modern Chinese legal culture. Drawing on a wide range of archival sources, Guo challenges the view that the prevalence of summary execution constituted merely instances of "lawlessness" and "abuses" of punishment. Guo argues by contrast that the approach of judicial economy, the competition between central and local governments, the continued trend of local militarization, and the ideology of popular justice all contributed to the "sanctioned" practice of summary execution. Moreover, Guo asserts that after the late 1830s, the practice of summary execution transformed from merely "expediency" in judicial procedure to extensive "exclusion" of local roughs or subversives that were perceived as evil or worthless. In 1853, when China was enmeshed in the Taiping Civil War, the Emperor Xianfeng further issued an edict to empower not only local officials but also local militia and elite groups to execute those they defined as "bandits" or "robbers" without further examination or report. The persecution of "bandits" and "robbers" and the mobilization of capital punishment continued to flourish even after the late Qing and Republican states centralized their power and introduced a Western legal system. Such practice blurred the boundary between legitimate violence and illicit violence. Regimes and various local actors manipulated capital punishment, which was supposedly the exclusive prerogative of the state. Furthermore, the practice nourished the demand for quick justice among the populace and arguably even laid the foundation for the culture of capital punishment during the 1960s and the Cultural Revolution, in which millions of people were summarily killed by Communist cadres and by ordinary people. Guo argues that the development of summary execution in China provides an intriguing comparison between Chinese history and Western experiences. On the one hand, China's trajectory of criminal justice diverged from its Western counterpart in the process of state-building and modernization. On the other, China's experience of summary execution in some respects resembles the history of popular support for rough justice and lynching in nations such as the United States.

In his chapter, Frank Jacob carefully examines another significant manifestation of collective violence in Asian history: the mass atrocities committed by Japanese soldiers against Chinese in the Rape of Nanking in 1937 and 1938. First analyzing at length the contentious historiography and historical evidence surrounding this pivotal episode of collective violence performed by agents of the Japanese state, Jacob then closely examines the violence perpetrated at Nanking from a theoretical perspective, arguing that it displayed both dynamics of state-sponsored macro-violence such as warfare and genocide as well as some qualities of extralegal micro-violence, such as lynching.

Focusing on medieval Nepal, Yogesh Raj argues that existing sociohistorical accounts of lynching and other extreme forms of collective cruelty are inadequate for developing "a credible historical account" due to what he considers their "narratological bias." Raj asserts that the problematic nature of the Event Catalogues, the main methodological innovation in these accounts composed by scholars of European rioting and American lynching, "call for a radically different approach to historiography." Using Newari medieval records of lynching, Raj argues for "employing analogy, and not argumentation, to develop a deeper historical understanding of lynching in Nepal and across societies."

In her chapter, Nandana Dutta examines the turn to collective violence, especially lynching, in postcolonial India, tracing it to "the forms of agency that emerged in the peculiar understanding of issues of modernity, the rule of law, and the indigenous Gandhian form of self rule known famously as swaraj during and after the Independence movement." Dutta reflects on the connotations of the word *lynching* as it has been used in recent years in India to refer both to the taking of life by a mob or group, and to also refer to occasions of mob fury/action where death may not actually occur but the dynamics of the individual/mob victim-perpetrator relationship are similar. Noting the influence of American culture in the spread of the term *lynching* in India, Dutta argues that Indian collective violence "has emerged alongside or in the wake of movements for autonomy, identity, and territory that have become independent India's most significant problem because these provide both occasion and site for the exercise of agency in the form of extralegal violence."

Turning to Africa, Nicholas Rush Smith's chapter explores collective violence in postapartheid South Africa, where vigilante violence involving an attempt to necklace alleged criminals has been common. That the *necklace*—placing a gasoline-filled tire around the neck of a victim and setting it alight—is frequently deployed is surprising, Smith asserts, because the struggle against apartheid was, in important ways, a struggle for a procedural rights-based legal system, something necklacing undermines. Moreover, necklacing was originally developed as a tool to sanction political threats under apartheid, whereas today it is primarily used as a technique to punish criminals. Why, Smith asks, is necklacing still practiced twenty years after the dawn of democracy given that it was first implemented as part of the struggle against apartheid? Smith's chapter argues that citizens deploying the necklace challenge the postapartheid state's-rights–based legal system, which South Africans often argue enables insecurity and immorality to proliferate; rhetorically and ideologically, this in some ways parallels the criticisms that American lynchers often made of procedural, due process rights. Through its spectacular violence, the necklace dramatizes these critiques of the democratic legal order much like it dramatized critiques of the apartheid state. To make this argument, Smith closely examines two cases: the apartheid-era killing of Maki Skhosana and a postapartheid lynching in Khutsong in which six people were killed, three of whom were necklaced.

Finally, turning to the Middle East, Shaiel Ben-Ephraim's and Or Honig's chapter focuses on the lynching and mob violence between Jews and Arabs in the area known as mandatory Palestine, and later as the State of Israel and the occupied territories. Ben-Ephraim and Honig seek to answer two questions: when and why has lynching and mob violence occurred, and how has it affected the development of the Zionist-Palestinian conflict? The chapter focuses on two periods of intercommunal conflict in which lynching and mob violence took place: the British Mandate period (1920–1948), and the period following the eruption of the first Palestinian Uprising "Intifada" (1987) until today. Ben-Ephraim and Honig find that the main variable determining the use of lynching attacks was the level of institutionalization of national political movements. When there are organized institutions and society is more organized, organized forms of violence such as uprisings or terrorism tend to be more prevalent since society or elements of it can be mobilized to act in a more systematic fashion. Lynching and mob violence reflect a lack of political institutionalization because the leadership possesses the ability to incite, yet lacks the tools to restrain or guide, the violence it inspires. By contrast, when the national movements are well institutionalized, Ben-Ephraim and Honig argue, more spontaneous acts of violence tend instead to take the form of sporadic acts of vengeance.

In sum, the volume's essays demonstrate that lynching cannot be dismissed as a phenomenon peripheral to global history. To the contrary, even as it displays much local variation, summary group violence matters to scholars of various regions and nations as a key index of contested state formation, as a brutal, culturally powerful collective expression of social values, such as communal identity, ethnicity, race, gender, sexuality, class, political and legal legitimacy, and understandings of criminal justice in opposition to or in tension with evolving structures of state authority. We cannot understand the history of state formation, social values, criminal justice, and developing notions of "rights" in the United States and other societies (mob violence invariably abridges the procedural, due process rights of its victims) without understanding how lynching—and the varied responses of those communities that have been targeted by lynchers—has punctuated the uneven pathway of the development of the state, notions of criminal justice, and concepts of civil rights in particular nations.

Notes

1. For the history of the term *lynching* and the rhetoric surrounding it in the United States, see Christopher Waldrep, *The Many Faces of Judge Lynch: Extralegal Violence and Punishment in America* (New York: Palgrave Macmillan, 2002); Christopher Waldrep, ed., *Lynching in America: A History in Documents* (New York: New York University Press, 2006). For the spread of the word *lynching* around the world, see William D. Carrigan and Christopher Waldrep, eds., *Swift to Wrath: Lynching in Global Historical Perspective* (Charlottesville: University of Virginia Press, 2013), 1–9.

2. For efforts at understanding lynching and other forms of collective violence in structural and theoretical terms across world cultures and eras, see Roberta Senechal de la Roche, "Collective Violence as Social Control," *Sociological Forum*, Vol. 11, No. 1 (March 1996), 97–128; Senechal de la Roche, "Why Is Collective Violence Collective?" *Sociological Theory*, Vol. 19, No. 2 (July 2001), 126–144; Senechal de la Roche, "Toward a Scientific Theory of Terrorism," *Sociological Theory*, Vol. 22, No. 1 (March 2004), 1–4; Donald Black, "Violent Structures," in Margaret A. Zahn, Henry H. Brownstein, and Shelly L. Jackson, eds., *Violence: From Theory to Research* (Newark: Lexis-Nexis/Anderson Publishing, 2004), 145–158; Mark Cooney, *Is Killing Wrong? A Study of Pure Sociology* (Charlottesville: University of Virginia Press, 2009); Bradley Campbell, "Genocide as Social Control," *Sociological Theory*, Vol. 27, No. 2 (June 2009), 150–172; Charles Tilly, *The Politics of Collective Violence* (Cambridge, U.K.: Cambridge University Press, 2003); David Pratten and Atreye Sen, eds., "Global Vigilantes: Perspectives on Justice and Violence," and Ray Abrahams, "Some Thoughts on the Comparative Study of Vigilantism," in Pratten and Sen., eds., *Global Vigilantes* (New York: Columbia University Press, 2008), 1–19, 419–442. Senechal de la Roche's work is especially useful for distinguishing among categories of collective violence such as lynching, rioting, vigilantism, and terrorism. For a cogent discussion of the issues involved in studying lynching and collective extralegal punishment from a global perspective, including a useful problematization of the role of state authority and Max Weber's conception of the state monopoly upon violence, see Manfred Berg and Simon Wendt, "Introduction: Lynching from an International Perspective," in Berg and Wendt, eds., *Globalizing Lynching History: Vigilantism and Extralegal Punishment from an International Perspective* (New York: Palgrave MacMillan, 2011), 1–18, esp. 6–9, 13–15; Max Weber, "Politics as a Vocation" (1919), reprinted in H. H. Gerth and C. Wright Mills, eds., *Max Weber: Essays in Sociology* (London: Routledge, 1970), 77–128. For an

interesting effort at a comparative analysis of lynching across global cultures, albeit one that unnecessarily and erroneously downplays the significance of race in lynching in the American South, see Robert W. Thurston, *Lynching: American Mob Murder in Global Perspective* (Farnham, U.K.: Ashgate, 2011), and Thurston, "Lynching and Legitimacy: Toward a Global Description of Mob Murder," in Berg and Wendt, eds., *Globalizing Lynching History*, 69–86. For collective violence prior to modern eras, see Scott Morschauser, "'Vengeance Is Mine': Lynching in the Ancient Near East," and Brian P. Levack, "Witch Lynching Past and Present," in Carrigan and Waldrep, eds., *Swift to Wrath*, 15–49, 49–67; Sara Forsdyke, "Street Theater and Popular Justice in Ancient Greece: Shaming, Stoning, and Starving Offenders inside and outside the Courts," *Past and Present*, No. 201 (November 2008), 3–50; David Nirenberg, *Communities of Violence: Persecution of Minorities during the Middle Ages* (Princeton, N.J.: Princeton University Press, 1998). For extralegal punishments, including collective murder, in early modern France and among the Russian peasantry in the nineteenth century, see William Beik, "The Violence of the French Crowd from Charivari to Revolution," *Past & Present*, No. 197 (November 2007), 75–110; Stephen P. Frank, "Popular Justice, Community and Culture among the Russian Peasantry, 1870–1900," *Russian Review*, Vol. 46, No. 3 (July 1987), 239–265. For *linchamientos* (lynchings) in contemporary Latin America, see Angelina Snodgrass Godoy, "When 'Justice' Is Criminal: Lynchings in Contemporary Latin America," *Theory and Society*, Vol. 33, No. 6 (December 2004), 621–651; Daniel M. Goldstein, *The Spectacular City: Violence and Performance in Urban Bolivia* (Durham: Duke University Press, 2004); Christopher Krupa, "Histories in Red: Ways of Seeing Lynching in Ecuador," *American Ethnologist*, Vol. 36, No. 1 (February 2009), 20–39; Jim Handy, "Chicken Thieves, Witches, and Judges: Vigilante Justice and Customary Law in Guatemala," *Journal of Latin American Studies*, Vol. 36, No. 3 (August 2004), 533–561. For non-state violence in recent decades across the varied regions of sub-Saharan Africa, see Bruce Baker, *Taking the Law into Their Own Hands: Lawless Law Enforcers in Africa* (Aldershot, U.K.: Ashgate Publishing, 2002); Tilo Grätz, "Vigilantism in Africa: Benin and Beyond," in Berg and Wendt., eds., *Globalizing Lynching History*, 207–223.

3. For extended treatment of these matters, see Michael J. Pfeifer, *The Roots of Rough Justice: Origins of American Lynching* (Urbana: University of Illinois Press, 2011), and Pfeifer, "Extralegal Violence and Law in the Early Modern British Isles and the Origins of American Lynching," in Berg and Wendt, eds., *Globalizing Lynching History*, 19–34.

4. Michael J. Pfeifer, *Rough Justice: Lynching and American Society, 1874–1947* (Urbana: University of Illinois Press, 2004), 15, 22–24, 68–86, 139–147. For discussions of the evolution of the legal and rhetorical context for the racially motivated extralegal violence that came to be known as "hate crime" in the 1980s, see Waldrep, *Many Faces of Judge Lynch*, 185–191; Christopher Waldrep, *African Americans Confront Lynching: Strategies of Resistance from the Civil War to the Civil Rights Era* (Lanham, Md.: Rowman and Littlefield Publishers, 2008), 113–127.

5. For treatment of these developments, see Pfeifer, *Rough Justice*, 122–147.

1 Lynching, Public Violence, and the Internet in Indonesia

LAURENS BAKKER

In Indonesia, public violence is a means to intervene in society that is applied by state as well as non-state actors. It functions to further the interests of individuals, organizations, and groups, as a tool to establish or emphasize authority, and to substantiate claims to power. It is also a way to provide security and reestablish peace, and a source of fear that inspires submission or curbs resistance. The practice of *lynching*, by which I mean the public murdering or injuring of individuals without recourse to due process of law, is a regular occurrence in Indonesia. Varney (2008: 344) points out how the frequency of lynchings between 1994 and 2004 in four Indonesian provinces studied by Welsh (2008) make the frequency of lynchings in the American South between 1882 and 1930 pale by comparison.[1] While these places and eras differ considerably, they both concerned regime changes that went beyond mere elite rotations as they also included new social norms, economic tensions, and struggles over authority. While in a Weberian idea of state-based order such capital punishment would be the monopoly of the state and be governed by the rule of law, such tensions see dominant groups use lynchings to suppress challengers and assert their power in social and economic affairs. In Indonesia, both state and non-state actors argue the legitimacy of their acts of public violence, if not through the law, then by custom, religion, or societal support. Lynching serves to punish, deter, and confirm authority. Yet while punishment can be meted out by an anonymous, faceless mob, lynching as proof of power requires for the lyncher and the lynching to be made known as widely as possible.

The role of violence in Indonesia is the subject of a considerable number of academic publications, many of which have addressed such diverse issues as historical continuation (e.g., Colombijn and Lindblad, 2002; Davidson, 2009); the role of government (see Hüsken and de Jonge, 2002; Van Klinken, 2007; Aragon, 2013); the influence of religion and ethnicity (Bertrand, 2004; Sidel, 2006; Wilson, 2008); and social and economic inequality (Barron et al., 2004; Tadjoeddin, 2014). While a comprehensive discussion of this literature is beyond my purposes in this chapter, we should note a number of its central elements in order to contextualize the events discussed below.

First among these is the realization that the usage of violence by the rulers in power to sustain a "regime of fear" has a long history in Indonesia (Schulte Nordholt, 2002) and remains an ongoing issue. Whereas state violence has decreased in the past decade, this practice is continued by non-state actors acting for patrons or furthering their own agenda (see Wilson, 2006; Bakker, 2015). Second is the decrease of violence by the government. The resignation in 1998 of President Suharto marked the end of over three decades of governance by his New Order regime, which made liberal use of state violence (police and the army) as well as of non-state violence (thugs and gangsters), depending on legitimacy and context of the action, to suppress discontent and opposition. While today's government is far more law-abiding in its usage of violence, it also fails to control non-state organizations now applying the "regime of fear" strategy. The third issue pertains to the identity of those killed by the mob: they need to be placed outside of the local community and pose a threat to its security or well-being (see Bråten, 2002; Colombijn, 2002). As anonymous nonlocals, their status and human dignity are uncertain and fragile, making them much more susceptible to the exceptionally brutal violence that is applied to restore social order. A horrendous and humiliating public death is a punishment, but it also signifies the superiority of the community over the dangerous outsider who was overcome. Finally, the causes of such violence differ widely between cases. They might pertain to issues of security or be religious, ethnic, or social in nature, or to a lack of economic means and development perspectives (cf. Peluso, 2007; Tadjoeddin and Murshed, 2007).

In this chapter, I use these elements to explore the goals that the performance of public violence, and especially murders, serve in establishing and maintaining authority in the gray area between state and society. I begin by discussing the roles of state and non-state violence in Indonesia in order to identify the parameters of "normal" practice and go on to discuss the societal effects of three murders—one a low-profile street lynching and the other two high-profile killings that made the national and international media. I go on to consider the effect of popular digital media to generate attention for violence before offering some concluding thoughts on the function of public murder in Indonesian society today.

The State and Violence

Indonesia's founding fathers declared independence from the Netherlands in 1945, after three years of Japanese occupation and with four years of fighting returning colonial forces ahead. National history emphasizes the participation in these battles of citizens who, often armed with bamboo spears only, organized to fight the colonial troops. Independence was attained through civilian mass violence, and such civilian violence remained of crucial assistance to the national army in dealing with rebels and separatists who threatened the unity of the nation. For civilians to take up arms or use violence when this is seen as "proper" or "just" is an inherent part of Indonesian national history and identity. While the army and government dispose of such authority as well, they have not replaced it—not in the least because both have been known to fail to defend citizens' interests or even to act against them.

Indonesia has known protracted civil wars, regional wars, uprisings, and separatist movements. The *PRRI/Permesta* rebellion was fought in Sulawesi and Sumatra between 1956 and 1961, while the *Darul Islam* (Islamic State) movement was defeated by central government in 1962 after sustained fighting in Java, Sulawesi, Kalimantan, and Aceh. Each of these movements involved leaders who had risen to the fore in the war for Indonesian independence, thus requiring the nation's population to accept that one-time co-fighters could become adversaries who rejected the hard-won nation. A major reconsideration of the nation's community took place in 1965, when allegations of a failed coup attempt by the communist party caused the killing of perhaps half a million real or alleged members and supporters (Cribb, 2000: 181). The army, administration, and civilian militias closely collaborated in identifying and killing suspected communists, thus effectively ending the influence and existence of the largest communist party in Asia outside of China. It was ensured that the "communists' betrayal" was widely known and that communities were aware of, and frequently assisted in, making local communists pay with their lives. At times, this involved the mutilation of victims before or after their execution (cf. Farid, 2005).

General Suharto, who had overseen the anticommunist purge, assumed presidential power in 1967. His New Order government brought a period of three decades of relative calm during which brutal and massive violence was occasionally applied by the regime against those going against New Order notions of what Indonesia and Indonesians should be like. A well-known example is the annexation of East Timor upon its independence from Portugal in 1975. The regime of terror maintained by the Indonesian military and civilian vigilante allies served to inspire fear and submission as much as to discourage support for the Timorese resistance (see Moore, 2001). In Java and Sumatra the killings of gangsters and criminals between 1982 and 1985, and of practitioners of black magic and traditional Islamic leaders in East Java in 1998, likewise inspired fear in the population. Dead, mutilated bodies would be found in the morning on the streets, in garbage dumps, or floating in the river, but certainly at places where they would eventually be discovered. The gangsters were killed by "mysterious shooters" (*penembak misterius*, hence the *petrus* killings); the magicians and religious leaders were rumored to be murdered by equally mysterious masked men in black who became known as *ninja*, although the killings were in fact frequently committed by local residents (Herriman, 2007). Even today, rumors of sightings of ninja or groups of mysterious men hiding near towns or villages cause fear and unrest, and locals have gone so far as to kill suspected ninjas (Herriman, 2010). During both killing campaigns it transpired that the mystery killers were affiliated with the army. This serves to illustrate the lawlessness with which the regime could choose to operate and terrorize: dead, mutilated bodies were left for the public to find and recognize as symbols of the power of a regime that could act with complete disregard of accountability and legal process.

Suharto's abdication from the presidency in 1998 took place as a result of strong calls for democracy among demonstrations and violence in Jakarta. As his successor implemented new laws decentralizing considerable regional administrative and fiscal authorities to the lower levels of government, regional conflicts broke out in—among others—West and Central Kalimantan, the Moluccas, Central Sulawesi, Aceh, and Lombok. Images of destruction and displacement, of beatings, killings, and the bodies of murdered individuals came out of these conflicts and traveled the world through the internet. Some parties benefited from media attention. Ethnic Dayak in Kalimantan, for instance, referred to their past as head hunters to decapitate the corpses of ethnic Madurese and parade the heads through the streets or display them at public locations. Photographs were published by various newspapers and helped to spread the Dayak's brutal image. Migrant Madurese left Kalimantan en masse. By contrast, the army and police—the forces of the state—were largely absent from these conflicts. Whereas New Order reactions would likely have been swift and brutal, the new government's emphasis on ending authoritarianism and promoting democracy made commanders adopt passive stances. Both the application of violence and the maintenance of "order" were largely taken up by non-state actors who established themselves as authorities, fighters, and protectors of the population, thus displaying citizens' continued capacities to establish control over society through non-state violence. In Indonesian history, both state and non-state thus have been responsible for violence that served to protect, intimidate, or both. Violence is the prerogative of those with the power and authority to use it, rather than that of designated actors.

Violence by Society

Non-state, citizen violence in settling conflicts, meting out punishments for social infringements, and dealing with burglars and thieves is historically entrenched in the local community. Distrust of the judicial system, which would not recognize the acts committed as crimes or let the perpetrators off with light sentences, as well as of the police who might, as one respondent put it, require payment to arrest the perpetrators and then allow the arrestees to pay for being let off, are weighty reasons for not expecting these authorities to deal with cases properly. The punishments meted out by society, either by spontaneous mobs having caught a thief red-handed or by a group carrying out a planned punishment of an adulterer or black magician, are, however, often cruel and—from the perspective of modern law and human rights—out of proportion. Consider the following example of the punishment of a recidivist petty thief, related to me in the city of Tangerang in 2010 by a participant in the mob:

> Yes, this happened in May, two months ago. We punished this thief, he had been stealing things for years. He lived with his uncle in the next village. His uncle is rich, he gave him work, but this guy would not work! He just sat around and refused the work people offered. He was a bit simple, but his uncle looked after him so he did not have to steal. He was caught stealing sandals at the mosque. People came, more and more, and they beat him up. They did not stop. Then he was tied behind a motorbike by one arm and one leg, and dragged up and down the street. Then he was dragged to the edge of town. People had phoned the police, but they would not come. Their station was too far away, and they said they would come if the thief was dead. People tore of his clothes and poured a jerrycan of gasoline over him, and burned him to death. Later the police came and took the body away, but the authorities were involved. The gasoline was provided by a guy from city government.

This killing appeared to be a case of a local community finally losing patience with a known ne'er-do-well, and doing away with him thoroughly and painfully. Colombijn (2002), discussing such lynchings (*keroyokan*) in Indonesia, points out that such acts are one possible outcome; he also refers to cases where thieves are handed over to the authorities but the spontaneity of the event and the well-known script cause matters to proceed almost automatically. The identification of the lynchee as a criminal, an outsider damaging the interests of the community, legitimizes dehumanization and provides participants with all the reason necessary to carry out the act. Welsh describes how the post–New Order power vacuum increased instances of local violence and suggests that, next to local communities dealing with criminals and dangerous outsiders, struggles over power and the settling of scores were likely part of this as well. She distinguishes between community justice and assault/murder as drivers of the violence and suggests that premeditation is likely in cases dealing with revenge, gang warfare, and ninja killings, as well as punishing such norm violators as witches and adulterers. To understand violence, then, cases should be considered individually and in their individual contexts.

The relation between the level of violence and its purpose thus becomes a central issue, even though I do not intend to argue that a clear and balanced line between the two has to exist. In a series of discussions on the subject with journalists in Jakarta, East Kalimantan, and North Sulawesi in the summer of 2014, my interlocutors frequently expressed their mystification about the brutal violence deployed. One person pointed out how he had assumed that the harsh dealings with criminals had to do with low levels of education, poverty, and perhaps sadism, until, a few months earlier, a burglar had been caught in his own upper-middle-class neighborhood. The neighbors had tied him up, phoned the police, and then proceeded to burn the flesh off the burglars' feet. These people were educated, well-off, and known to him as friendly and caring. He could not explain their actions except as a combination of stress, anger, and fear.

Fear is also likely to be a major driver behind the large number of organized, semimilitary vigilante groups that have come into existence along ethnic or religious lines and provide local security and order in lieu of, or in assistance to, government. My journalist informants felt that the presence of these vigilantes had not resulted in an increase of violence (with some exceptions; see next section).[2] The violent potential each of these groups embodies creates a standoff and maintains a balance between the groups' political and economic interests (see Bakker, 2015). At times, however, these groups must remind society that their potential for violence is real. To do so, they act upon infringements that society can recognize as such. In line with the "regime of fear," the identity of the actors must be known in order for the group to maintain its reputation, yet this requires justification in a way that will be recognized by society as legitimate. I now turn to analysis of two instances of such publicly enacted, and subsequently publicly mediated, violence.

The Cikeusik Ahmadiyyah Killings

The issue of religion, and specifically political and societal considerations as to the nature of Islam and its place in the nation, is well-established in the Indonesian public debate. While the Indonesian Constitution stipulates freedom of religion, blasphemy is prohibited and made punishable under the Penal Code. The Blasphemy Law, while not prohibiting other religions per se, limits recognized religions to a total of six. Some 85 percent of the population are Muslim. The vast majority are Sunni, with a small number of Shiites. While this means that Islam is the nation's largest religion, its adherents differ in cultural, social, and political dispositions of their faith while further ethnic, customary, and economic differences make this majority by no means a single united whole. Rather, and possibly unique to the Islamic world (cf. Van Bruinessen, 2012: 125), Indonesian Muslims are divided over a limited number of large religious associations, notably *Muhammadiyah* and *Nahdlatul Ulama*, whose outlooks range from traditionalist to modernist. These organizations run different institutions, mosques, schools, and unions with chapters throughout the nation and have political parties associate with them. The highest representative organ of Islam in Indonesia is the government-endorsed Indonesian Council of Islamic Scholars (*Majelis Ulama Indonesia*, hereafter MUI) in which the mentioned associations are represented. The MUI acts as a vehicle to bring Muslim interests under government attention, as well as vice versa. While Islam in Indonesia is generally seen to be fairly tolerant,[3] a more radical and conservative faction that criticizes mainstream Islam as too modern and too liberal has been steadily on the rise since New Order control ended (see Feillard and Madinier, 2011; Van Bruinessen, 2013). During the first years of the twenty-first century, several well-organized Islamic terrorist attacks shocked the nation, returning in early 2015. At the same time, hard-line Muslim vigilante groups such as *Front Pembela Islam* (Islamic Defenders Front, FPI) and *Forum Umat Islam* (Islamic Community Forum, FUI) began to carry out attacks on bars, liquor shops, brothels, and other such sources of vice but also closed church buildings from further use by their congregations. While support and sympathy for terrorist attacks is very limited among the Indonesian population, these vigilante groups enjoy more respect and support. Wilson (2014: 249) has suggested that the groups constitute "pragmatic Islamic militancy," by which he refers to a militancy that appeals to the Muslim urban poor that make up most of the members not because of its "comprehensive and coherent ideological or political programme . . . [but]. . . . through the particular combination of normative Islamic practice, tradition and social conservatism, aggressive rhetoric, together with opportunities offered for the pursuit of instrumentalist livelihood strategies, strategic advantage in local contestations over resources and space and the expressing of a broad range of grievances and resentments." In other words, it is a militancy that uses a discourse of furthering and defending Islam to initiate actions that serve interests beyond religious issues alone and offers space to rebellious youngsters and those at the bottom of the economic ladder. This discourse works to focus societal discontent and anger and, as such, converges societal, religious, and popular dissent into a strong and aggressive power.

On February 6, 2011, an angry mob of hundreds, armed with sticks and machetes, attacked the home of a man named Suparman, in Cikeusik in the province of Banten, West Java.[4] Suparman was a follower of Ahmadiyyah, a Muslim sect originally from British India, with some 400,000 followers in Indonesia. A text message had been circulating for about two weeks among local residents to assemble and evict the Ahmadis from the area, as they were considered to be apostates who had left the true teachings of Islam. A known and identifiable individual urging this action, also by text message, was a local Islamic scholar who also was the chairman of the local FPI chapter.

The threat was known to local authorities, and in the morning local police picked up Suparman and most of his family as well as some visiting friends—all Ahmadis—and took them to the local station for protection. In the meantime, the house would be guarded by police personnel as well as by a group of seventeen men from the Ahmadiyyah men who had come up from nearby Jakarta and Bogor to protect the house and property from damage by the expected mass. The police force numbered some 115 individuals, among them two platoons of rapid response officers. At 10:30 A.M. a crowd of hundreds arrived and bypassed the outnumbered police with shouts of "Police get out of the way! These are unbelievers!" (Yasra et al., 2011: 16). The crowd was held back by the Ahmadiyyah defenders who threw stones and used bamboo sticks, but the more numerous attackers also threw stones and several produced machetes from under their clothes, with which they physically attacked the small group. A second wave of attackers arrived minutes later and joined in as well, bringing their number up to an estimated 1,500 (Yasra et al., 2011: 18). The defenders were overwhelmed, and most fled for their lives as their cars and the buildings were demolished. Just before eleven o'clock, the police managed to secure the battered body of one Ahmadiyyah defender, after which they left the scene. The crowd stayed on and continued to beat, cut, and jump on the naked bodies of two other Ahmadiyyah defenders who had been killed. The violence was cheered on by the crowd with shouts of *Allahu akbar* following each hit.

The case was widely reported in the national and international press and numerous visual recordings of the event, made by members of the crowd using their hand phones, were uploaded to the internet. A simple search of "ahmadiyyah" and "Cikeusik" will provide the reader with vivid footage of events, particularly of the mutilation of the two corpses and the cheering crowd. Importantly, footage was also recorded by an Ahmadiyyah cameraman who decided not to interfere but to document what was happening. These recordings clearly identify the individual attackers hitting and abusing the Ahmadiyyah members and show that the efforts made by the authorities to prevent or stop the violence were very limited indeed.

Violence against Ahmadiyyah followers was not new, and the Cikeusik attack was not the last. Ahmad (2007) mentions a total of thirty-five attacks between 1993 and 2005, while Yasra et al. (2011: 18–19) list fifteen instances of attack or administrative measures against Ahmadiyyah communities throughout Indonesia. A quick and superficial news search for 2006 to 2014 lists at least seventeen other instances of violence, while Kahmad (2012) reported fifty-six cases of anti-Ahmadiyyah violence following the 2011 issuance of a Gubernatorial Regulation banning the organization in West Java. While much of such violence took place in that province, the small island of Lombok also stands out as Ahmadis there were driven from their homes in 2005 and 2006 and have been forbidden to return unless they converted to mainstream Islam first. While some converted and others left the island, some forty families have since been living in refugee shelters with state authorities ignoring their appeals for help (Ong, 2013). Violence against Ahmadis is, as Breidlid (2013) argues, in danger of becoming legitimate.

Such legitimization is rooted in the position of Ahmadiyyah in Indonesian society.[5] The movement reached Indonesia in 1925, and by 1930 both Muhammadiyah and Nahdlatul Ulama had declared Ahmadiyyah to be deviant and outside of Islam. Mainstream Muslim critics generally agree that since Ahmadis call themselves Muslims, they are apostates and even heretics (cf. Burhani, 2014). Their criticism concerns a number of issues of Ahmadiyyah doctrine (see Platzdasch, 2011). First of these is the status of Mirza Ghulam Ahmad, the founder of Ahmadiyyah, who, the critics argue, is seen by Ahmadis as a prophet, or even as the Mahdi. This would make him a prophet after the prophet Mohammed, who—in the Koran—is named as the "Seal of the Prophets" (*Khātam an-Nabiyyīn*), the final prophet of Islam. Critics of Ahmadiyyah also maintain that the Ahmadis have their own holy book, the *Tadzkirah*, next to or instead of the Koran, and that the towns of Qadiyan (in India) and Rabwah (in Pakistan) rather than Mecca and Medina, are their holy towns.[6] Furthermore, Ahmadi's denouncement of jihad as a physical struggle and their belief that Jesus Christ survived his crucifixion and moved to Kashmir in India afterward, are considered controversial and out of line with the teachings of Islam.

Ignoring this discussion on Ahmadiyyah's Islamic identity, the Indonesian government had declared the organization to be lawful in 1953. Throughout the following decades, Indonesian Ahmadis faced little open hostility, yet pressure on the movement increased steadily worldwide. In 1980, the MUI issued a *fatwa* (legal opinion under Islamic law) declaring Ahmadiyyah to be deviant and outside of Islam. However, the government again paid no heed to the clergy's opinion, and the official status of the organization remained unchanged. In 2005, after the fall of the New Order, the MUI issued a second fatwa, in which it referred explicitly to a 1985 decision by the international Organisation of Islamic Conference (OIC), which declared those accepting Mirza Ghulam Ahmad as prophet and his visions as truth to be apostates.[7] In the fatwa, the MUI pointed out that the government was obliged to stop the spread of the Ahmadiyyah ideology, stop Ahmadiyyah activities, and close their centers because their beliefs and dogmas are not in accordance with Islam. Ahmadis calling themselves Muslims therefore were considered apostates.[8] In the elucidation to the fatwa the MUI emphasized that carrying out actions against the Ahmadiyyah was a task of the government in its position as representatives (*ulil amri*) of God and his prophet, and that the MUI would not justify actions by others. Nevertheless, the elucidation closed with an impressive listing of Islamic vigilante groups who had pledged their support for the fatwa.

Tensions continued to build. In a February 2008 meeting of FPI, FUI, Hizbut Tahrir, and other hard-liner groups, the secretary general of FPI urged Muslims to kill Ahmadiyyah members, pointing out that the Ahmadis destroyed Islam and that killing them therefore was self-defense and halal. He claimed that while the killings would be said to go against human rights, the Human Rights Declaration was "cat shit" (*tai kucing*) to him. He himself and the other leaders would take full responsibility for any Ahmadiyyah killings, urging their followers to state that they acted under orders in case they were stopped by the authorities (Platzdasch, 2011: 9–10; Burhani, 2014: 134). While his speech got considerable attention in the media, the government refrained from sanctions. The seriousness of the FPI secretary's words became clear on the first of June 2008, when a consortium of activists, NGOs, moderate Muslims, and members of other religions celebrated Pancasila Day—a yearly commemoration of the national state ideology—by holding a march to support religious freedom.[9] The participants assembled at Indonesia's national monument in Jakarta, where they were attacked by some 400 Islamic vigilantes of FPI, FUI, and similar groups. The vigilantes accused the consortium of supporting Ahmadiyyah and injured some thirty of its leaders so severely that they needed to be hospitalized. FPI's leader and several other members received prison sentences of up to eighteen months for instigating or taking part in the attack, but the organizations were not disbanded or limited in any other way.

A first national government reaction on the Ahmadiyyah issue came on June 9, 2008, a week after the Pancasila Day violence. The Minister of Religious Affairs, the Attorney General, and the Minister of Home Affairs put out a joint decision that emphasized that religion is an inalienable human right but also that it is forbidden for anyone to engage in interpretations or teachings of a religion practiced in Indonesia that deviates from the main principles of that religion.[10] The authorities found that the Ahmadiyyah considered themselves to be Muslims, yet recognized another prophet after Mohammed and that they therefore deviated from the main interpretation of Islam, which was causing social unrest. The Ahmadiyyah were ordered to stop their deviations and refrain from proselytization. If they failed to do so, they would be liable to sanctions under existing law. Furthermore, the authorities reminded society at large to keep the peace and refrain from taking the law into their own hands. The decision was a disappointment to Islamic hard-liners who considered nothing but a ban on Ahmadiyyah and compulsory dissolution of its organization as suitable. The decision essentially prohibited the Ahmadiyyah from publicizing their faith, but did nothing to stop them from continuing worshipping and practicing among themselves.

Ironically, Indonesia's current freedom of speech and democratization stimulated manifestations of anti-Ahmadiyyah sentiment and violence. Crouch (2009) lists some nineteen decisions and prohibitions on provincial, regional, and municipal levels in West Java, Lombok, West Kalimantan, and parts of Sumatra that all limit or forbid Ahmadiyyah activities. Although these essentially go against the freedom of religion set out in the Constitution, their enforcement is not countered by the national government. Administrative decentralization made it possible for hard-line preachers to bypass the control of central government by focusing on local settings rather than the nation as a whole, and for regional governments to suppress and drive out Ahmadiyyahs and other religious minorities (Nastiti, 2014: 13–14). It is a worrisome finding (Nastiti, 2014: 13) that attacks of Ahmadiyyah property—or, for that matter, on Ahmadi individuals—rarely lead to the arrest of the attackers.

The online availability of ample video material depicting events, victims, and attackers at Cikeusik led to a trail in which twelve men were accused under various provisions of the Penal Code of inciting hatred through text messages, organizing the crowd, assault leading to serious injury and death, destruction of property, mistreatment, and participating in assault. As Crouch (2012) pointed out, based on these provisions the prosecution could have sought sentences of up to twelve years, but instead recommended sentences of seven months for ten of the defendants and five and six, respectively, for the two others, who were minors. The prosecution argued that the Ahmadis had provoked the attack by pelting the crowd with stones and exacerbated the incident by filming events and distributing the footage through the internet. By contrast, the prosecution sought a sentence of nine months for the single Ahmadi on trial, as he was said to have incited the seventeen Ahmadis to fight the crowd and resist the police, which had ordered the Ahmadis to leave. All attackers were sentenced to periods between three and six months in jail, while the Ahmadi received a sentence of six months on charges of resisting the police and, ironically, of assault. He did not appeal as that could well have resulted in a lengthier sentence (see Ulum, 2011a and 2011b).

The mutilation and humiliation of the dead Ahmadis in Cikeusik is a strong illustration of the righting of what is seen as a social vice by mob justice. While no legal basis for such action existed and the small community in Cikeusik could hardly be interpreted as a threat to the majority of mainstream Muslims there, the attack cleansed the community and showed its unity. It also showed the mobilizing capacity of FPI and its willingness to take on heresy, even if that defied government authority. At a higher level of analysis, however, the Cikeusik killings provide a strong illustration of the contestation of power between state and non-state actors. Hicks (2014) pointed out how, if the killings are seen in the context of contestation between religious authorities, the role of the state vis-à-vis the non-state hard-line groups is not defined just by its absence (in its failure to protect the Ahmadis) but also by its active involvement (in confirming the Ahmadis's deviance and so competing with the non-state hard-liners over authority). In other words, next to the outcomes in terms of state and non-state power relations in Cikeusik and Banten, the Ahmadiyyah killings and their legal and procedural consequences strongly illustrate how these public killings were made into a competition over societal power between government and hard-line Islamic challengers.

The Cebongan Prison Raid

On March 19, 2013, a fight took place in Hugo's, a well-known Yogyakartan nightclub, between a customer and a bouncer who worked at a neighboring club.[11] The bouncer came into Hugo's followed by three friends, members of an ethnic Timorese gang as well as of Kotikam, a powerful local vigilante-cum-criminal outfit. CCTV footage of the fight shows how these four crowded around the customer, who was initially still seated at his table, drove him into a corner, and hit, kicked, and stabbed him while club-goers close by looked on and others—although it is impossible to say whether they were aware of what was going on nearby—unconcernedly continued their evening's enjoyment.[12] As the customer died from the wounds he suffered in the fight, the police immediately arrested the bouncer and his friends. It then became clear that the unfortunate nightclub visitor was a former sergeant in Kopassus, the Indonesian army's special forces, whose unit was stationed in the nearby town of Kartasura. The bouncer, on the other hand, was a notorious member of Yogyakarta's crime scene and had served prison sentences for violence and rape.

For reasons of security and protection, the police moved the four arrestees from their city headquarters to Cebongan prison on March 22nd. Early the next morning, a group of men claiming to be police officers with instructions to collect the four arrestees arrived at the gate. Once the guard opened the gate, masked men stormed in with automatic guns at the ready. They quickly subdued the eight jailers, disabled the CCTV equipment, and methodically reconnoitered the complex until they came to the holding cell where the four arrestees were placed among some thirty other detainees. The armed men forced all prisoners to sit down on the left side of the cell and identify the four men that killed the Kopassus sergeant. These four were then placed at the right side of the cell and riddled with bullets. According to witnesses, the shooters then shouted "long live Kopassus!" (*hidup kopassus!*) before leaving the scene.

Although it was not clear who had carried out the killings, revenge retaliation by Kopassus seemed likely. The unit has a reputation for human rights violations during its deployment in East Timor, Aceh, and Papua, and for enjoying protection by the political elite. Moreover, a history of conflict and open violence between army personnel and the police made it unlikely that the colleagues of the sergeant would be kept from their revenge by the killers being in police custody.[13]

The killings in the Cebongan prison attracted considerable national and international attention and were discussed and depicted in bloody detail in Indonesian media. Images of the corpses punctured with bullet wounds on the floor of the cell, as well as later ones showing them dressed and displayed in their coffins awaiting burial, were televised in news broadcasts and have become permanently available on the internet. Suspicions that the killers were Kopassus became ever more vocal: first, because of their elite equipment and the efficient manner in which the raid was carried out; and second, because all of them had the muscled and fit build of trained soldiers. Yet, whereas this attention made it widely known that those who kill a Kopassus member cannot escape their own death, not even if they are in the protection of the police, it also highlighted that if Kopassus personnel had indeed carried out the killings, they apparently still considered themselves exempt from the rule of law. This was a painful conclusion after years of political, judicial, and army reform. Kopassus initially reported that all personnel stationed at Kartasura had been in their barracks at the time of the raid on the prison (Sunaryo, 2013), yet a national army headquarters investigation found otherwise. On the investigators' first day at Kartasura Kopassus barracks, eleven noncommissioned officers came forward and reported that they had carried out the raid. A twelfth NCO was indicted for failing to report the raid. The soldiers stood trial in the Yogyakarta military court, which sentenced the three prime suspects to jail sentences of between twelve and six years as well as dismissal from the army, while the nine other suspects received jail sentences of between 21 months and four months and 20 days for complicity and failure to report the raid to superior officers (Prabowo, 2013).

As the trial progressed from the first hearing to the reading of the verdict in September, support for the soldiers became more vocal. In Yogyakarta, local groups hanged banners praising the soldiers' action and Kopassus in general, and organized rallies and demonstrations in Yogyakarta and nearby towns. Supporters maintained that the killings were not premeditated but spontaneous actions, and that such killings of known criminals were a service to society. The National Human Rights Commission, which was carrying out its own research into the prison killing and was critical about the military's swift acceptance of the confessions of the soldiers and their apparent unwillingness to consider involvement of higher-ranking officers, found demonstrators in front of its office who claimed that the Commission was only trying to attract good press for itself because it paid hardly any attention to illegal killings of criminals otherwise (Prasetya, 2013).

The army also showed its support for the soldiers on trial. Kopassus Commander Major General Sutomo pointed out that if anyone was to blame, it was he. For had not the army instilled a knightly (*ksatria*) attitude in the soldiers that brought them to take the law into their own hands (*main hakim sendiri*) and carry out "dark justice" where the weak law system appeared to be failing? And, furthermore, did not the soldiers take responsibility as they freely confessed their deeds knowing fully well that they would then have to face the consequences? (Hidayat, 2013). President Susilo Bambang Yudhoyono, a former army general himself, pointed out that the soldiers' actions were not justified but was quoted in the media as stating: "The soldiers appear to act responsible, knightly, and are ready to receive whatever legal sanction might follow. To me that is a relief, it's a knightly characteristic, to take responsibility for one's actions. These are true soldiers who have to be shown to all the Indonesian people" (Rosarians and Seo, 2013).[14]

The president's statement attracted considerable criticism. Members of parliament wondered whether "knightly" is a suitable label to use if the main element of the action is the illegal killing of thugs. If such extrajudicial killings could be justified, a member found, the state surely was experiencing a legal crisis (Asril, 2013). In public, however, much more support was visible for the Kopassus soldiers than for those arguing for upholding the law. Representatives of the National Human Rights Commission who emphasized the violation of the victims' human rights found themselves chased off the court's premises by Kopassus supporters. In media opinion pieces as well as in demonstrations, the idea that the killing violated the victims' human rights was ridiculed, and overruled by the idea that the soldiers had cleansed the city of these criminal elements.

It seems, however, that, as with the Ahmadiyyah killings, public opinion was diverted from the essence of the events: the shooting of unarmed, locked-up police arrestees by national army soldiers. Not only was the action in breach of Indonesian Human Rights Law, Criminal Law, and Military Law, it was also a clear infringement by elements of the army of police authority. To overlook or ignore these matters by giving preference to the soldiers' dubious chivalry—shooting an unarmed, locked-up opponent does not appear to quite fit that ticket, even if he is a criminal—would indeed signal a crisis of the law.

As such, the pro-Kopassus protests also served strategic and political purposes. It is quite likely that the protests hampering activities of the National Human Rights Commission had more to do with their desire to research the involvement of higher Kopassus officers, than with "spontaneous" public anger. The protesters in front of the Commission's office in Jakarta, for instance, were dressed in FKPPI regalia (see Prasetya, 2013), which is a military-backed "youth" organization that violently defends the interests of its overlords against societal criticism. Many protesters in Yogyakarta had the physique and haircuts of soldiers, even if they were not in uniform, while others sported the colors and uniforms of organizations that were rivals of Kotikam, the vigilante outfit to which the four murdered criminals belonged. Supriatma (2014) analyzed the killings along local political lines, and showed that whereas the killed criminals had acted as personal bodyguards to a sultan-pretender of Yogyakarta, all groups supporting the current sultan had thrown their weight behind the Kopassus soldiers: first, Supriatma argues, because such a common case helped the leaders maintain unity among the members; and, second, because their support for Kopassus in these difficult times could provide them with a powerful ally in the future.

As with the Ahmadiyyah killings, the Cibongan prison raid provides us with insights into authority as a quality based upon—or between—society and the state, and that can be obtained through displays of public violence. Using this perspective, the raid shows two important outcomes: first, the effect of the killings in local-level *realpolitik*; and second, the sentencing of the soldiers by the legal regime of the national state. Locally, the killings were placed and explained in the context of a power struggle between supporters of different factions within the royal family. Things might have stayed there, had NGOs and the media not picked up on the involvement of the Kopassus soldiers—namely, their pride in their vengeance and their stance toward the consequences. The case seems to show that the military is no longer outside the reach of the law. The perpetrators have to submit to the judiciary and face the consequences of their actions. This is an important difference from the petrus killings (discussed earlier), in which the killers were known to belong to the military, but were not brought to justice. It remains to be seen, however, whether the soldiers will be let off with a lighter sentence in years to come, and the involvement of senior officers remains unsolved. Justice is being served, but whether this is done comprehensively is uncertain. However, the support—political and otherwise—for the soldiers and the chivalrous image that has been ascribed to them shows that these execution-style killings nevertheless retain a degree of legitimacy in society. Even if Kopassus is currently supported by the criminal rivals of the murdered, the notion of soldiers avenging their colleague and submitting to the consequences has wide-ranging sympathies among the Indonesian population. The fact that they meted out justice according to their own standards and judgment, rather than await the result of police investigations and ensuing legal proceedings, sits in a tradition of illegal army violence. Societal approval shows that the killings met notions of justice among parts of the population and that trust in due legal process remains limited. Importantly, however, it also indicates the likelihood that such a reaction is expected from Kopassus soldiers, violent actors with a reputation and status that needs to be maintained in order to remain valid.

Virtual Violence: The Internet

On June 3, 2013, a suicide bomber carried out an attack on central police headquarters in Poso. Riding a motorbike, he drove into the compound where officers stood assembled for morning inspection. The bomb proved faulty and killed only the bomber, seriously damaging his body but leaving his head and face intact. The Poso region in Central Sulawesi is considered by Indonesian authorities to be the basis of some of Indonesia's most active jihadi groups and although their membership is quite small, activities such as this bombing are cause for serious concern.[15]

Public reactions in the media showed fear and outrage, but on the internet the failure of the attack and its deviousness were also heavily ridiculed in messages and postings dealing directly with the bomber. Pictures of his bloody and only vaguely recognizable body with his mostly unscathed head at the top that had been taken and uploaded by those present at the scene were circulated widely. Although it was a (failed) suicide attack and, as such, not a killing or a lynching, usage of and reactions to these pictures strongly resemble those to photographs of American lynchings in the nineteenth and early twentieth century, showing deterrence and ridicule. They echo Colombijn's observations of Indonesian lynchings (mentioned earlier) that the identification of the lynchee as a criminal, an outsider damaging the interests of the community, legitimizes dehumanization and provides participants with all the reason necessary to carry out the act. Such pictures, then, prove to the world that local society is willing and capable of restoring order in this way.

On Facebook, a posting of a picture of the mangled corpse of the Poso suicide bomber on the page of Brigade Manguni, a Christian militia in nearby North Sulawesi, attracted dozens of likes as well as some twenty-four comments mocking the bomber and his failed attempt: "He made his own bomb, he detonated himself, he killed himself. What can I say, this is suitable for anyone this stupid. Hahahaha!!" "Hahahaha ... Did this guy not understand the meaning of the life that God has given?" "One of those again, anarchist barbarians! Good entry into Paradise and your orgy with 72 angels! Hahahah" "Horrible behaviour that ended in a mess. Congratulations yeeeehhh." "He is going to have trouble in this state when he feels carnal desires for those women once in Paradise, the women will get a lot of meat, but otherwise . . ."

The commenters see the bomber's fate and the physical state of his remains as a suitable ending to his murderous attempts, as in the displays of the remains of lynchees. For Brigade Manguni members, Christians who fear to be targeted by jihadis themselves, the bomber's fate showed divine judgment and justice, as graphically depicted in the state of his remains. Members told me how only God could have prevented the bomber from killing anyone but himself and that this powerful result of the invocation of God's anger should be shown to humanity as a reminder not to engage in such sinful deeds. To them, sending around the bloody and horrible result that the bomber brought upon himself was nothing if not just. As the pictures of his sad remains spread over the internet, they served to ridicule his action, goal, and memory, and to confirm the restoration of calm and normality in society.

Since the fall of Suharto in 1998, and the various local wars of that era, a steady stream of pictures and films of killings, beheadings, and mutilated corpses has been circulating in Indonesia through email, telephones, and internet uploads. Such recordings were regularly shown to me by members of local vigilante groups in Kalimantan, Jakarta, and Sulawesi to illustrate either how successful they had been in protecting society by killing its enemies, or to show the depravity of the opponents against whom they guarded the local population. The value of such recordings as actual proof of either one or the other position is debatable if no individuals, organizations, or circumstances can be identified. A single, specific clip showing the corpse of a decapitated male held in a standing position by the lower arm tied to a tree branch, was shown to me as an example of ethnic Dayak violence against Madurese settlers in Kalimantan, but also as the corpse of a Muslim fighter tied up by victorious Christians in Poso. In 2008, about two years after the first time I was shown this video, I happened to receive a longer version, this time with the explanation that it illustrated Muslim victory over Christians in Poso. This time, the video continued after the initial image of the corpse tied to the tree by showing other corpses and separated heads, and a conversation could be heard in what a colleague identified as Thai, thus likely placing the event as part of the unrest in southern Thailand, since none of the groups claiming the death had suggested to me that they had Thai members among their ranks. My various contacts, however, were not that easily convinced when I pointed out the opposing claims and the language issue to them. Each maintained that the other groups' claim to the clip simply was a lie, and one maintained that the longer version, which he knew as well, must have been dubbed by Thais for their own usage. The message of the clip, that one's organization was capable of carrying out the violence shown, was a powerful symbol of the strength of that organization and one that therefore was not given up easily.

The wars in Chechnya, Iraq, and—more recently—Syria have added considerably to the images and clips circulating in Indonesia, but whereas the ethnic appearance of individuals and the natural surroundings generally made it immediately clear that the events did not involve Indonesians or take place in Indonesia, I was also shown such videos as proof to claims that Middle-Eastern jihadis were coming to fight in Indonesia. In north Sulawesi, Christina Brigade Manguni members used such claims by Indonesian Muslim militias to argue their ongoing importance as guarantors of local security. They also upload videos of unidentified violence in the Middle East, but claim that these depict Kurdish *Peshmergas* on their way to fight the Islamic State. In a summer 2014 upload to the internet, a Brigade Manguni leader argued that a video of a mass execution of Iraqi soldiers by Islamic State fighters—stills of which had featured in Western media days before—was in fact of Israeli soldiers being shot by IS troops. He knew this to be so, as it was stated at the hard-line Islamic website from where he got the clip. This seriously worried him as he considered Israel to have the most modern and best-equipped army in the region, and he therefore used the clip to argue the relevance of his own militia to local government officials. This resulted in a tightening of his militia's relation to the provincial governor and the local military commander. Two weeks later, he informed me that some of his men were to receive training with newer weapons from the military and that the governor was considering awarding the militia a permanent financial contribution.

Movie clips and pictures hence have a dual role in the establishment and maintenance of authority through public violence. The images can be said to display the results of violent actors' actions: punishing wrongdoers, re-establishing order, and displaying their potential to do so through clips of supporters or of their own people and arms. Likewise, such images can illustrate the danger that threatens society and against which its violent actors stand prepared.

Conclusion

The role of brutal violence, mutilation, and the display of the result, in situ or through recorded images distributed through the media and the internet, are powerful means of influencing Indonesian society. This is not new. Throughout Indonesian history, the application of violence by state and non-state actors has worked to establish control over an area or to protect the security of the community. Violence is not the prerogative of the state and when the state was controlled by a powerful party, such as the New Order regime, these rulers did not allow their violence to be controlled by the law but instead opted to use their access to violence to apply a "regime of fear." In this chapter, I show that the decentralization and democratization instigated by the successors to this regime realized a more legitimate government as well as a stronger control on the actions of its "strong arm," yet also allowed for the renewed appropriation of violence by multiple non-state actors. Non-state violence is an element of Indonesian patriotism, and its current applicators echo this sentiment. Engaged in close dialogue with society, they maintain that their actions protect and defend the population from infringements by malignant elements operating carefully within the protection of the national law. As the state does not "suitably" punish Ahmadiyyah or the killers of a Kopassus sergeant due to the limits as well as the protection of the law, it is up to soldiers, militias, and citizens to administer "proper justice." This is a dangerous and highly undesirable side effect of the withdrawing state.

The state is found wanting. When the police still fail to offer protection or show up to arrest petty criminals, even when phoned, the continuation of violence and lynching by local citizens may not come as a surprise. The practice puts out a warning to other criminals: enter at your own peril, for we will have our vengeance. Security remains a local issue and justice not the domain of the government.

In such an environment, fear and opportunity go hand in hand. Where murder and lynching signify the power of the perpetrators and provide them with the ability to create fear through displays of violence, the authority of the government suffers and non-state violent actors establish authority through societal support for their actions. Both elements have been boosted considerably by the arrival of the internet and mobile phones. The distribution of images creating fear as well as of those depicting the meting out of justice and its horrific results has become a matter of a few clicks. The meting out of public violence, and even more the control of its message and significance, thus is not simply a way to get even or substitute for failing government authorities. If done well, it rallies support and evokes popular appreciation in a way that the rule of law and human rights drives do not yet seem to be able to answer.

Acknowledgments

This work was supported by the Netherlands Organisation for Scientific Research [grant number 463-08-003] as part of the research project "State of Anxiety: A Comparative Ethnography of Security Groups in Indonesia." The author would like to thank Knut D. Asplund of the University of Oslo and Gerry van Klinken of the KITLV (Royal Netherlands Institute of Southeast Asian and Caribbean Studies) and of the University of Amsterdam for insightful comments on an earlier version of this chapter. Any mistakes or shortcomings are the sole responsibility of the author.

Notes

1. Varney reports a yearly average of 500 victims for Indonesia and 100 for the southern United States.

2. This is, however, a point open to contestation. Notably, regional media have been requested by local authorities not to publish news about lynchings and other violence,

as this might create feelings of insecurity among the population. Because ignoring the request would sour relationships with local officials, many regional media concede.

3. See Fealy et al. (2006) and Pringle (2010) for more elaborate discussions on Indonesian Islam.

4. The version of events presented here is based on Yasra et al. (2011) and KontraS (2011).

5. See Zulkarnain (2005) and Crouch (2009) for an in-depth discussion of the history of the Ahmadiyyah movement in Indonesia.

6. Ahmadis to whom I spoke in Indonesia disagreed with these issues: they stated that *khātam* may mean *seal*, but also means *jewel* in Arabic, and hence does not have to indicate that Mohammed was the final prophet. They maintained that the Koran was their holy book and the *Tadzkira*—which they considered a non-Ahmadi term—was a collection of writings to guide one's life, not a holy book. Neither Qadiyan nor Rabwah was, according to them, a city holy in a similar sense as Mecca and Medina.

7. Decision of the Organisation of Islamic Conference Number 4 (4/2) of December 22–28, 1985.

8. Fatwa Majelis Ulama Indonesia no 11/munas VII/MUI 15/2005 on *Aliran Ahmadiyah*.

9. See Astuti (2008) and Crouch (2009: 12–15) for more in-depth discussions of the Monas Incident.

10. Joint Decision of the Minister of Religion, the Attorney General, and the Minister of Home Affairs No. 3 of 2008, No. KEP-033/A/JA/6/2008, No. 199 of 2008 on Warnings and Instructions to Adherents, Members and/or Board Members of the Ahmadiyah Indonesia and Members of Society.

11. The rendition of events presented here is based on Jamaludin et al. (2013), Sunudyantoro et al. (2013), and Supriatma (2014).

12. The CCTV recordings from Hugo's are available at, among others, http://www.youtube.com/watch?v=XXbMbK_gzCA, last visited August 15, 2014.

13. An example just preceding the raid on Cebogan prison is the burning of a police station and the injuring of seventeen officers in South Sumatra by soldiers in early March 2013 in retaliation for the shooting of soldiers by a police officer two months earlier (Hendrawan, 2013). In a February 2014 interview, Indonesian Chief of Staff of the army, General Budiman, explained this rivalry as emanating from jealousy, big egos, and too much esprit de corps, but also from competition over control of "dirty" (*haram*) sources of money (Widaya, 2014).

14. "*Para prajurit tampil bertanggung jawab, kesatria, dan siap menerima sanksi hukum apa pun. Bagi saya itu melegakan, itu sifat kesatria, bertanggung jawab atas apa yang dilakukan. Itulah prajurit sejati yang harus ditunjukkan kepada seluruh rakyat Indonesia.*"

15. See Chernov-Hwang et al. (2013) and Jones and Solahudin (2014) for in-depth discussions of the terrorist threat in Poso.

Works Cited

Ahmad, Munawar (2007). "Faith and Violence," *Inside Indonesia* 89. Retrieved July 25, 2014, from http://www.insideindonesia.org/.

Aragon, Lorraine (2013). "Development Strategies, Religious Relations and Communal Violence in Central Sulawesi, Indonesia: A Cautionary Tale." In: William Ascher and

Natalia Mirovitskaya (eds.), *Development Strategies, Identities and Conflict in Asia*, 153–182. Basingstoke: Palgrave Macmillan Ltd.

Asril, Sabrina (2013, April 8). "Pantaskah 11 Anggota Kopassus Disebut Kesatria?" *Kompas.com*. Retrieved July 25, 2014, from http://www.kompas.com/.

Astuti, Fatima (2008). "Fallout from Jakarta's Monas Incident: What Is to Be Done with Fringe Groups?" *RSIS Commentaries* 64.

Bakker, Laurens (2015). "Illegality for the General Good? Vigilantism and Social Responsibility in Contemporary Indonesia." *Critique of Anthropology* 35 (1).

Barron, Patrick, Kai Kaiser, and Menno Prasad Pradhan (2004). *Local Conflict in Indonesia: Measuring Incidence and Identifying Patterns*. Washington D.C.: Worldbank.

Bertrand, Jacques (2004). *Nationalism and Ethnic Conflict in Indonesia*. Cambridge: Cambridge University Press.

Bråten, Eldar (2002). "Against Community, beyond Humanity: Grasping 'Violence' in Java." In: Frans Hüsken and Huub de Jonge (eds.), *Violence and Vengeance. Discontent and Conflict in New Order Indonesia*, 11–30. Saarbrücken: Verlag für Entwicklungspolitik Saarbrücken GmbH.

Breidlid, Torhild (2013). "The Legitimization of Violence against the Ahmadiyya Community in Indonesia." *Kawistara* 2, 117–226.

Burhani, Ahmad (2014). "Hating the Ahmadiyya: The Place of 'Heretics' in Contemporary Indonesian Muslim Society." *Contemporary Islam* 8, 133–152.

Chernov Hwang, Julie, Rizal Panggabean, and Ihsan Ali Fauzi (2013). "The Disengagement of Jihadis in Poso, Indonesia." *Asian Survey* 53 (4), 754–777.

Colombijn, Freek (2002). "Maling, Maling! The Lynching of Petty Criminals." In: Freed Colombijn and Thomas Lindblad (eds.), *Roots of Violence in Indonesia*, 299–330. Leiden: KITLV Press.

Colombijn, Freek, and Thomas Lindblad (eds.) (2002). *Roots of Violence in Indonesia*. Leiden: KITLV Press.

Cribb, Robert (2000). "From Petrus to Ninja: Death Squads in Indonesia." In: Bruce B. Campbell and Arthur D. Brenner (eds.), *Death Squads in Global Perspective: Murder with Deniability*, 181–202. New York: St Martin's Press.

Crouch, Melissa (2009). "Indonesia, Militant Islam and Ahmadiyah: Origins and Implications." *ARC Federation Fellowship "Islam, Shariah and Governance" Background Paper Series* No 4.

——— (2012). "Criminal (In)justice in Indonesia: The Cikeusik Trials." *Alternative Law Journal* 37 (1), 54–56.

Davidson, Jamie (2009). *From Rebellion to Riots. Collective Violence on Indonesian Borneo*. Singapore: NUS Press.

Farid, Hilmar (2005). "Indonesia's Original Sin: Mass Killings and Capitalist Expansion, 1965–66." *Inter-Asia Cultural Studies* 6 (1), 33–16.

Fealy, Greg, Virginia Hooker, and Sally White (2006). "Indonesia." In: G. Fealy and V. Hooker (eds.), *Voices of Islam in Southeast Asia*, 39–50. Singapore: ISEAS Publications.

Feillard, Andree, and Remy Madinier (2011). *The End of Innocence? Indonesian Islam and the Temptation of Radicalism*. Honolulu: University of Hawai'i Press.

Hendrawan, Parliza (2013, March 7). "Ini Kronologi Penyerangan TNI AD ke Mapolres OKU." *Tempo.co*. Retrieved July 18, 2014, from http://www.tempo.co/.

Herriman, Nicholas (2007). "'Sorcerer' Killings in Banyuwangi: A Re-Examination of State Responsibility for Violence.'" *Asian Studies Review* 31 (1) 61–78.

——— (2010). "The Great Rumor Mill: Gossip, Mass Media, and the Ninja Fear." *Journal of Asian Studies* 69 (3), 723–748.

Hicks, Jacqueline (2014). "Heresy and Authority: Understanding the Turn against Ahmadiyah in Indonesia." *South East Asia Research* 22 (3), 321–339.

Hidayat, Rachmat (2013, April 6). "Sikap Danjen Kopassus Ksatria." *Tribunnews.com*. Retrieved July 25, 2014, from http://www.tribunnews.com/.

Hüsken, Frans, and Huub de Jonge (eds.) (2002). *Violence and Vengeance. Discontent and Conflict in New Order Indonesia*. Saarbrücken: Verlag für Entwicklungspolitik Saarbrücken GmbH.

Jamaludin, Jajang, with Sunudyantoro, Pito Agustin Rudiana, Shinta Maharini, and M. Syaifullah (2013). "Malam Jahanam di Cibongan." *Tempo*, April 1–7, 76–83.

Jones, Sydney, and Solahudin (2014). "Terrorism in Indonesia: A Fading Threat?" *Southeast Asian Affairs*, 139–147.

Kahmad, Dadang (2012). "Religious Radicalism and Cultural Change." *Inside Indonesia* 107. Retrieved July 25, 2014, from http://www.insideindonesia.org/.

KontraS (2011). *Negara Tak Kunjung Terusik. Laporan Hak Asasi manusia Peristiwa Penyerangan Jama'ah Ahmadiyah Cikeusik 6 Februari 2011*. Jakarta: KontraS. Retrieved August 25, 2014, from http://www.kontras.org/data/laporan%20cikeusik.pdf.

Millie, Julian (2012). "One Year after the Cikeusik tragedy." *Inside Indonesia* 107. Retrieved July 25, 2014, from http://www.insideindonesia.org/.

Moore, Samuel (2001). "The Indonesian Military's Last Years in East Timor: An Analysis of Its Secret Documents." *Indonesia* 72, 9–44.

Nastiti, Aulia (2014). "Discursive Construction of Religious Minority: Minoritization of Ahmadiyya in Indonesia." *Deutsches Asienforschungszentrum Asian Series Commentaries* 19.

Ong, Iwan (2013, February 5). "Warga Ahmadiyah Lombok Sudah 7 Tahun Mengungsi." *Kompas.com*. Retrieved July 25, 2014, from http://www.kompas.com/.

Peluso, Nancy Lee (2007). "Violence, Decentralization and Resource Access in Indonesia." *Peace Review: A Journal of Social Justice* 19 (1), 23–32.

Platzdasch, Bernhard (2011). *Religious Freedom in Indonesia: The Case of Ahmadiya*. National University of Singapore Institute of Southeast Asian Studies Working Paper: Politics and Security Series No 2.

Prabowo, Dani (2013, September 5). "Vonis Kasus Cebongan Dinilai Proporsional." *Kompas.com*. Retrieved July 25, 2014, from http://www.kompas.com/.

Prasetya, Eko (2013, April 12). "Dukung Kopassus, puluhan pria berbaju loreng demo di Komnas HAM." *Merdeka.com*. Retrieved July 25, 2014, from http://www.merdeka.com/.

Pringle, Martin (2010). *Understanding Islam in Indonesia: Politics and Diversity*. Honolulu: University of Hawai'i Press.

Rosarians, Fransisko, and Yohanes Seo (2013, April 6). "SBY Bilang Pelaku Penyerangan LP Cebongan Kesatria." *Tempo.co*. Retrieved July 18, 2014, from http://www.tempo.co/.

Schulte Nordholt, Henk (2002). "A Genealogy of Violence." In: Freed Colombijn and Thomas Lindblad (eds.), *Roots of Violence in Indonesia*, 33–62. Leiden: KITLV Press.

Sidel, John (2006). *Riots, Pogroms, Jihad. Religious Violence in Indonesia*. Ithaca N.Y.: Cornell University Press.

Sunaryo, Arie (2013, March 23). "Grup 2 Kopassus: Tidak ada anggota yang keluar pada Jumat malam." *Merdeka.com*. Retrieved July 25, 2014, from http://www.merdeka.com/.

Sunudyantoro with Shinta Maharani, M. Syaifullah, and Yohanes Seo (2013). "Tumbang di Depan Punggawa." *Tempo*, April 1–7, 84–85.

Supriatma, Antonius (2014). "Defending Murder." *Inside Indonesia* 115. Retrieved July 25, 2014, from http://www.insideindonesia.org/.

Tadjoeddin, Mohammad (2014). *Explaining Collective Violence in Contemporary Indonesia: From Conflict to Cooperation*. Basingstoke: Palgrave Macmillan Ltd.

Tadjoeddin, Mohammad, and Syed Murshed (2007). "Socio-Economic Determinants of Everyday Violence in Indonesia: An Empirical Investigation of Javanese Districts, 1994–2004." *Journal of Peace Research* 44 (6), 689–709.

Ulum, Wasi'ul (2011a, July 28). "Penyerang Ahmadiyah Cikeusik Divonis 3 Sampai 6 Bulan Penjara." *Tempo.co*. Retrieved July 18, 2014, from http://www.tempo.co/.

——— (2011b, August 15). "Kepala Keamanan Ahmadiyah Divonis 6 Bulan Penjara." *Tempo.co*. Retrieved July 18, 2014, from http://www.tempo.co/.

Van Bruinessen, Martin (2012). "Indonesian Muslims and Their Place in the Larger World of Islam." In: Anthony Reid (ed.), *Indonesia Rising. The Repositioning of Asia's Third Giant*, 117–140. Singapore: ISEAS Publications.

——— (2013). "Introduction: Contemporary Developments in Indonesian Islam and the 'Conservative Turn' of the Early Twenty-First Century." In: Martin van Bruinessen (ed.), *Contemporary Developments in Indonesian Islam. Explaining the "Conservative Turn,"* 1–20. Singapore: ISEAS Publications.

Van Klinken, Gerry (2007). *Communal Violence and Democratization in Indonesia: Small Town Wars*. London: Routledge.

Varney, Ashutosh (2008). "Analyzing Collective Violence in Indonesia: An Overview." *Journal of East Asian Studies* 8, 341–359.

Welsh, Bridget (2008). "Local and National: Keroyokan Mobbing in Indonesia." *Journal of East Asian Studies* 8, 473–504.

Widaya, Indra (2014, February 26). *Kompas.com*. Retrieved July 25, 2014, from http://www.kompas.com/.

Wilson, Chris (2008). *Ethno-Religious Violence in Indonesia: From Soil to God*. London: Routledge.

Wilson, Ian (2006). "Continuity and Change. The Changing Contours of Organized Violence in Post-New Order Indonesia." *Critical Asian Studies* 38 (2), 265–297.

——— (2014). "Morality Racketeering: Vigilantism and Populist Islamic Militancy in Indonesia." In: Khoo Boo Teik, Vedi Hadiz, and Yoshihiro Nakanishi (eds.), *Between Dissent and Power. The Transformation of Islamic Politics in the Middle East and Asia*, 248–274. Basingstoke: Macmillan Publishers Limited.

Yasra, Setri, with Sunudyantoro, Anton Septian, and Agung Sedayu (2011). "Fear and Loathing in Banten." *Tempo*, February 16–22, 12–19.

Zulkarnain, Iskandar (2005). *Gerakan Ahmadiyah di Indonesia*. Yogyakarta: LKiS.

2   A Different Kind of War

Summary Execution and the Politics of Men of Force in Late-Qing China, 1864–1911

WEITING GUO

In March 1853, when the Qing Empire was stuck in the suppression of the Taiping Rebellion, the Xianfeng emperor issued an edict to all governors and officials:

> Recently, the Sichuan and Fujian Governors reported their progress in suppressing banditry. Chen Jinshou (陳金綬) also reported the disturbing behaviors of the disbanded militants from Guangdong. I therefore issued an edict requiring these governors to suppress the bandits with full force. Once bandits have been captured, governors shall conduct a brief investigation and execute them on the spot (*jiudi zhengfa* 就地正法). I also ordered local officials, militia (*tuanlian* 團練), gentry, and ordinary people to execute villains without exception (*gesha wulun* 格殺勿論). In the midst of bandit suppression, outlaws from every locality might take advantage of the unrest to rob and disturb civilians. If we fail to take strict measures, how can we restore order and reassure the public? I hereby command all provincial governors, together with their subordinates, to make all attempts to capture the bandits. If they detect any mobs gathering and robbing others, they should interrogate them and execute them on the spot. All these measures are to ensure that justice is served properly to deter further wrongdoing. I also reiterate that all militia, local elites, and ordinary people should join the suppression campaign and execute all villains promptly. Only if we do so will gangsters show restraint and peace be restored.[1]

While Xianfeng had previously warranted summary execution for specific regions and banditry cases,[2] this was the first time he had issued a comprehensive command that required all officers and local militia to inflict the death penalty in a thorough manner. In the following century, China witnessed the largest number of summary executions annually in its history. The extensive use of this extraordinary procedure, in conjunction with regular public executions by political regimes, local officials, and militia, had considerable influence on modern Chinese legal culture. Prior to the explosion of the Taiping Rebellion, a number of Qing emperors had also resorted to summary execution.[3] The Qianlong reign (1736–1795) witnessed an initial boom in summary executions, as the prosperous empire encountered increasing social conflicts, tax resistance, and frontier unrest. The ambitious Qianlong emperor initiated a series of punishment of "rootless rascals" (*guanggun* 光棍),[4] "wicked people" (*diaomin* 刁民), political dissidents, and deserting soldiers through the quickened and militarized procedures of "king's order" (*wangming* 王命), "banner-plaque," (*qipai* 旗牌), and "submitting a routine memorial and carrying out execution at the same time" (*yimian juti yimian zhengfa* 一面具題，一面正法).[5] Contrary to the practice of summary execution during and after the Taiping Rebellion, the quickened procedure of execution during this period primarily operated on bureaucratic communication and the majority of cases were under the monarch's surveillance.

In the subsequent Jiaqing reign (1796–1820) and Daoguang reign (1820–1850), the imperial court continued to institutionalize the summary execution procedure through the enactment of a number of substatutes.[6] However, the limited use of summary execution and formal troops made the Qing government appear defenseless and inefficient in the face of the disastrous Taiping Rebellion. The devastation of prosperous regions and the expanding Heavenly Kingdom of the Taiping, together with its "heterodox" orientation incorporating Christian ideology that scared the authorities, posed a tremendous challenge to the endangered empire. Learning from the Jiaqing emperor's suppression of White Lotus rebels, Xianfeng clearly knew that the forces of the militia, *baojia* (保甲), and village braves (*xiangyong* 鄉勇 or *yong* 勇) could help the government expel the bandits. Throughout the battles against the Taiping, Xianfeng followed his predecessor's footsteps and eventually facilitated what Philip Kuhn calls the process of "local militarization."[7]

The influence of summary execution went far beyond the Taiping Rebellion. After the fall of the Taiping Kingdom in 1864, summary execution was an element in the power conflicts between central and regional governments over the regulation of authority over punishment. The Qing court attempted to restore the regular procedure for the death penalty, but financial constraints and emerging social unrest forced the court to retain the regional official's power of quick execution. Following the humiliating Boxer Rebellion of 1900, the imperial center faced stronger pressure from reform-minded officials and intellectuals. It was forced to abolish execution by slow-slicing (*lingchi* 凌遲)

and other cruel punishments.⁸ Yet it further extended the use of summary execution to "allow the populace to witness the execution and thus make them feel vigilant and prudent."⁹ The following decades witnessed the introduction of a Western legal system that tended to protect the defendant's right to a fair trial. But the Republican state, regardless of its political orientation in Beijing, Nanjing, and Chongqing, continued the use of summary execution in a series of campaigns against "banditry," "local strongmen" (*tuhao* 土豪), "evil gentry" (*lieshen* 劣绅), and those acting "counterrevolutionary" (*fangeming* 反革命) or "endangering the Republic" (*weihai minguo* 危害民國). The mobilized justice reached its height under the party-state system of the Nationalist Party (*Guomindang* 國民黨, a.k.a. KMT) and the Chinese Communist Party (*Zhongguo gongchandang* 中國共產黨, aka CCP). Eventually, such mobilized justice, featuring the style of "enemy-hunt" persecution, laid the foundation for the collective violence during the 1950s and the subsequent Cultural Revolution (1966–1976).

It is not surprising that summary execution, which allowed convicts and loosely defined "bandits" to be summarily killed, has long been regarded as a "barbaric and cruel institution."[10] Many studies attribute the flourishing of summary execution to the plight of China, in which overpowered governors and intensified warlordism plunged the Chinese people into dire suffering. Some scholars notice its complex context and its linkage with social unrest, political struggle, and financial constraints. Yet these scholars criticize its "lawlessness," "arbitrariness," and even "feudalist" characteristics, which hampered the judicial reforms in the early twentieth century.[11] Only a few scholars, particularly Suzuki Hidemitsu and Thomas Buoye, have started to place summary execution in the broader context of the rise of informal punishments since the late eighteenth and early nineteenth centuries.[12] However, most scholars focus on institutional and political contexts behind the rise of summary execution. Few have explored its correlation with a broader trend of social transformation, particularly the epidemic of men of force that either helped the state suppress bandits or became the targets of summary execution. As a result, little is known about how such an exceptional institution was linked with Chinese society and the gradually expanded network of armed forces.

In order to fill this void, this chapter explores the history of summary execution during the post-Taiping period in the light of the culture of violence and, in a broader sense, the politics of exclusion that allowed regimes and community members to expel the "society's enemy" through both legal and illicit measures. Challenging the conventional view that presumes violence as merely "deviance" or "disorder," recent scholars, particularly Mark Lewis,

Barend ter Haar, David Robinson, William Rowe, and David Der-wei Wang, have noted that various forms of violence had been "sanctioned" by both the state and ordinary people, while illicit force had long been an integral component in Chinese society.[13] Rowe's observation fits particularly well in the case of summary execution. He points out that order ("men of force," such as local strongmen and militia leaders) and disorder (often rather casually labeled "bandits") existed in a "rough, negotiated equilibrium" and that criminals, rebels, and the modern-era "class enemies" have "routinely been demonized in order for the bloody act visited upon them to be legitimated."[14]

Moreover, throughout the late nineteenth and early twentieth centuries, the punishments enacted by the state were not simply the state's prerogative. Instead, local militia and armed groups frequently participated in the process of "state violence" through state-sponsored campaigns, "local militarization," or what Rowe terms "demonic violence."[15] As David Robinson points out, even during the relatively peaceful period of the mid-Ming, the "patronage network" of violence had been built between imperial court and local society.[16] Based on an abundant resource of violence network, together with the rise of social powers and an increasingly diverse local society, nineteenth-century China witnessed not only what Philip Kuhn calls "local militarization" but also what he terms the "parallel hierarchies of militarization," in which "the same kinds of linkages and the same levels of organization would [then] be visible within both the orthodox, gentry-dominated Confucian culture and the various heterodox, secret-society–dominated sectarian subcultures."[17] The militarization eventually led to a culture in which, according to Diana Lary, "soldiers and bandits were indistinguishable" (*bing fei bufen* 兵匪不分) and that blurred the boundaries between legality and illegality.[18] As a result, as this chapter argues, summary execution as a death penalty practice profoundly influenced by both formal and informal forces was not merely a product of "chaotic time." Instead, it was an integral part of the equilibrium of a wide variety of legitimation processes and a product of social and political transformations before the advent of disastrous warfare.

Previous studies on Chinese summary execution usually focus on the abuse of power in the practice of summary execution and rarely notice how the extended network of violence facilitated the rise of this institution. Before the Taiping Rebellion, the rise of local military organizations had become a visible trend and the Qing government had established its collaboration with local militia. On the other hand, by the end of the eighteenth century, the explosive population had created a series of social problems, including the increased vagrants and "rootless rascals," the emerging migration and the conflicts between indigenous and migrants, and rampant litigation and popular protests.¹⁹ The multitier reviewing system and the enactment of new capital crimes worsened the already-delayed executions at the annual Autumn Assizes, making what Thomas Buoye calls "lingering imprisonment" a real epidemic in all levels of prisons.²⁰ All these problems enhanced the anxiety of authorities and compelled the imperial center to approve summary executions against serious crimes and unruly subjects. Ironically, during the nineteenth century, while the state extended its authority through the use of militarized judicial procedure, the emerging underclass and men of force continued to prevail and challenged the state's authorities.²¹ Due to the financial constraints and overwhelming banditry across the nation, the imperial center and regional authorities adopted summary execution and relied on *baojia* and militia to deter crimes and expel unlawful subjects. While the government feared its collaborating forces would join in banditry and rebellion, the patronage network of violence continued to fill in with gangs of orthodox and heterodox organizations. In essence, militia as an organization of local toughs and several local elites inevitably met the problems of managing their own militants. Some militants drifted around and committed robbery with the weapons acquired from militia. This, in turn, made the government continuously adopt severe punishment to sweep the braves outside the legitimate organizations. In the end, the epidemic of men of force, the continued campaign against "heterodox" braves, the demand for efficient punishment, and the coexistence of "legal" and "illegal" elements had jointly structured what I call the "economy of punishment"—the distribution and management of penal resources related to crime and the network of violence.²² As this chapter argues, the economy of punishment not only constituted an important response to the trend of local militarization but also impacted Chinese criminal justice throughout the late nineteenth and early twentieth centuries.

The term *economy of punishment* also builds a dialogue between China and other countries and extends our discussion in a global and comparative sense. During the late nineteenth and early twentieth centuries, when China underwent its largest campaign of rough justice, it was not alone as Europe, the United States, and various nations also encountered similar trends. In Europe and Latin America, popular justice and mobilized purges occurred while the states gradually established a monopoly on legitimate force. During the late nineteenth and early twentieth centuries, the practice of lynching was popular in a number of regions in the United States, in which the masses summarily killed presumed criminals through extralegal measures. Recent studies of American lynching also challenge the perspective of American exceptionalism that narrowly defines lynching as an American practice.²³ This chapter echoes this perspective by pointing out that the rise of Chinese rough justice constituted a parallel development in the history of violence around the globe. However, China's case also differed from its Western counterpart in that its widespread men of force had become a significant element of the formal establishment and local governance. They were targets of the government's suppression in some occasions, but they could also convert themselves into members of public service. This is not merely particular to the nineteenth century. During the first half of the twentieth century, Chinese authorities also continuously "soaked up" (*shoubian* 收編) local illegal forces, while the latter collaborated with other elements that may have had conflicts with the government. The highly eclectic nature of legal and illegal elements reveals a distinct process of Chinese state-building and society-making. Whether or not they were soldiers or bandits, legal and illegal forces interacted with one another and mutually achieved legitimization through the process.[24]

Drawing on a wide array of primary sources, including the Veritable Records of the Qing Dynasty (*Qing shilu* 清實錄), local gazetteers, and newspapers, this chapter explores the rise of summary execution in the light of the web of braves in late Qing China. The Qing dynasty's summary execution law targeted a wide variety of offenders, including sect members, smugglers, and "roaming braves" (*youyong* 游勇). Each of these groups had varied contexts and thus resulted in different responses from state and society. While this chapter focuses on the punishment of the roaming braves, it also provides an overview of summary execution law and its various targets. As the following analysis reveals, the war against roaming braves was part of a greater trend toward summary execution. However, it also differs from the trend in some ways, particularly because the Qing authorities manipulated the epidemic of "braves" in their governance and local defense. In 1905, the *Chinese and Foreign Daily* (*Zhongwai ribao* 中外日報) reported that "the authorities called them 'roaming braves' because they intended to kill them.... These people were disbanded soldiers when our country had no warfare. They turned from ordinary people to braves, and then turned from braves to wanderers. It is all because of the state's policies."[25] While the Qing authorities extensively hunted and executed these wanderers, they continued to absorb local bullies into their defense and local security systems.

In the following sections, I first discuss how authorities legitimized summary execution based on a judicial economy approach. While keeping summary execution a temporary procedure that was valid only for several years, both imperial center and regional officials continuously extended the laws in order to punish crime in a prompt and efficient manner. The second section further explores how the Qing government approached the problem of roaming braves and eventually enacted a summary execution law for these illegitimate men of force. On the other hand, as the third section points out, the Qing government continued to recruit braves to its military forces, but when soldiers deserted or were disbanded by the troops, they were labeled by the authorities as roaming braves and were usually suppressed by the government. Many officers arbitrarily accused local people of being disbanded braves. In many occasions, braves and vagrants were hurriedly killed because officials intended to cover up scandals or simply punish those who did not obey their commands. In the fourth section, I examine how local militia, while being immersed in the suppression and quick execution, continued to engage in violence against bandits and roaming braves. Local officials did not wish local militia to excessively execute the criminals as they did in the civil war, but they also relied on these local armed groups to help detect and capture the vagrants. The final section offers an in-depth exploration of a Ningbo riot that shows how both government and society demanded quick justice and rejected the reform that bestowed legal rights to criminal defendants. It was such sentiments and the government's demands that brought the practice into the reform period, when the practice of summary execution and the coexistence of legal and illicit forces continued to structure the politics and legal culture in the subsequent Republican period.

Legitimizing Laws that Broke the Rules

While the Qing court relied on summary execution in the battles against the Taiping rebels and emerging armed forces, the extensive use of this exceptional institution also posed a number of new threats to the Qing state. During the Ming and Qing Dynasties, Chinese criminal justice had reached a height of centralization. Capital cases were required to go through multiple levels of reviews, including the final sanction by the monarch. This centralized system secured the emperor's power of killing and prevented abuse of power at the local level.[26] During the Taiping Rebellion, the rising power of governors largely changed the existing judicial system. The Xianfeng emperor's policy left the governors to avoid the regular distinction between bandit leaders and followers and execute all convicts without any exception.[27] The imperial court even allowed governors to impose taxes for the supply of their armies, enhancing the power and financial independence of each province.[28] During the latter half of the Taiping Rebellion, the Xianfeng emperor further extended indiscriminate execution to cases of robbery, smuggling, resisting arrest, and coin counterfeiting.[29] While the exact number of executions remains unknown, thousands of ordinary people were reportedly killed annually in war-ravaged regions.³⁰ Many officials urged the throne to punish governors who disregarded human lives "like playing with toys," but the throne prioritized urgency while admitting that the punishment of officials might only thrill other officials and trigger a new crisis rather than resolving the problem.³¹

During the late 1860s, when the Qing defeated the major forces of the Taiping and Nian rebels, initial reforms attempted to abolish summary execution. In 1869, the Tongzhi court issued an edict stating that the previous summary execution laws were expedient and merely temporary measures. However, while the court required all judicial officers to resume the regular judicial reporting procedure, it permitted that the regions involved in the war could continue to use the militarized procedure.³² Even such a compromise approach did not gain support from the majority of the governors. As the Board of Punishment later admitted, it was difficult to abolish summary execution because, even after the war, regional governments still relied on it to suppress theft and robbery.³³ In order to keep summary execution an exceptional practice, the Qing court granted each province only a few years to carry out summary execution. Nevertheless, many governors continued to request extensions, and the Qing court, while fully aware that harsh laws could help secure its rule, continued to extend the laws for each province.³⁴

To a certain extent, the continued renewal of summary execution laws reflected the imperial strategy over the power of killing. By keeping the regular statutes unchanged, the imperial court retained its discursive tradition of "circumspection in punishment" (*shen xing* 慎刑) while allowing its subordinates extensive power to kill potential threats on its behalf. The governors had to defend the need for using such punishment, and they would be criticized if they failed to use their power properly. The renewed policies required governors to submit reports periodically, securing the imperial control over summary execution.³⁵

In 1878, for instance, Zhejiang governor Mei Qizhao (梅啟照) reported a robbery case in which nine robbers mobbed a government office and caused the death of a government staff member. The Board of Punishment quickly cited the policy of summary execution and suggested that the governor execute the robbers on the spot. Mei may have expected the suggestion. The Qing court had recently denounced him for ignoring local robbery cases,³⁶ so he probably used the robbery case to demonstrate that he had handled this one more seriously.³⁷ Any local upheaval could make him lose his position, and he had to demonstrate his competence. In this regard, the extension of governors' power did not necessarily negate monarchical power, although the limited resources provided by the center, together with the intensified turmoil that challenged imperial authority, eventually forced governors to rely on their own resources to survive.

In 1879, the imperial court approved a guideline (*zhangcheng* 章程) drafted by the Board of Punishment stipulating that summary execution applied only to the cases where bandits and robbers were captured far from the provincial capital. In such cases, prefectural authorities could execute suspects without sending them to the province, but a postexecution report with interrogation record should be submitted for further supervision.[38] The guideline represented an official response to the debates on the legitimacy of summary execution. Instead of restricting the use of summary execution, the guideline reinforced the institution. Moreover, the guideline implied that local magistrates encountered difficulties in both prison management and the conveyance of prisoners, a problem that began to be visible in local judicial administration over a century earlier.

The financial constraints on the practice of criminal justice surfaced in the mid–eighteenth century, when the empire underwent a tremendous population increase and economic growth. Although bestowed only limited resources under what Philip Huang terms "centralized minimalism,"[39] local officials encountered increasing difficulties in handling the increased judicial backlog. A wide range of informal and flexible measures was thus created in the local operation of judicial administration.[40] The issue remained unresolved during the nineteenth century, and the Daoguang emperor criticized Zhejiang and Jiangsu officials for ignoring piracy and banditry due to the lack of funds for conveying criminals.[41] It was also during the Daoguang reign that the government explicitly legitimized the use of summary execution for reasons of finance and prison management. In 1848, Commissioner Lin Zexu (林則徐) defended the practice of summary execution on the grounds that conveyance was costly and dangerous as the prisoners usually took this chance to escape and sometimes their companions would rescue them during the conveyance.[42] During the latter half of the nineteenth century, several famous governors-general, including Zeng Guofan (曾國藩) and Li Hongzhang (李鴻章), provided similar reasons for the continuation of summary execution.[43] Due to the prevailing support for summary execution, the imperial center had little room for removing it. In an imperial edict issued in 1898, the court condemned local officials for seeking convenient and expedient approaches, while admitting that the scant regard for human lives was unavoidable given the problems in judicial practice.[44]

Moreover, while the civil war intensified local political struggles, the existing problem of "judicial backlog" (*ji'an* 積案) worsened following the fall of the Taiping Kingdom. Endless disputation emerged between competing groups that had fought during the lingering civil war. The disbanded fighters also became a new social problem, causing severe robbery and banditry across the nation. Roughly after the late 1860s, the increasing number of crimes and litigations forced several governors to start a new "cleaning up judicial backlog" campaign (*qingsong* 清訟). After some governors successfully "cleaned up" accumulated judicial cases, the Qing court publicly praised them and encouraged other provinces to follow their example.

Zeng Guofan's *Ten Regulations on Cleaning Up Judicial Backlog in Zhili* (*Zhili qingsong shiyi shitiao* 直隸清訟事宜十條, published in 1869) was one of the earliest official publications on this issue. The regulations encompassed a wide range of dimensions, including robbery and banditry cases (Article 7). Zeng stipulated that his subordinates should divide robbery and banditry cases into two categories: one involving lesser severity and less stolen money, and the other greater severity and more stolen money. Prosecution of the former followed the regular reporting procedure, while the latter had to be reported to Zeng for his consideration of the application of *military judicial procedure* (*junfa congshi* 軍法從事), a synonym for summary execution. The reason to resort to summary execution, according to Zeng, was to "threaten the bandits and take away their courage."[45] Moreover, as Zeng repeatedly emphasized, any delay in the suppression of banditry would allow these villains to "remain out of the law's reach and never fear the law."[46]

Despite the support from the imperial court, the campaign to clean up judicial backlog was primarily a regional matter. Given the limited funds from the central government and the accumulating judicial cases, the provincial authorities had to clean up these cases by themselves. After the Zhili regulations, several provinces imitated Zeng's model of "cleaning up cases." Zhejiang Province, for example, issued a *Guideline on Cleaning Up Judicial Backlog* (*Zhejaing qingsong zhangcheng* 浙江清訟章程, published in 1878), reiterating that it was the officials' responsibility to sweep out crimes and accumulating litigations. One of the precedents cited a Taizhou case involving summary execution for the offense of robbery at sea. The interpretation following the case warned local officials and yamen runners to capture all felony criminals and punish them in a prompt manner.[47] Like Zhili's and other provinces' regulations, Zhejiang's guideline suggested that the regional government had routinized the practice of summary execution in an attempt to deter outlaws and to clean up accumulated cases. In addition, through the promotion of "cleaning up judicial backlog," the provincial authorities summarily finalized a number of felony cases without reporting them for further review.

The extension of summary execution continued after the Qing initiated its judicial reform under the name of "New Policies" (*xinzheng* 新政). Under pressure from the public following the Boxer Protocol of 1901, the Qing court appointed a number of reforming officials to revise imperial law. In 1905, the imperial court abolished a set of cruel punishments, including death by slow slicing, display of the severed head (*xiaoshou* 梟首), and mutilation of remains (*lushi* 戮屍).[48] Roughly at the same time, the Board of Punishment rejected a suggestion to extend summary execution to government clerks and doormen.[49] On the surface, the Qing government intended to be benevolent in the use of the death penalty. However, the Qing court would not abolish summary execution because it had become the only useful instrument in bandit suppression after the abolition of cruel punishment.[50]

To the reforming officials, the largest problem of summary execution came from its erosion of the emperor's power and the combination of legal and military powers. In 1906, the Bureau of Government Organization (*Bianzhiju* 編制局) suggested the introduction of a Western system of separation of powers. It also suggested that the "issue of military power" (*junquan wenti* 軍權問題) should not be confused with the "issue of legal power" (*faquan wenti* 法權問題), claiming that "the power of killing should belong to the emperor."[51] This suggestion faced strong criticism from the governors-general.[52] Yet the imperial court had regarded law as an indispensable part of its centralization program. The opposition of the governors-general demonstrated that a unified punishment system could not penetrate to the lower level of the imperial bureaucracy. First, the court had to consolidate its own military and punishment systems in order to ask its subordinates to follow the rules and supervision from the central government. In August 1908, the newly established Ministry (*Lujun Bu* 陸軍部) announced four supplementary provisions, most of which concerned summary execution. The provisions extended the scope of military law from military affairs to ordinary offenses. It also strengthened the legal grounds of the administrative official's power of capital punishment.[53]

In the last four years of the dynasty, the imperial center enacted a series of new laws introducing Western institutions. District courts were gradually established in some regions. The new court and prosecution system quickly caused dissatisfaction among local officials. The administrative officials could not imagine having to send criminals to court after arresting them. Some provinces even started to prohibit summary executions because of the new system of separation of executive and judicial powers.[54] The Qing court expected judicial and military centralization, but its measures created uncertainty and extra costs to local governments. The battles between administrative and judicial officials over the power of summary execution continued to increase. The reforming officials frequently condemned summary execution for its harmful effect upon "judicial independence."[55] Yet many local officials rejected sending summary execution cases to the district courts.[56] Some governors even argued that as "the quality of the Chinese people was extremely uneven," it was necessary to perform summary executions to manage those unqualified people.[57]

Actually, the establishment of new courts achieved only part of the imperial center's goal of centralization. The new courts extended the state's law to the local bureaucracy and gradually removed part of the local official's power over capital punishment. However, it did not help local governments gain more strength to cope with the growing upheavals and revolution. The imperial center expected that the courts and laws could help it manage local officials and society, but the continuous problem of banditry and revolutionary uprisings made the imperial court complain that "while the court frequently issued imperial edicts about judicial reform, the country still had no people who wished to abide by law."[58] However, another project of the court, strengthening the military and the unification of military justice, had succeeded to a certain degree. This project even resolved the conflict between administrative and judicial branches because the Ministry and governors-general discovered that once the power of summary execution belonged to military justice, the problem of "the administration's intervention into judicial practices" would be resolved.[59] This relocation finally resolved the problem of the ambiguous role of summary execution in the preceding half-century. Although the reconsolidation of summary execution through the establishment of military justice was not able to save the falling dynasty, it continued to play an important role in criminal justice and influenced the interplay between law and politics during the Republican era.

Debating the Policy for the Roaming Braves

In the summer of 1864, the Qing general Zeng Guofan submitted an imperial memorial requesting the court to dissolve his Xiang Army.[60] The army had just defeated the Taiping rebels and recovered the city of Nanjing. Over a decade of fighting, the military had reached over 120,000 soldiers at this point.[61] The large army carried heavy expenditures. Many militants were underpaid and riots occasionally broke out.[62] The limited supplies from the court even made the underpaid soldiers engage in a smuggling business or join the banditry groups. What further annoyed Zeng was the suspicion regarding his loyalty.[63] By the end of the Taiping Rebellion, he had become the most powerful official in the nation. No one could ever contend with his military power. Even the court was wondering if he would reduce his power by himself.

While the financial constraint and political conspiracy seemed to have overwhelmed Zeng's mind, the diverse background and the potential criminal tendency of his soldiers constituted another critical issue that could have destroyed his career during the restoration period. Initially based in Hunan Province, Zeng recruited a wide variety of braves from different places during the process of suppression. The soldiers included local bullies, secret society members, smugglers, and surrendered rebels.[64] In 1859, Zeng enacted a regulation for his army, empowering his subordinate commanders to summarily execute any soldier with a connection to secret societies, particularly those conveniently labeled as Gelaohui (哥老會).[65] These strict laws did not stop illicit activities. Many soldiers continuously engaged in robbery and smuggling. Some escaped from the army and joined the enemies or bandit groups. Frequent changes of identities made it difficult to distinguish a friend from a foe.[66] Zeng could only dissolve these soldiers and select what he needed for future defense.

The dissolution of the Xiang Army created a large flood of roaming braves. Zeng kept only a few braves and reassigned them to his new navy troops, the Yangtze Navy Brigade (*Changjiang shuishi* 長江水師). He retained part of Zuo Zongtang's (左宗棠) troops and Li Hongzhang's Huai branch. The latter became the main force in the suppression of the Nian Rebellion and then was largely disbanded after the war.[67] Following the Sino-French War (1883–1885) and the Sino-Japanese War (1894–1895), the Qing government further disbanded a large number of mercenaries.[68] Hundreds of thousands of roaming braves had no household, no taxation records, and even no place to go. Many of them joined secret societies and mobster groups and reportedly committed robbery, murder, human trafficking, and smuggling.[69] Some local officials provided land cultivation jobs for the disbanded braves, but a number of braves who had previous military ranks did not accept such a degrading and humiliating arrangement.[70] Due to the strict punishment enacted by the government, many braves hid in the mountains and begged on the street when they were hungry.[71] The epidemic of this wandering group quickly impacted local governance and social order. As the famous scholar and reformist Liang Qichao (梁啟超) observed, "roaming braves continuously killed and robbed civilians; they were fond of making trouble; they viewed raising a revolt as their general diet."[72]

The Qing government had long been aware that braves could become a threat to the state. Recruiting local mercenary members might prevent these strongmen from joining the rebel forces, but they could easily become uncontrollable if circumstances changed and turned unfavorable to them. The extensive use of summary execution was also a way of warning militia leaders, suggesting that any betrayer would be severely punished with the help of other militia. As Zeng Guofan once revealed, the "brutal suppression without care for human lives was to make people fear [Zeng] much more than they feared the bandits."[73] However, it was also such brutal killing that drew criticisms against Zeng. His braves committed robbery and even massacred women, elders, and children during the battles.[74] He also admitted that both the Qing army and the local militia had abused the power of killing, resulting in the death of a large number of innocent people.[75] Both militia and summary execution were double-edged swords. Zeng and other governors relied on these two institutions while also acknowledging their shortcomings. They adopted somewhat competing strategies not only to maintain local security but also to ensure that the growing men of force would be their friends rather than their enemies.

Near the end of the warfare, many officials started to suggest that the Qing court should pay close attention to the braves. In 1862, Hunan Governor Mao Hongbin (毛鴻賓) suggested that military commanders should be careful about any brave who applied to leave. The Tongzhi court responded to Mao's memorial and announced to all officials:

> Ever since the outbreak of this war, hundreds of thousands of braves were recruited as imperial soldiers. These braves shared their hatred of the same enemy with us. Many of them killed bandits and accomplished a great achievement. Yet some of them became involved in banditry and were looked down upon by their fellows. After they received merits and secured their military ranks, they took these achievements as their protectors. . . . These unruly braves gradually formed factions and disturbed the order of local communities. All military commanders and local authorities should strictly control these braves and investigate their activities so that chaos can be prevented.[76]

However, while the Qing court had guarded against the spread of roaming braves, it had not decided if it should accommodate these wanderers even after the imperial troops released hundreds of thousands of soldiers. Both harsh and moderate approaches were taken, and the authorities had gradually strengthened the investigation of roaming suspects. The problem, then, was the lack of legal grounds to punish roaming braves. In the cases involving the Gelaohui and "fierce smugglers" (*sixiao* 私梟), local authorities could summarily execute the suspects since the state had previously extended the indiscriminate execution not only to robbery but also to smuggling, sectarian activities, resisting arrest, and coin counterfeiting.[77] However, in cases where the braves were simply wandering around, officials could not execute them unless they had previous criminal records, such as deserting from the army or joining banditry. Many officials and literati had expressed sympathy toward vagrants. A large number of wanderers merely committed theft and extortion. Some suffered privations and were forced to take a risk in running smuggling businesses.[78] As a result, it was difficult to determine if these wanderers should be executed when they had not committed crimes but might yet cause disturbance to local communities.

Although the Qing court had not yet enacted a summary execution law for roaming braves, the monarch and governors had repeatedly elaborated the necessity of executing these wanderers. In September 1864, two months after the recovery of Nanjing, the Jiangning military general Fuminga (富明阿) disbanded his troops in the south and headed north to assist in the suppression of Gansu bandits. The emperor reminded him to capture all the disturbing roaming braves along his trip to the north, and make sure "no [roaming braves] escaped unpunished."[79] In the same year, the Hunan Governor Yun Shilin (惲世臨) permitted local militia to execute roaming braves without prior report. He argued that "only through these strict precautions will the roaming braves not fulfill their wishes; these measures could also make them repent and turn them into good people."[80] Two years later, when Zeng Guofan was battling against Nian rebels, the emperor reminded Zeng and his collaborating generals that "there were many defeated troops, and thus it's necessary to use massive military force to suppress all these braves."[81] In 1867, fearing the spread of Gelaohui, the Tongzhi court also commanded all officials to summarily execute any roaming brave who had contact with bandits.[82]

Some governors considered moderate approaches, including sending braves to cultivate land. However, these approaches could not stop braves from wandering around.[83] In some cases, the braves' disturbance to local communities even forced local people to become "bandits." In February 1868, the General of Uliastai, Deleke Duoerji (德勒克多爾濟), reported from the suppression frontlines of Mongolia that many of the "bandits" were actually refugees. A number of soldiers had escaped from the troops. They robbed local communities and forced local people to resist against the imperial army. In response, the Tongzhi court ordered the military to provide funds for disbanded soldiers to return home. At the same time, the imperial center also directed local authorities to expel all these roaming braves.[84] This response revealed the paradoxical approaches taken by the imperial court. Borrowing the words of the court, the imperial policy was to "neither push [roaming braves] too harshly nor tolerate their rampaging."[85]

The Qing court once again considered the policy that they had promoted before—recruiting these wanderers into the imperial military system. The Taiping Rebellion proved that this policy could not only supplement the weakening standard force but also place the unruly braves under the control of the military. The imperial center also knew that the wide expansion of braves was more an institutional issue than a mere social problem. Several months after Deleke Duoerji's report, the chief executive for the Minister of War, Li Yanghua (李揚華), challenged the existing policies by proposing an entirely different approach. Concerning both finance and public security issues, Li argued that many troops lied about the number of their braves so that the government could grant them more money for salaries. Such behavior was certainly intolerable within the government's system, particularly when the government was unable to afford the huge military expenditure. However, the original military force of the empire, the Green Standard Army, had been weakening for decades and wasted more money than the recruited braves. Given that the large number of disbanded braves would exacerbate the already worsening social problems, Li suggested that the imperial court "selectively replace" (*tiaobu* 挑補) the weakening Green Standard Army with roaming braves.[86]

The financial issues with the Green Standard Army had existed for many years. Only a few years earlier, Zeng Guofan criticized the state for "feeding the Green Standard Army for two centuries" although it was still unable to resist against the rebels.[87] The government was gradually unable to afford the salaries and even had no funds to upgrade and repair weapons.[88] During the Taiping Rebellion, the Green Standard Army also experienced scandals concerning lying about the amount of rice for soldiers.[89] Weighing between the braves and standard forces, the emperor wondered what the governors thought of Li's suggestion.[90] Replacing problematic troops with yet another problematic army might not be a good idea, but the replacement might help improve national defense at less cost. The emperor then forwarded his correspondence with Li to the governors. He knew that previous emperors had disbanded regular forces after significant battles. He was just not sure if it was appropriate to replace the formal troops with roaming braves, who had been a serious trouble to the military and local communities.

Probably because Li's suggestion criticized the governors for rounding up the number of braves, there were no immediate responses during this heated moment. Governors had been frequently granted the authority to command regular armies, but they had to avoid any suspicion of scandal. The emperor was cautious about this issue. He knew that some governors-general would disagree with Li. Four years earlier, when Zeng Guofan decided to disband his

Xiang Army, the imperial censor Chen Tingjing (陳廷經) had suggested that the court replace regular soldiers with disbanded braves. Zeng immediately responded and criticized the idea of "selective replacement":[91]

> Recently, many officials suggested replacing regular soldiers with selected braves. I respectively disagree with this idea. The main reason is that the ration of braves was two times that of cavalries and three times that of garrison soldiers. The cavalries had only a few vacancies, and the garrison soldiers received only one *liang* of ration—it's totally insufficient to live on. Who would like to travel thousands of *li* to just fill the vacancies and receive little money? Most of my honest Hunan braves would not like to serve as a Sanjiang Green Standard Army soldier. Only a few of them might be interested in filling the vacancy, and these interested braves must be idle, lazy, and wandering around without going home.[92]

Zeng suggested the court send these braves back to their native places. For the regular soldiers, he argued that each brigade should recruit new soldiers from its locality. "This will be the best plan for the long future," Zeng stated.[93]

Zeng's reluctance to transform his braves into regular soldiers was closely related to the recruitment institutions. Ever since the latter years of the Taiping Rebellion, the Ministry of War had commanded the provinces to follow the recruitment procedures and fill up the required quota for each jurisdiction.[94] Such recruitment had to follow the formal regulations in terms of management and dismissal. Contrary to this, the recruitment procedure for the braves was flexible, and the disbanding of these braves was relatively easy. Military officers could either fire braves or make up inflated figures to the court, whereas in regular troops such behavior was far more difficult. In 1871, the Ministry of War official Hu Jiayu (胡家玉) offered his belated response to Li Yanghua's suggestion. He agreed the actual number of braves was between 50 and 80 percent of the reported number. He argued that disbanding soldiers could not only save money for the military but also reduce the levies of local communities:

> If we calculate the salary based on the Xiang Army's regulations, a thousand braves will take 5,800 *liang*, ten thousand braves will need 58,000 *liang*, and one hundred thousand braves need 580,000 *liang*. If it's two hundred thousand braves, the salaries will reach 14 million or 15 million *liang*. . . . All these expenditures, including the salaries of bureau staff, the labour fee paid to the petty officials, and the rations for the garrison braves, come from the taxes squeezed out of ordinary people. Not to mention that local authorities had a wide array of levies and taxes with a multitude of names and all sorts of traps.[95]

When the nation's coffers were increasingly deficient, both central and regional governments were reluctant to turn the braves into formal soldiers.

The operation of the Green Standard Army not only enhanced the state's financial burden but also involved complex interactions between various regional authorities, including Governors, Regional Commanders (*zongbing* 總兵), Provincial Military Commanders (*tidu* 提督), and the Residence Military Commander (*zhufang jiangjun* 駐防將軍).[96] The management of braves was relatively flexible, but regional officials had to impose heavy levies for maintaining the armies, and this could draw resistance from local people. The best policy was to disband both regular soldiers and military braves and then execute the disbanded braves who were wandering around. Only a few officials would show sympathy toward roaming braves. Such sympathy rarely received support from other officials.

In 1875, the Viceroy of Liangjiang, Liu Kunyi (劉坤一), suggested that the court command the governors to be merciful and recruit roaming braves. Citing the regulation of Jiangxi, Liu argued that this policy could be extended to other provinces. Since finances were a major concern of regional authorities, Liu suggested reducing the salaries to half of the amount of regular pay. The new emperor, Guangxu, who was then under the influence of Empress Dowager Cixi, expressed concern about the hardship of roaming braves. He commanded governors to recruit braves, but he also reiterated that this was "entirely at the governor's discretion" and that governors should never tolerate any vicious brave.[97] Liu's approach was quickly criticized. Among others, Li Hanzhang criticized that the recruitment would increase military expenditure without preventing these braves from disturbing local security.[98] Li's argument was based on his experiences fighting against roaming braves.[99] As with Zeng Guofan and Hu Jiayu, Li didn't believe that recruitment could turn these "wild" elements into good ones.[100]

In fact, the 1875 debate was more about the possibility of a nationwide policy than the discussion of "merciful recruitment" at half-priced salaries. Before this, as the Guangxu emperor stated, roaming brave policy was "entirely at the governor's discretion." Liu Kunyi was probably the first governor to ask the court to assign a policy to other governors regarding the roaming brave arrangement. Even the imperial center, which had asked Liu to adopt summary execution in the cases of bandits and unorganized soldiers, did not extend this policy nationally.[101] The throne forwarded Liu's opinion to all the governors, probably in the hope that governors could have a say before adopting another governor's suggestion.

In the following years, the Qing court continued to approve summary execution on a case-by-case basis. In 1882, the imperial center finally set its policy toward the roaming braves. In response to the continued flourishing of unorganized braves, the Qing court approved the revision of the summary execution guideline. The new guideline continued to apply "execution on the spot" to "local bandits" (*tufei* 土匪) and "thieves on horseback" (*mazei* 馬賊), while adding "roaming braves" and "sect bandits" (*huifei* 會匪) as targets of summary execution.[102] The co-appearance of roaming braves and sect bandits reflected the rationale behind the legislation, which was to prevent unorganized strongmen from joining local sects and rebel groups. In the eyes of the center, their military backgrounds, vagrantlike status, and frequent collective action made these braves more dangerous than the regular individual robbers who, unlike roaming braves, were allowed to receive full and elaborate judicial review as long as they had not committed other serious crimes at the same time.

Although the 1882 guideline derived from the idea that summary execution should be restricted to certain types of cases, it granted governors solid legal grounds on which to execute roaming braves. In the last decades of the Qing dynasty, the official policy of treating roaming braves was to kill them on the spot. However, as the following sections reveal, the determination of roaming braves was largely at the local official's discretion. The suppression of these wanderers inevitably involved abuse of power. Moreover, a number of the organized braves did not act much differently from the roaming braves except for their legitimate affiliation and the power of suppressing illegitimate braves. The blurred boundary between the two constructed a distinct culture of summary execution, which utilized extreme punishment on the one hand and extracted resources from the violence network on the other.

Hunting for the Dangerous Toughs

When the Tongzhi court exhorted the governors to keep a wary eye on wandering toughs, it probably had little knowledge about how officials identified and captured these drifting men. Roaming braves, as Yun Shilin pointed out, "drifted from place to place and, their gathering and departing was extremely uncertain."[103] Yun and other governors repeatedly reported how difficult it was to combat such ghostly and drifting groups. They required *baojia* and militia to patrol every corner of their guarding areas. They also prevented wanderers from connecting with other bandits.[104] Apparently, a large-scale hunt for roaming braves and the unorganized toughs was taking place in the nation.

In 1886, for example, the *Shen Bao* (申報) reported the achievements of the new Zhejiang Governor, Wei Rongguang (衛榮光). The first achievement of Wei's new policy that many people "craned their necks and waited to see," as *Shen Bao* described it, was the intensive campaign of "expelling roaming braves." Wei commanded his subordinates to inspect every teahouse, bistro, inn, and temple. He reiterated that disbanded veterans had received redundancy payments and should never stay away from their home. If they stayed overnight and were caught by officials, they were to be executed right away even if they had committed no felony crime. Anyone who hid these braves or withheld their information from the authorities would also be seriously punished.[105] In essence, Wei's approach did not differ from his predecessor governors of the province.[106] It was intriguing here that the populace and the newspaper editors viewed the punishment of unorganized braves as an important index in defining good officials.

Due to the consistent efforts of the governors, the prefectures and counties in Zhejiang also issued a series of regulations regarding the punishment of roaming braves. In an 1887 Zhejiang announcement, the Surveillance Commissioner reiterated the significance of the *baojia* policy and stipulated a detailed classification of different people. The "vagrants" (*liuyu* 流寓 and *youmin* 遊民) had to be registered with the *baojia* system with a local guarantor. The "*kemin*" (客民; literally "guest people," sometimes interchangeable with the term "Hakka") constituted a separate category within the *baojia* and its leader was required to collaborate with native leaders in the maintenance of order. In contrast, the "roaming braves" were to be expelled, and no one from this category was allowed to stay in the city overnight. The regulation pointed out that some "refugees" (*nanmin* 難民) were previously military braves. Thus, the authorities had to interrogate these people and expel them once it was confirmed they were roaming braves.[107] The differentiation between vagrants and roaming braves reflected the fundamental logic of the Qing government. Roaming braves' backgrounds made them violent and pugnacious. They were difficult to capture, and they were used to the game of cops and robbers. Sometimes these braves acted like vagrants, and sometimes they were like rebels. In some cases, they even pretended to be military officers, which was the most intolerable act in the eyes of the authorities.[108]

Similar to many "bandit suppressions," the hunt for roaming braves inevitably involved local politics and abuse of power. Ordinary people did not merely fear the disturbance of roaming braves. They feared everything related to this ghostly group, including being charged with hiding braves or having connections with them. The severe punishment compelled people to find a way to protect themselves. In many cases, roaming braves were not very different from vagrants or ordinary people. Teahouses and hotels usually detected suspects by their "Huguang accent," an accent that had been reportedly spoken by many Xiang Army's braves. In Hangzhou, some teahouse owners suspected those who spoke Wenzhou or Taizhou dialects and acted in a different way toward ordinary people.[109] Such identification measures were inevitably arbitrary, and the results could bring disaster to the suspects, as the punishment was summary execution.

In 1883, a monk at the Huanglong Cave (*Huanglongdong* 黃龍洞), one among various caves that had long attracted tourists outside the Qiantang Gate of Hangzhou, met a military officer demanding to inspect his cave. The officer had a Huguang accent. He dressed in imperial robe and hat and commanded eight soldiers. Claiming to have the order of Zhejiang Governor Liu Bingzhang (劉秉璋), the officer said that he intended to check whether any roaming brave, bandit, or unauthorized weapon was hiding in the area. These words terrified the monk. He kneeled down and argued that there were no such things in the cave. The officer was apparently unsatisfied with this answer. He commanded his soldiers to search the cave, discovering a western-style gun, a pack of gunpowder, a long spear, and several daggers. The monk then quickly kneeled down again, stating that these weapons were for hunting animals only. The officer was extremely angry. He threatened to send the monk to the governor's office. Fearing serious punishment, the monk agreed to pay 80 *yang* dollars to the officer. Since there were only 40 dollars in the cave, he signed a note promising that he would pay the rest in ten days. After the officer and soldiers had left, the monk went to see a Hunan military official to check whether there was any inspection in the area. He quickly realized that there was no such officer in the camp, and the governor had never issued such a command. In ten days, when the fake military officer came back to the cave, the monk ordered ten strong men to catch him. They sent him to the military camp while the pretend soldiers, who all seemed to be roaming braves, escaped arrest.[110]

The Huanglong Cave case not only reveals that braves attempted to impersonate officers[111] but also demonstrates the popular fear of the charge of being associated with braves. People feared to get involved in an official's investigation because the judicial process might bring disastrous treatment and severe punishment. On the other hand, government inspection was inevitably arbitrary, particularly because of the difficulty of identifying braves. Accents and the possession of weapons were the most common elements considered in the interrogation. In actual practice, local officials might abuse punishment in order to report their achievements to superior officials. As Tan Sitong (譚嗣同) noted in 1897, the interrogation utterly disregarded human lives:

> When the authorities found a vagrant, they first confirmed if he was a military brave. If he were, he would be executed on the spot. Then the local officers could report to their supervising officials that they had killed several roaming braves [as though they had made certain achievements].[112]

In general, military authorities and local administrators rarely gave sufficient investigation to those without influential supporters. Many common criminals were falsely accused of being roaming braves.[113] The extensive expulsion further enhanced the possibility of abuse. In May 1877, a robbery occurred in Changxing County, Zhejiang. On the night of May 2nd,[114] several armed mobsters robbed the house of the Hu family. Hu Youmao (胡有毛) was fatally injured by the robbers. His son, Hu Shungou (胡順狗), was hidden in the dark and could see that half of the robbers were military braves. The next day, Hu Shungou reported the case to the magistrate. On May 4th, two captured roaming braves confessed the crime and stated that soldiers in the Chu Army conceived the entire plan. The magistrate then turned to the Chu Army camp and found five soldiers involved in the robbery. The five braves quickly admitted their offense and also confirmed the identity of several other accomplices.

The Vice Commander of the Chu Army, Neng Changfu (能常富), then tried to make a compromise with Hu, but the latter rejected it. Finding his compromise did not work, Neng insisted that the two roaming braves were the principal offenders. He did not follow the regular procedure of conveyance and detained the suspects in his camp. He had Zhang Chengyuan (張成元) pretend to be provincial messengers and claimed that the wanderers were responsible for the crime, and the five soldiers should be released. The magistrate declined to release the soldiers since they had made confessions. A provincial officer then interrogated the soldiers, and the soldiers repeated their confession. At this point, the military officer Zhu Mingliang (朱明亮) suddenly threatened the soldiers, stating that such an offense would result in beheading, at which point the five soldiers quickly withdrew their confessions. They were returned to the camp without any punishment. In order to match the number of the accused listed in the records of the investigation, the military captured another three wanderers to join the two captured earlier. The five roaming braves then became the accused and were sent for review and sentencing.[115]

Furious at the adjudication, Hu Shungou brought the case to the capital in October. The imperial court sent the imperial censor to investigate. It also required the Zhejiang Governor Mei Qichao to investigate the responsibilities of Neng Changfu and Zhu Mingliang.[116] While the result of this case remains unknown, it suggests that the politics of labeling consistently appeared in the persecution of roaming braves. Both authorities and ordinary people presumed that roaming braves were felony offenders. They particularly could not bear that these braves sometimes served as military soldiers and sometimes acted as bandits. Such sentiment enabled local officials to manipulate the truth during the judicial process. The summary execution policy also allowed the authorities to make up achievements in the reports to higher officials.

Moreover, while a large portion of disbanded braves wandered around by themselves without joining any organization, many of them turned to organized groups to seek safety and make a living. The majority of these organizations derived from the need for mutual help. The practices of these popular organizations did not necessarily result in revolt and rebellion.[117] Nevertheless, in keeping with the trend of increasing braves and social unrest, brotherhood societies were inevitably involved in local conflicts and illegal activities, including banditry, rebellion, and later on in the revolution that facilitated the fall of the dynasty.

One of the most significant phenomena was the fast spread of Gelaohui and the large number of braves it recruited following the fall of the Taiping Kingdom.[118] The Gelaohui was based on the centuries-long tradition of local organizations among peripheral groups and ethnic minorities in Sichuan, Hunan, and Hubei. The predecessor of this organization incorporated a wide range of resources from predatory groups in the eighteenth century, and then in the mid–nineteenth century it became known as *Gelaohui*.[119] Although the Gelaohui had developed certain hierarchical structures and specific religious rituals, it had a relatively high level of flexibility in terms of organization and activity.[120] Members could move and spread their business to other regions. This was particularly favorable to roaming braves, who had been used to a life of relocation and changing identities. Braves usually moved and acted together with their closest brothers in the organizations. They moved from one place to another in order to find new sources of profit and escape government persecution. Gelaohui members spread around all kinds of places, including cities, villages, mountains, and river ports. Their actions also varied. Some of them conducted illegal trade, and others engaged in robbery.[121] Sometimes they acted just like normal vagrants in the hope that the authorities would take mercy on them and provide famine relief or accommodation.[122]

In 1876, the Shitai County Magistrate arrested a group of six people whom he perceived to be ne'er-do-wells (*wulairen* 無賴人). Some of these people were craftsmen. Others ran small businesses. The magistrate commanded his subordinates to search their houses, and they discovered a white cloth printed with the words "Daxing Mountain Songbo Tang" (*Daxingshan songbo tang* 大興山松柏堂). Seizing on the word *tang*, the magistrate held this group to be "Gelao sect bandits." According to their confession, the group leader, Xu Gui (徐貴), was previously a brave in the military. He reportedly gathered several roaming braves to join the sect, asking all his followers to listen to his words and the commands from their headquarters on the Mountain of Nine Dragons (Jiulongshan 九龍山; Jiulong Mountain), a mountain at the borders of Zhejiang, Jiangxi, and Fujian provinces where many bandits and local marginalized groups gathered. Xu further confessed that he avoided using the term *Gelao* in the group's name because this term was highly sensitive. He stated that his group had created a secret way of communication, using invisible ink that could be seen only after immersion in alcohol.[123]

This arrest quickly caught the attention of the *Shen Bao*, one of the largest Chinese-language newspapers, which was founded in 1872. During its founding years, the newspaper extensively cited imperial edicts and the government-sponsored *Peking Gazette* (*Jing Bao* 京報). The reports inevitably contained a large number of negative terms about executed criminals, and the contents were based on the imperial authority's perspective.[124] From about 1876, *Shen Bao* started to increase the number of original reports about cases involving bandit suppression. This case was one of them, and the reporter explicitly compared this incident with another case he had recently reported. After a close comparison of the cases, the reporter stated that the slogans and commanding system of the two groups were very different. The members of Xu's group were mere pickpockets and petty pilferers and should not be treated in the same way as sect bandits were treated. Unfortunately for Xu and his followers, the magistrate did not further investigate this case. The six convicts were summarily executed after the county yamen received the command from the provincial government. The reporter sighed over such quick execution for a case that should have been retried. He supposed the strict punishment was to deter subversives, as rumors spread so fast that the Gelaohui were quickly informed of any summary execution.[125]

To a large extent, Gelaohui could not be perceived as a unified or homogeneous group because its divisions were involved in different regions' local politics and social relations. Local officials and local elites conveniently labeled their opponents as sect bandits. This label clouds our understanding of the variations in different regions and their changes over time. During the Taiping Rebellion, the intensified local struggles made competing groups incriminate the other side as Taiping rebels and sect bandits. The term *Gelaohui* was also used distortedly during the post-Taiping era, particularly when the authorities intended to suppress a group that they deemed as a threat. Similarly, the label of "roaming braves" was casually and arbitrarily applied throughout the last decades of the Qing dynasty. People suspected all sorts of strangers, including those enrolled in militaries and even those conventionally labeled as *Hakka* people. The population growth after the eighteenth century created a large flood of vagrants, migrants, and "shed people" (*pengmin*

棚民), particularly in Zhejiang, Jiangxi, and Fujian provinces.[126] The authorities clearly knew that many roaming braves did not commit serious crimes, but the increasing crimes forced them to take certain measures. Regional authorities continued to rely on summary execution, especially because of the increasing number of bandits, the emergence of revolutionaries, and the risky and costly conveyance of prisoners. The imperial court eventually adopted a severe approach after a series of debates on the policies regarding roaming braves.

Battles among Men of Force

Since the Qing government commanded all militia and *baojia* to participate in the suppression of roaming braves, the battles inevitably involved excessive killing and even enhanced rivalries among local communities. This was particularly common during the Taiping Rebellion, when villagers and braves—both organized and unorganized—constantly engaged in feuds and warfare. Local government did not always tolerate private suppression. It had to at least comprehend what was going on and why locals killed the suspects. In 1856, when the civil war was still in its height, local militia at the Baihe County of Shaanxi Province brutally killed over ninety roaming braves in a battle. The county magistrate was astonished by the efficiency of militia, but he exhorted the militants to refrain from indiscriminate killing.[127] In 1859, villagers at the Nankang Prefecture slaughtered four roaming braves and left the corpses at the residence of Tang's family. The Nankang Prefect cautiously investigated this case because the villagers seemed to plant it on Tang's family and their motives remained unclear.[128] Local officials clearly knew that many militias killed these braves not only for suppression but also for revenge or private conflict. In many cases, different branches of militias fought against each other, and their action was not far different from those of bandits and roaming braves.[129]

In 1881, *Shen Bao* reported a case of banditry in eastern Zhejiang. As the reporter argued, ever since the large-scale disbanding of the army, braves existed everywhere, and they tirelessly committed robbery and banditry. Many braves were essentially bandits, although their acts differed from the latter in that they drifted around and never stayed in one place. They sometimes gathered in the name of militia and helped locals to resist against bandits, but they continued to disturb communities and exploit money from local people.[130] In 1889, *Shen Bao* posted a similar report, criticizing military braves for connecting with sectarian members and boat bandits. The report argued that "it was all because of the organization of militia that taught these men unkind behaviors and gave them skills of killing people."[131] In some cases, both locals and government officials felt nervous when they saw a large group of military braves gathered together.[132] Apparently, many locals and elites compared military braves and militia to those they were supposed to suppress. These militants possessed a legitimate power of killing, and no one dared to challenge them except those with weapons and strong political resources.[133]

Moreover, a number of militia did not return their weaponries to the government and they refused to disband their members after the task of suppression was completed. Many weapons were in braves' possession. Some of these braves left their militia and used their weapons to rob local communities. Having such uncontrollable collaborators, local government was embarrassed but had no better solution. In 1883, a native of Shanghai was robbed and stabbed by eight roaming braves. According to *Shen Bao*, these robbers either acquired their swords from militias or from the gradually accessible weapon market.[134] In 1887, another robbery case broke out in southern Anhui. This time, over 160 roaming braves were involved. Their weapons were primarily from their previous militias.[135]

In general, the public not only supported but also expected the officials to sweep out the pugnacious braves. Newspaper reports reiterated the necessity of using summary execution for felony crimes.[136] Thanks to the rise of news media, the popular sentiment against roaming braves and the vivid accounts of disbanded veterans were recorded together as both text and image. The famous *Dianshizhai Pictorial* (*Dianshizhai huabao* 點石齋畫報), a new Shanghai-based magazine, recorded several illustrations regarding the activities of roaming braves. In a drawing titled "Tiger and the Buffalo Monster Ran out of the Cage" (*hu si chu xia* 虎兕出柙), the pictorial editor told a story about how roaming braves "spread around the villages and increased the incidents of robbery."[137] A group of robbers broke into and robbed a Beijing house. One of them even intended to rape a lady. The lady struggled and bit the robber on the right wrist. The next day, the family reported the case to the Beijing Gendarmerie, and the latter promised to investigate the case. After the Gendarmerie's commander arrived in the house, the lady found that the bandits were among the troops. She told the commander that the one who intended to rape her was one of his soldiers, and asked him to check all the soldiers' wrists. The rapist was then found, and the commander felt very embarrassed. He asked the family to conceal this scandal from the public. He then commanded his subordinates to conciliate the case and deal with the aftermath.

As the title of the illustration suggests, the editor asserted that the commander had allowed his bandits-turned-soldiers to "run out of the cage." The editor stated,

> Our military was built to battle against the bandits, not to hide bandits in the troops. Ever since the roaming braves spread around the villages, the incidents of robbery increased. The cases usually could not be tracked down, and the authorities still asserted that the offending braves had been disbanded. These braves were supposed to be the ones who captured bandits, but they committed banditry themselves. . . . In this [house-breaking and rape] incident, the commander neglected the problem beforehand and then intended to conceal the fact afterwards. The tiger and the buffalo monster had run out of the cage. Who should be responsible for this?

While the nature of roaming braves was not far different from those hired by the military and local militia, newspapers and popular narratives usually depicted them as petty criminals. In an illustration entitled "The Escort Threw the Dart," a group of roaming braves were roaming and hiding in the narrow ways and alleys. When an apprentice of a rice shop carried 80 *yang* dollars for buying goods, they came out and robbed him of the money. The apprentice cried for help. A street escort quickly came out and threw a dart at the robbers. The dart hit a robber and shot the money he carried out of his hand. The escort quickly took the money and returned it to the apprentice.[138]

The scene of this incident resembled many other narratives. These braves drifted around and hid in small alleys. They looked like petty thieves and acted like aggressive robbers. All of these braves looked sly, repulsive, and cowardly, while the escort was portrayed as muscular, upright, and sincere. Braves robbed on the street during the day and fled away before the crowds. All of these behaviors were hateful to the public. People could not believe these gangsters dared to commit crimes in such an impudent way. As will be discussed in the next section, the masses usually demanded timely justice against the roaming braves. Such sentiment resembled the dart of the escort, which, as the *Dianshizhai Pictorial* said, arrived at a "timely and appropriate moment."[139]

Militia certainly were one of the most stable collaborators of the authorities. In the trend of local militarization, militia gained its legitimacy from both government and local society. However, its actions could not stay aloof from local politics and social relations. Sometimes, militia appeared reluctant to suppress the groups as officials expected them to do. The underlying cause varied from case to case. But the correlation between militia and other groups usually played a role, and the leaders of militants had to calculate the benefit they would gain from suppressing a targeted criminal. In an 1885 case of Fuzhou, a group of twenty to thirty roaming braves broke into a prison and rescued several criminals who had previously worked with them in the military. The nearest militia quickly detected this incident. Having thought it was a feud between local groups, the militia decided not to take any action because, as its post officer stated, "it was unnecessary to interfere with the matters among common people."[140] The braves and prisoners then successfully fled. The local government had no choice but to set a price for capturing these criminals. No one knew if the officer's statement revealed the major concern of the militia. Yet it was quite apparent that local armed groups were not actively involved in suppression if the action could not deliver any benefit and perhaps even bring them troubles in terms of local politics and social relations.

Certainly, on most occasions, militia suppressed roaming braves for the purpose of local defense. They had to do it particularly because local government left the task to them and even reduced the number of formal troops. In the autumn of 1901, a Guangxi merchant shipped two hundred boxes of opium and tobacco from Liuzhou to Xiangzhou. When his shipping boat approached the neighboring Wuxuan County, a group of two hundred roaming braves came out and robbed all the goods. The merchant was also abducted by the robbers. All these robbers carried Mauser guns. No villager dared to resist them. When the county government heard of this, it felt helpless because more than half of the county's braves had been disbanded. The Defense Officer Liang Jiazhi (梁家治) quickly contacted local militia leaders and ordered the two nearest militias, Changqing Militia (長慶) and Changshun Militia (長順), to prepare for the defense along the way. The leader of Changqing Militia, Wu Ziqing (吳子卿), was assigned to watch the robbers' movements. For reasons unknown, the robbers encountered Wu and asked him to recruit porters to help them move the goods. Wu then quickly informed other militias. They hid in the places where robbers would bring their captured goods. Soon, the roaming braves appeared. The militias quickly grabbed a chance to attack them, but the enemy's fire was too intense. Liang and his fellows had only simple weapons, and they even had to use hand-to-hand combat. After a fierce battle, Liang and his fellows took back more than twenty boxes of goods. They detected the robbers' next destination, attacked them on the road, and took the robbers' guns. The strong weapons helped the militia kill a number of braves. The rest of the gang fled and let the merchant get away.[141] The militias eventually defended their communities. Their soldiers were apparently outnumbered by the enemies, but they still managed to achieve the victory.

The Ningbo Riot of 1911

After the Qing government initiated the new wave of judicial reforms in 1901, the imperial court encountered numerous challenges from both officials and the populace. The entire nation was unfamiliar with the new system, which downplayed the role of morality and emphasized rules and separation of powers. The abolition of cruel punishments in 1905 forced the authorities to reinforce the use of summary execution. Further complicating matters was the intensified social and political upheaval. Throughout the late nineteenth and early twentieth centuries, the rise of elite activism and the subsequent trend of local factionalism enhanced uncertainty among different social groups.[142] Food riots occurred across the nation.[143] The indemnities brought by the Boxer Protocol of 1901 enhanced the financial burdens of both government and ordinary people. The so-called "local self-governance" campaigns (*defang zizhi* 地方自治) after 1905 even became a new arena for elites and governments to impose taxes on local residents. It was a period when the tensions between different social groups and local officials frequently aggravated and extended fierce local conflicts. Any controversial policies would result in discontent as the populace gradually became dissatisfied with new changes and the worsened situation.

The 1911 Ningbo Riot reflected these tensions. In May 1911, when Ningbo's district court and prosecution office had been established for only half a year,[144] a robbery case triggered great turmoil in the city. The incident transpired on the first day of May.[145] Fang Desheng (方得勝), a roaming brave, banded together with other two fugitives, Ye Fubiao (葉福表) and Fan Laozong (范老總), to rob a money shop in the Quanjiawan region. On that morning, the three vagrants drifted around the region to look for a target. When they saw people exchanging currency at the Xindeshun Shop (新德順), they entered the shop, snatched the coins on the counter, and quickly ran away.[146] The shop's owner, Sheng Shanxiang (盛善香), could not catch the offenders. His neighbor, Bao Renbao (鮑仁寶), made attempts to stop them and was stabbed by Fang. A shoe-store manager witnessed the situation and grappled with the assailant. He, too, was stabbed by Fang and then fell down in the street. Fang and Ye ran away and threw their daggers into a brook. A policeman, Peng Fuchen (彭福臣), heard about this and hurried to the spot. He and the villagers finally caught Fang but were unable to locate Fang's fleeing companions in the ensuing search.[147]

Fang, a twenty-eight-year-old male from Xiangshan County, was sent to the prosecution office for preliminary procedures. The prosecutor conducted a quick investigation and then sent him to court for a preliminary trial. During the trial, Fang confessed that he was once a soldier at the Shaoxing military training unit in 1904. He was laid off by the military and was ordered to return to his hometown. In the following years, Fang wandered around different cities.[148] Three years earlier, Fang appeared to have committed larceny in Shanghai after he left the army.[149] During the trial, however, Fang refused to admit involvement in any prior crime. He asserted that he had only recently moved to Ningbo on April 25 and then resided in the front of the New City God Temple. During a short stay in Ningbo, he met Ye Fubiao and Fan Laozong. On the date that they committed the robbery, they chatted about their miserable life in front of the temple. Fang proposed a robbery, and the two companions agreed to join. They then committed the crime that ultimately brought him to trial.[150]

The preliminary trial judge summoned Sheng Shanxiang to confront the suspect and quickly sent the case to formal trial. From the report of the Ningbo court and prosecution published in June 1911, it appears that the prosecutor did not accuse Fang in writing but instead orally accused him. In the formal adjudication, the judge adopted the evidence collected in pretrial procedures. He ruled that Fang was not a soldier when he committed the crime, thus the court needed to adhere to the regular statutes. He further reasoned that according to Qing law, a "robbery" (*qianduo* 搶奪) case where three or more offenders were involved and had used weapons to injure the owners of the lost belongings (*shizhu* 事主) was analogous to a case of "theft with force" (*qiangdao* 強盜).[151] In this case, the injured neighbor, Bao Renbao, was not "the owner of the lost belongings," but the judge asserted that a neighbor injured at the gate of a shop should be regarded as no different from an owner injured at his shop. The court then concluded that Fang should be sentenced to "immediate strangulation" (*jiao lijue* 絞立決).[152] According to the Great Qing Code, those who committed "theft with force" and obtained property should be beheaded, not strangled. Furthermore, the Code stipulated that the leader of the offense of "daylight robbery" who injured others should be sentenced to "beheading with delay" (*zhan jianhou* 斬監候) rather than "immediate strangulation."

Complicating the application of the law in this case was that, earlier in 1911, the imperial court had enacted the "New Criminal Law of Great Qing" (*Da Qing xin xinglü* 大清新刑律), which did not allow execution by beheading. The court did not mention which laws it cited, but it is clear that it did not follow the Great Qing Code and its accompanying substatutes. Neither "immediate strangulation" nor "beheading with delay" were to be executed until the Board of Law had reviewed the case. That is to say, the court did not need to request permission for summary execution from either the High Court or the provincial government.

As Fang was not to be executed summarily, he still had some time before his execution. He was sent to the Yin County prison for detention. However, the events that followed shocked not only the officials but also the entire city and province. While Fang was tried in court, some residents gathered around the court building and called for his summary execution. They were angered when the judgment was announced. They shouted at the officials, asking them to immediately behead the criminal in front of them. The prosecutor told the crowd that Fang would be executed regardless of what procedures were applied. Furious at this answer, thousands of people flooded into the court. They damaged signs and vandalized the reception room, patrol room, guest room, and investigation room. They also broke windows, doors, and the officials' carts. The riot in the court building lasted for seven hours.[153] The crowd yelled, "It is a daylight robbery! If the offender is not immediately executed on the spot, we can also rob a rice shop, too!" Soon after, mobs attacked two rice shops in front of the drum tower and took most of the rice. They claimed that they would continue robbing rice shops around the city. The owners of the nearby rice shops heard about this and quickly closed down the market as a demonstration (*bashi* 罷市).[154] The riot was about to worsen, and the officials became anxious and unsure of how to handle the city's rising turmoil.

To the citizens of Ningbo, the riot over Fang Desheng was not new. In May 1906, thousands of short-term workers at rice shops protested against the shops and asked them to raise their salary. Many workers found it hard to make a living, while the shops earned a great fortune through raising the price of rice. Some rioters destroyed the rice shops and attacked the officials who came to mediate the conflict. The County Magistrate, with the approval of the Provincial Governor, arrested one of the rioters, Ye Changcai (葉昌才), and quickly executed him. The crowd then stopped their protest and returned to their work, but the tension between workers and rice shop owners remained.[155] In February 1907, the price of rice increased again. The County Magistrate was afraid that poor people would protest, thus he reduced the price of the lower-quality rice and maintained the price of higher-quality rice.[156] Rice prices and living difficulties had always been one of the most important issues of popular protest.[157] The execution of rioters was one among many solutions for such incidents, while the execution of criminals at times had the effect of extinguishing rising outrage.

When the riot broke out after Fang's trial, the officials in front of the crowd did not know how to cope with the situation. The prosecutors sent telegrams to provincial governors asking for military support. The troops came over quite late, and only sixteen soldiers in total were sent.[158] Both the County Magistrate, Zheng Lirong (鄭禮融), and the head of the Ningbo District Court, Jin Minlan (金泯瀾), came over. Jin found the situation was beyond his control and asked the judges to send Fang Desheng to the crowd and "let them decide how to punish him." Fang was almost handed over to the rioters, but the judges interceded, stopped Jin, and returned Fang to the court building. Fang was then sent to the county prison under the protection of some security crews.[159] The crowd moved to the prison and vowed to destroy the county yamen building. The prosecution office sent telegrams to the Governor and the Board of Law. No one replied. The police arrested three members of a mob that had robbed rice shops, but the protest did not cease.[160]

At seven o'clock that night, rain suddenly started pouring down and the crowd started to leave. The prosecutors tried again to contact higher officials to seek help. This time, Ningbo Prefect Deng Benkui (鄧本逵) made a short visit to the prosecution office and promised to deploy troops to protect the court building and the prison. He then quickly left. The Police Commissioner, Liu Cailiang (劉采亮), also came to the court, but the crowd had left much earlier.[161] No one else came over during the night. Even the crowd did not gather again after the rain. It was a peaceful night indeed. However, no one really knew what would transpire the next day.

The next morning, at around eight o'clock, the prosecutors finally heard news about the reaction of Ningbo-Shaoxing-Taizhou Circuit Intendant Sang Bao (桑寶) toward this incident. What surprised them was that Fang Desheng had been summarily beheaded under the "surveillance" (*jianshi zhengfa* 監視正法) of Sang, Deng, and Zheng. The three officials had obviously discussed how to deal with this case beforehand, but they never informed the court and prosecutors of their decision in advance.[162] The angry prosecutor-in-chief Wang Yunian (汪郁年) quickly went to the county yamen building to confront Magistrate Zheng Lirong. Zheng admitted that he did not receive any approval from the Provincial Governor, but he had received a telegram of authorization from Sang. He also reported to the Governor that the riot had been pacified and he had asked the rice merchants to supply the poor with rice. This made Wang and his colleagues feel humiliated because the administrative officials had not respected their ruling and authority. Subject to an open condemnation of the actions of the administrative officials, all the judges and prosecutors resigned from their posts. They condemned the officials for summarily beheading the criminal without informing the court in advance. They opted to resign and cease operating the courts because such "illegal behavior that invaded the authority of the court" had "made the court's ruling invalid."[163]

All these events, from the Fang robbery to the resignation of the court, transpired within twenty-four hours. Trials and prosecutions were shut down for the first time in the city. Many people found nowhere to bring their lawsuits. Even the three arrested rioters had nowhere to be sent for further investigation.[164] The dramatic development of this incident caught the attention of the media. *Shen Bao* followed the aftermath of this incident on a near-daily basis. Noting the conflicts between the administrative and judicial branches, it expressed worry about the future of judicial reform.[165] Since *Shen Bao* had exposed the provincial officials for not responding to the calls of the judges and prosecutors, the Provincial Governor, Zeng Yun (增韞), certainly felt disgraced.

As the highest official of the province who was in charge of the establishment of new-style legal infrastructures, Zeng was fairly aware of the conflicts between the new system and the old bureaucrats at the local level. Magistrates once complained to him that prosecutors enjoyed stronger powers than magistrates, while the magistrates bore more responsibilities than the prosecutors.[166] Only four months before the riot, a new order from the Commission on Studying Constitutional Government restricted summary execution to those who "called each other and formed a gang, resisted against government troops, and acted like rebels."[167] In April, the *New Criminal Law of Great Qing* further prohibited the use of beheading and required all banditry cases to go through new procedures.[168] Apparently, the use of beheading in Fang's case violated the newest law on criminal procedure. The governor needed to find a way to explain why he had tacitly approved such an execution.

Zeng quickly sent telegrams to both judicial and administrative branches. In his telegrams to the administrative officials, Zeng condemned them for not informing the judiciaries before the execution. In the telegram to the judicial officers, Zeng stated that he had ordered administrators to investigate the rioters. He then asserted that judges and prosecutors should stay at their post and he would not approve their resignations.[169] Zeng cited the *Current Criminal Law of Great Qing* (enacted in 1909), in which both strangulation and beheading were allowed, and that in the case of banditry by soldiers, the leader should be sentenced to immediate beheading. He also asked the Police Commissioner Liu Cailiang to resign to show that the major responsibility was with Liu and no one else.[170] Under Zeng's influence, the Zhejiang Department of Justice (*Tifa si* 提法司) asserted that the main issue was "foolish rioters" who refused to listen to reason. The judges correctly applied the law, and there was no need for them to resign.[171]

The court and prosecutors also had some words to say. They made a public announcement explaining how ordinary people distrusted their judgment. Since the new Westernized law protected defendants' rights, people always presumed that the new court was lenient to criminals and even tolerated banditry. They disrespected both judges and prosecutors. When prosecutors performed autopsies, people even disrupted and insulted them. Moreover, during the riot, administrative officials did not support the court. The court was isolated, and the law was not respected. As a result, the judges and prosecutors had no other choice but to resign from their position.[172]

For reasons unknown, the judges and prosecutors quickly resumed their posts after two days. Most people were more concerned about maintaining public security than applying the law correctly. Although the media had expressed concern about the future of judicial reform, they did not support the resignation of judicial authorities. Most of their reports were about the riot and the recovery of local order. The administration's invention in judicial power was not journalists' major concern. In a later report from the Provincial Governor to the Prime Minister of the Imperial Cabinet, the Governor explained that in Ningbo, "Chinese and foreigners mixed together and rascals and hooligans filled up the city." The rising price of food and the shortage of silver further exacerbated the situation.[173] The reply from the Prime Minister to the Provincial Governor also asked the Governor to "squelch the riot seriously and never let any trouble start."[174] Of course, these were the perspectives of the officials, but such perspectives were prevailing among officials and elites across the nation. After these reports, no one mentioned the incident except for the provincial representatives.[175] A few months later, the 1911 Revolution started. All of these conflicts about summary execution, Western-styled law, and the masses remained unresolved. They were to become the problems of the Republican era.

From the case of Fang Desheng, one can see that summary execution was upheld as a common procedure to deal with robbers and rioters. The new laws and court system restricted the application of summary execution procedures, but the officials and the masses were still inclined to employ such procedures. In fact, throughout the entire reform period, the authorities never wished to surrender such a useful institution. What made events further complicated is that if the officials did not carry out executions as the crowd demanded, a riot could occur and challenge the authority of the government. This is the irony of summary execution: it was not merely a tool of the officials but also a discursive weapon of the ordinary people. The officials could always find a way to legitimize their action of maintaining the exceptional summary execution procedures, but they could hardly legitimize riots by the masses in the name of demanding justice in a prompt manner.

Conclusion

From the practice of summary execution in late Qing China, one can see how exceptional punishment was systematically sanctioned by the state, regional government, and local people. Originating as an expedient measure to address social problems and political upheaval, the institution gradually became a tool that expelled certain groups of people, including the braves that had long served as the collaborators of the state throughout the trend of local militarization. The extreme punishment and the widespread coercion of men of force jointly constituted China's distinct trajectory of "local militarization" and the growing culture of rough justice. This culture, as this chapter argues, blurred the boundary between "legality" and "illegality" and further revealed how these two coexisted in the making of modern Chinese legal culture.

Moreover, continued warfare facilitated the spread of men of force, while the reaction of the state and society consistently extended their exclusion. The epidemic of organized and unorganized toughs legitimized the use of exceptional punishment, which was applied so extensively that it came to appear as if it were a regular procedure. The government's campaign reinforced the popular imagination against bandits and roaming braves. Newspaper reports further spread such ideas to many classes of people. These influences jointly constructed Chinese rough justice and differentiated China's trajectory from many other countries. During the Nationalist era (1927–1949) and the early decades of the People's Republic of China, summary execution continued to be an important part of political propaganda and mobilization. The late Qing practice of summary execution laid the foundation for later developments, systematically shaping popular sentiment for the use of violence or quick execution against politically labeled villains or "society's enemy."

Notes

I'd like to thank Professors Thomas Buoye and Yiching Wu for their valuable comments on my chapter.

    1. *Da Qing Wenzong Xian (Xianfeng) Huangdi Shilu* 大清文宗顯皇帝實錄, in *Da Qing lichao shilu* 大清歷朝實錄 (Taipei: Huawen, 1964 reprint), Xianfeng, 88: 165a.

    2. *Da Qing Wenzong Xian (Xianfeng) Huangdi Shilu*, 55: 737a; *Da Qing Wenzong Xian (Xianfeng) Huangdi Shilu*, 72: 946b; *Da Qing Wenzong Xian (Xianfeng) Huangdi Shilu*, 85: 112a; *Da Qing Wenzong Xian (Xianfeng) Huangdi Shilu*, 86: 116b.

3. In addition to the procedures of "instant execution without any time restriction" (*budaishi* 不待時), "instant execution without full adjudication" (*buyiting* 不以聽), "respectfully invoking the king's authority of executing criminals" (*sujiang wangzhu* 肅將王誅), and various forms of "actions in militarized manners" (*junxing congshi* 軍興從事), one noted origin of the institution of Chinese summary execution was the Shangfang Sword (*shangfang jian* 尚方劍 or 上方劍, also known as *shangfang baojian* 尚方寶劍, *zhanma jian* 斬馬劍, and *duanma jian* 斷馬劍), whose name derived from the Qin-Han officials manufacturing palace commodities and weaponry. Since the Tang dynasty, the imperial court increasingly rewarded the Shangfang Sword, banner (*sheng* 旌), and tally (*jie* 節) to prestigious officials. As *Ming Shilu* reveals, the Shangfang Sword was frequently used during the late Ming. For the early development of summary execution in Chinese history, see Weiting Guo, "The Speed of Justice: Summary Execution and Legal Culture in Qing Dynasty China, 1644–1912" (PhD diss., University of British Columbia, forthcoming), Ch. 1. For the procedure of "king's order" and the Qianlong emperor's reform on summary execution, see Guo, "Speed of Justice," Ch. 2.

4. For the development of "rootless rascal" laws, see Guo, "Speed of Justice," Ch. 2; Zhang Guanghui 張光輝, "Ming-Qing xinglü zhong de 'guanggun zui'" 明清刑律中的"光棍罪," *Asian Studies* 아시아연구, 5 (2008): 147–160. For the translation of *guanggun*, see Matthew Sommer, *Sex, Law, and Society in Late Imperial China* (Stanford: Stanford University Press, 2000), 97.

5. For the development of summary execution laws during the Qing dynasty, see Guo, "Speed of Justice"; Suzuki Hidemitsu 鈴木秀光, "Gongqing wangming kao: Qing dai sixing panjue de 'quanyi' yu 'dingli'" 恭請王命考: 清代死刑判決的'權宜'與'定例', *Neimenggu shifan daxue xuebao* 內蒙古師範大學學報 38 (2009): 23–37; Suzuki Hidemitsu, "'Seishi sokkō shōbō' kō: Shindai kenryū kakeiki ni okeru shikei saiban seido no ichi kōsatsu" 請旨即行正法'考: 清代乾隆嘉慶期における死刑裁判制度の一考察, *Senshū hōgaku ronshū* 專修法學論集 97 (2006): 1–51.

6. See Zhang Shimin, "Qing mo jiudi zhengfa zhidu yanjiu" (shang) (xia) 清末就地正法制度研究(上)(下), *Zhengfa luncong* 政法論叢 2012, No. 1 (2012): 46–57, and 2012, No. 2 (2012): 59–70; Suzuki Hidemitsu, "Gongqing wangming kao."

7. Philip A. Kuhn, *Rebellion and Its Enemies in Late Imperial China: Militarization and Social Structure, 1796–1864* (Cambridge: Harvard University Press, 1970).

8. For an analysis of this reform and its cultural and political backgrounds in a comparative perspective, see Timothy Brook, Jérôme Bourgon, and Gregory Blue, *Death by a Thousand Cuts* (Cambridge: Harvard University Press, 2008).

9. *Zhengzhi Guanbao* 政治官報 172, March 21, 1908, 7–8.

10. See Li Guilian 李貴連, "Wan Qing jiudi zhengfa kao" 晚清就地正法考, *Zhongnan zhengfa xueyuan xuebao* 中南政法學院學報 1994, No. 1 (1994): 81. Many scholars have criticized Li's thesis that summary execution originated during the Taiping Rebellion. Some scholars trace the origin to the late eighteenth and early nineteenth centuries, while others argue that summary execution dates back to at least the Ming dynasty.

11. Xiaoqun Xu, *Trial of Modernity: Judicial Reform in Early Twentieth-Century China, 1901–1937* (Stanford: Stanford University Press, 2008); Zhang Shimin, "Qing mo jiudi zhengfa zhidu yanjiu."

12. Suzuki Hidemitsu, "Zhangbi kao: qingdai zhongqi sixing anjian chuli de yixiang kaocha" 杖斃考: 清代中期死刑案件處理的一項考察, in *Shijie xuezhe lun zhongguo*

chuantong falü wenhua, 1644–1911 世界學者論中國傳統法律文化, eds. Zhang Shiming, Thomas Buoye, and Na Heya 娜鶴雅 (Beijing: Falü chubanshe, 2010), 209–234; Suzuki Hidemitsu, "Cong danxin dang'an kan qingchao houqi xingshi shenpan zhidu de yiban" 從淡新檔案看清朝後期刑事審判制度的一斑, conference paper, Academic Conference for Danxin Archive, National Taiwan University, Taipei, July 15, 2008; Thomas Buoye, "Death or Detainment: The Dilemma of Eighteenth-Century Chinese Criminal Justice," conference paper, International Workshop on Chinese Legal History/Culture/Modernity, Columbia University, New York, May 4–6, 2012. For the development of summary execution in the Republican era, see Xiaoqun Xu, "The Rule of Law without Due Process: Punishing Robbers and Bandits in Early Twentieth-Century China," *Modern China* 33, No. 2 (2007): 230–257.

    13. Mark E. Lewis, *Sanctioned Violence in Early China* (Albany: State University of New York Press, 1990); Barend J. ter Haar, "Rethinking 'Violence' in Chinese Culture," in *Meanings of Violence: A Cross-Cultural Perspective*, eds. Göran Aijmer and Jon Abbink (Oxford: Oxford University Press, 2000), 123–140; David M. Robinson, *Bandits, Eunuchs, and the Son of Heaven: Rebellion and the Economy of Violence in Mid-Ming China* (Honolulu: University of Hawaii Press, 2001); William T. Rowe, *Crimson Rain: Seven Centuries of Violence in a Chinese County* (Stanford: Stanford University Press, 2007); David Der-wei Wang, *The Monster that Is History: History, Violence, and Fictional Writing in Twentieth-Century China* (Berkeley: University of California Press, 2004).

    14. Rowe, *Crimson Rain*, 6–7.

    15. Ibid., 7.

    16. David M. Robinson, *Bandits, Eunuchs, and the Son of Heaven: Rebellion and the Economy of Violence in Mid-Ming China* (Honolulu: University of Hawaii Press, 2001), 2, 100–105, 163.

    17. Philip A. Kuhn, *Rebellion and Its Enemies in Late Imperial China: Militarization and Social Structure, 1796–1864* (Cambridge: Harvard University Press, 1970), 165–188.

    18. Diana Lary, *Warlord Soldiers: Chinese Common Soldiers, 1911–1937* (Cambridge: Cambridge University Press, 2010), 59.

    19. For the rise and institutionalization of popular protest during the mid-Qing period, see Ho-fung Hung, *Protest with Chinese Characteristics: Demonstrations, Riots, and Petitions in the Mid-Qing Dynasty* (New York: Columbia University Press, 2011). For the practice of capital appeal during the Qing dynasty, see Li Dianrong 李典蓉, *Qing chao jingkong zhidu yanjiu* 清朝京控制度研究 (Shanghai: Shanghai guji chubanshe, 2011); Jonathan K. Ocko, "I'll Take It All the Way to Beijing: Capital Appeals in the Qing," *Journal of Asian Studies* 47:2 (1988): 291–315.

    20. Thomas Buoye, "Death or Detainment: The Dilemma of Eighteenth-Century Chinese Criminal Justice," paper presented at the International Workshop on Chinese Legal History, Culture and Modernity at Columbia University on May 4–6, 2012.

    21. Guo, "Speed of Justice," Ch. 2.

    22. I am inspired by the concept of "economy of violence" created by David Robinson, which excellently captures the presence of violence in the shaping of Ming society or, more broadly, Chinese society during the late imperial and modern times. See Robinson, *Bandits, Eunuchs, and the Son of Heaven*, 2.

    23. See, for instance, Robert W. Thurston, *Lynching: American Mob Murder in Global Perspective* (Burlington: Ashgate, 2011); William D. Carrigan and Christopher Waldrep,

eds., *Lynching in Global Historical Perspective* (Charlottesville: University of Virginia Press, 2013); Manfred Berg and Simon Wendt, eds., *Globalizing Lynching History* (New York: Palgrave Macmillan, 2011).

24. The term *reverberate* is inspired by Paul Katz's work. According to him, judicial ritual and other elements of legal culture mutually shaped a wide "judicial continuum" that contained different options for achieving legitimization and dispute resolution in Chinese society. See Paul Katz, *Divine Justice: Religion and the Development of Chinese Legal Culture* (New York: Routledge, 2009), xi, 7, 47–60.

25. This paragraph first appeared on the *Chinese and Foreign Daily* (*Zhongwai ribao* 中外日報). It was reposted by the *Eastern Miscellany* (*Dongfang Zazhi* 東方雜誌). See *Dongfang Zazhi* 2:3 (1905): 66–68.

26. Na Silu 那思陸, *Qingdai zhongyang sifa shenpan zhidu* 清代中央司法審判制度 (Taipei: Wenshizhe chubanshe, 1992), 193–294.

27. *Da Qing Wenzong Xian (Xianfeng) Huangdi Shilu*, 159: 747a–747b; *Da Qing Wenzong Xian (Xianfeng) Huangdi Shilu*, 218: 412b–414a; *Da Qing Wenzong Xian (Xianfeng) Huangdi Shilu*, 283: 146a–146b.

28. *Da Qing Wenzong Xian (Xianfeng) Huangdi Shilu*, 121: 89b–90a.

29. Ibid., 230: 582a.

30. *Da Qing huidian shili* 大清會典事例 (Beijing: Zhonghua shuju, 1991 reprint), Xingbu, juan 850, Guangxu 7 nian, Vol. 9, 1231b–1232b; *Qingshigao* 清史稿 (Taipei: Dingwen, 1981), Liezhuan, juan 450, 11907–11908; Zhongguo diyi lishi dang'an guan 中國第一歷史檔案館, ed., *Qing zhengfu zhenya taiping tianguo dang'an shiliao* 清政府鎮壓太平天國檔案史料 (Beijing: Guangming ribao chubanshe, 1990), Vol. 2, 441.

31. *Da Qing Muzong Yi (Tongzhi) Huangdi Shilu*, 135: 177a–177b.

32. Ibid., 253: 523a–523b.

33. Ibid., 84: 746b–747a.

34. Zhu Shoupeng 朱壽朋, ed., *Donghua xulu (Guangxu chao)* 東華續錄 (光緒朝) (Shanghai: Shanghai jicheng tushu gongsi, 1909), 51–52, 55–56; Li Hongzhang 李鴻章, *Li Hongzhang quanji* 李鴻章全集 (Changchun: Shidai wenyi chubanshe, 1998), 1671.

35. Suzuki Hidemitsu, "Shinmatsu shūchi seihō kō" 清末就地正法考, *Tōyō bunka kankyūjō kiyō* 東洋文化研究所紀要 145 (2004): 35–38.

36. *Da Qing Dezong Jing (Guangxu) Huangdi Shilu*, 60: 831b.

37. *Xing'an huilan* (Taipei: Chengwen, 1968 reprint), Xinzeng xing'an huilan, juan 5, 4919.

38. *Da Qing huidian shili*, Xingbu, juan 850, Guangxu 7 nian, Vol. 9, 1231b–1232b.

39. Philip Huang, *Chinese Civil Justice, Past and Present* (New York: Rowman and Littlefield, 2009), 13–17.

40. Suzuki Hidemitsu, "Zhangbi kao"; Suzuki Hidemitsu, "Cong danxin dang'an kan qingchao houqi xingshi shenpan zhidu de yiban"; Buoye, "Death or Detainment."

41. *Da Qing Xuanzong Cheng (Daoguang) Huangdi Shilu*, 150: 297b–298a.

42. Ibid., 459: 792a–792b.

43. Zeng Guofan 曾國藩, *Zuben Zeng Wenzheng gong quanji* 足本曾文正公全集 (Changchun: Jilin renmin chubanshe, 1995), 1813–1819; *Shen Bao* 3143, January 28, 1882, 3–4.

44. Liu Jinzao 劉錦藻, *Qingchao xu wenxian tongkao* 清朝續文獻通考 (Taipei: Taiwan shangwu yinshuguan, 1987), 9880b.

45. Zeng, *Zuben Zeng Wenzheng gong quanji*, 1817.
46. Ibid.
47. *Zhejiang qing song zhang cheng* 浙江清訟章程, publisher unknown, 1878, rare book, call number 4896 3330, stored at Harvard Depository, Harvard University.
48. For the analysis of this reform and its cultural and political backgrounds in a comparative perspective, see Brook, Bourgon, and Blue, *Death by a Thousand Cuts*.
49. Zhu, *Donghua xulu (Guangxu chao)*, 5028–5029.
50. In 1908, Henan Governor Lin Shaonian (林紹年) also pointed out the important role of summary execution after the abolition of cruel punishments. See *Zhengzhi guanbao*, No. 172, March 21, 1908, 7–8.
51. *Shen Bao* 12201, April 11, 1907, 2–3.
52. Yuan Shuyi 苑書義, ed., *Zhang Zhidong quanji* 張之洞全集, Vol. 11 (Shijiazhuang: Hebei renmin chubanshe, 1998), 9563.
53. *Shen Bao* 12776, August 26, 1908, 4; *Shen Bao* 12963, March 9, 1909, 4.
54. *Shen Bao* 13747, May 19, 1911, 11.
55. *Shen Bao* 13766, June 7, 1911, 6; *Shen Bao* 13772, June 12, 1911, 6.
56. *Shen Bao* 13780, June 20, 1911, 12; *Shen Bao* 13747, May 19, 1911, 11.
57. *Xuantong zhengji* 宣統政紀, in *Da Qing lichao shilu*, 47: 854b–856a.
58. Ibid., 62: 1151a–1152a.
59. *Shen Bao* 13602, December 18, 1910, 4; *Shen Bao* 13622, January 7, 1911, 10–11; *Shen Bao* 13633, January 18, 1911, 5; *Shen Bao* 13663, February 23, 1911, 11; *Shen Bao* 13679, March 11, 1911, 11; *Shen Bao* 13708, April 10, 1911, 3–4; *Xuantong zhengji*, in *Da Qing lichao shilu*, 38: 679a–679b.
60. Zeng Guofan 曾國藩, *Zuben Zeng Wenzheng gong quanji* 足本曾文正公全集 (Changchun: Jilin renmin chubanshe, 1995), 1021–1022.
61. Xue Fucheng 薛福成, *Xue Fucheng xuanji* 薛福成選集 (Shanghai: Shanghai renmin chubanshe, 1987), 304–307.
62. For example, only three years earlier several soldiers in the troops of Hu Linyi (胡林翼) had rioted, carrying swords and requesting wages. The commander quickly executed the rioters. Hu Linyi 胡林翼, *Hu Linyi ji* 胡林翼集 (Changsha: Yuelu shushe, 1999), Vol. 1, 834.
63. Luo Ergan, *Luo Ergan quanji* 羅爾綱全集 (Shanghai: Shehui kexue wenxian chubanshe, 2011), Vol. 14, 158–166.
64. Liu Cheng-Yun 劉錚雲, "Xiangjun yu gelaohui" 湘軍與哥老會, in Zhongyanyuan jinshisuo 中研院近史所, ed., *Jindai Zhongguo quyushi yantaohui lunwenji (shang)* 近代中國區域史研討會論文集（上）(Taipei: Zhongyanyuan jinshisuo, 1986), 389–400.
65. Zeng Guofan, *Zeng Guofan quanji* 曾國藩全集 (Changsha: Yuelu shushe, 1994), Vol. 14, 466.
66. Surrendered soldiers had long annoyed Zeng's troops during the suppression. For example, in 1862, Taiping commander Tong Ronghai (童容海) led over 60,000 soldiers to surrender to the imperial forces. Zeng asked his subordinate commander Bao Chao (鮑超) to deal with Tong's surrender, keeping only 2,000 of Tong's braves and disbanding the rest. The Qing court then asked Zeng to retain more than 2,000 of Tong's soldiers because they worried that the large number of disbanded soldiers would soon become bandits. In some cases, the imperial center preferred using militia because they caused

fewer problems than surrendered troops in terms of postwar dissolution. See *Da Qing Muzong Yi (Tongzhi) Huangdi Shilu*, 35: 948b–949b.

67. *Da Qing Dezong Jing (Guangxu) Huangdi Shilu*, 402: 251b–252a.

68. Zhou Yuming 周育民, "Jiawu zhanghou Qingchao caizheng yanjiu (1894–1899)" 甲午戰後清朝財政研究 (1894–1899), *Zhongguo jingji shi yanjiu* 中國經濟史研究 1989, No. 4 (1984): 88–103; Luo Ergan, *Lüying bingzhi* 綠營兵志 (Beijing: Zhonghua shuju, 1984), 88.

69. *Da Qing Dezong Jing (Guangxu) Huangdi Shilu*, 20: 316a–316b.

70. Zhongguo diyi lishi dang'an guan 中國第一歷史檔案館, "Tongzhi nianjian gelaohui shiliao" 同治年間哥老會史料, *Lishi dang'an* 歷史檔案, 1998, No. 4: 32–43.

71. *Shen Bao* 118, September 14, 1872, 3–4.

72. Liang Qichao 梁啟超, *Yinbingshi heji* 飲冰室合集 (Beijing: Zhonghua shuju, 1989), 130.

73. Luo Ergan 羅爾綱, *Xiangjun bingzhi* 湘軍兵志 (Beijing: Zhonghua shuju, 1984), 54.

74. Taiping tianguo lishi bowuguan 太平天國歷史博物館, ed., *Taiping tianguo shiliao congbian jianji* 太平天國史料叢編簡輯 (Shanghai: Zhonghua shuju Shanghai bianjisuo, 1962), Vol. 3, 373, 387.

75. In fact, many had filed petitions against their opponents after the brutal killing, but the authorities refused to adjudicate these cases as judicial process would only lead to endless disputation and the rivalries would never be eased in the midst of a fierce civil war. See Zeng, *Zuben Zeng Wenzheng gong quanji*, 1145–1146.

76. *Da Qing Muzong Yi (Tongzhi) Huangdi Shilu*, 35: 929a–930a.

77. *Da Qing Wenzong Xian (Xianfeng) Huangdi Shilu*, 230: 582a.

78. *Shen Bao* 4535, November 27, 1885, 1.

79. *Da Qing Muzong Yi (Tongzhi) Huangdi Shilu*, 114: 547b–548a.

80. Yang Yiqing 楊奕青 et al., *Hunan difangzhi zhong de taiping tianguo shiliao* 湖南地方志中的太平天國史料 (Changsha: Yuelu shushe, 1983), 129–130.

81. *Da Qing Muzong Yi (Tongzhi) Huangdi Shilu*, 143: 370a–370b.

82. Ibid., 211: 738a–739a.

83. See, for instance, ibid., 112: 236a–237a.

84. Ibid., 260: 617a–617b.

85. Ibid., 262: 634b–635b.

86. Ibid., 247: 435a–435b.

87. Luo, *Luo Ergan quanji*, Vol. 14, 161.

88. Hsu Hsueh-chi 許雪姬, *Qingdai Taiwan de lüying* 清代台灣的綠營 (Taipei: Zhongyang yanjiuyuan jindaishi yanjiusuo, 1987), 67–68.

89. *Da Qing Muzong Yi (Tongzhi) Huangdi Shilu*, 116: 840a.

90. Ibid., 247: 435a–435b.

91. Zeng, *Zuben Zeng Wenzheng gong quanji*, 346.

92. Ibid., 346.

93. Ibid.

94. See, for instance, *Da Qing Muzong Yi (Tongzhi) Huangdi Shilu*, 107: 352b.

95. Gu Tinglong 顧廷龍 and Dai Yi 戴逸, eds., *Li Hongzhang quanji* 李鴻章全集 (Hefei: Anhui jiaoyu chubanshe, 2008), Vol. 4, 517–519.

96. For the finance and management of the Qing dynasty's military, see Yingcong Dai, "Military Finance of the High Qing Period: An Overview," in *Military Culture in Imperial China*, ed. Nicola Di Cosmo (Cambridge: Harvard University Press, 2009), 296–316.

97. *Da Qing Dezong Jing (Guangxu) Huangdi Shilu*, 20: 316a–317a.

98. Ibid., 24: 359a–360a. Wu Shanzhong argues that the main reason behind the disagreement was the governors' reluctance to return the military power to the imperial center. See Wu, "Kemin, youyong, yanxiao," 32–33.

99. *Shen Bao* 664, June 29, 1874, 9–10.

100. Wu Shanzhong 吳善中, "Kemin, youyong, yanxiao: jindai changjiang zhongxiayou, yunhe liuyu huidang jueqi beijing xintan" 客民·游勇·鹽梟-近代長江中下游、運河流域會黨崛起背景新探, *Yanzhou daxue xuebao* 揚州大學學報 1999, No. 5: 29–36.

101. *Shen Bao* 963, February 22, 1875, 3–4.

102. *Da Qing huidian shili*, Xingbu, juan 850, Guangxu 8 nian, Vol. 9, 1232b–1233a; *Qingshigao*, Zhi, juan 118, 4193.

103. Yang, *Hunan difangzhi zhong de taiping tianguo shiliao*, 129–130.

104. See, for instance, Liu Jun 劉浚 and Pan Zhairen 潘宅仁, *Tongzhi Xiaofeng xianzhi* 同治孝豐縣志 (Shanghai: Shanghai shudian, 1993), juan 8, 4–5.

105. *Shen Bao* 4856, October 21, 1886, 1–2.

106. Wang Wenbing 汪文炳, ed., *Guangxu Fuyang xianzhi* 光緒富陽縣志 (Taipei: Chengwen, 1983 reprint), juan 14, 14–15; Zhang Rui 張濬 and Wang Ruicheng 王瑞成, eds., *Guangxu Ninghai xianzhi* 光緒寧海縣志 (Taipei: Chengwen, 1975), juan 5, 12.

107. *Shen Bao* 5158, August 27, 1887, 2.

108. For an example, see the following discussion on Huanglong Cave.

109. *Shen Bao* 2918, June 17, 1881, 2; *Shen Bao* 3795, November 14, 1883, 2; *Shen Bao* 4829, September 24, 1886, 1; *Shen Bao* 5076, June 5, 1887, 2; *Shen Bao* 9391, June 8, 1899, 3.

110. *Shen Bao* 3795, November 14, 1883, 2.

111. There are many such cases. See, for instance, *Shen Bao* 3795, November 14, 1883, 2; *Shen Bao* 3880, February 4, 1884, 2; *Shen Bao* 6322, November 24, 1890, 9; *Shen Bao* 10919, September 12, 1903, 1–2; *Shen Bao* 11181, June 4, 1904, 3.

112. Tan Sitong 譚嗣同, *Tan Sitong ji* (Changsha: Yuelu shushe, 2012), 368–369.

113. Yao Shide 姚詩德, *Guangxu Baling xianzhi* 光緒巴陵縣志 (Nanjing: Jiangsu guji chubanshe, 2002), juan 35, 1249; Jonathan K. Ocko, *Bureaucratic Reform in Provincial China: Ting Jih-ch'ang in Restoration Kiangsu* (Cambridge: Harvard University Press, 1983), 33–35.

114. Dates here correspond to the lunar calendar: May 2, 1877 (the third year of Guangxu's reign) in the lunar calendar converts to June 12 in the Western calendar.

115. *Shen Bao* 1728, December 10, 1877, 2; *Shen Bao* 1755, January 10, 1878, 5–6; *Shen Bao* 2040, December 16, 1878, 3–5; *Da Qing Dezong Jing (Guangxu) Huangdi Shilu*, 60: 831a–831b.

116. *Shen Bao* 1755, January 10, 1878, 5–6; *Shen Bao* 2040, December 16, 1878, 3–5.

117. Daniel Overmyer, *Folk Buddhist Religion: Dissenting Sects in Late Traditional China* (Cambridge: Harvard University Press, 1976); David Faure, "Secret Societies, Heretic Sects, and Peasant Rebellions in Nineteenth Century China," *Journal of the Chinese University of Hong Kong* 5, No. 1 (1979): 189–206; David Ownby, *Brotherhoods and Secret Societies in Early and Mid-Qing China* (Stanford: Stanford University Press, 1996); David Ownby,

"Chinese Hui and the Early Modern Social Order: Evidence from Eighteenth-Century Southeast China," in *"Secret Societies" Reconsidered: Perspectives on the Social History of Early Modern South China and Southeast Asia*, eds. David Ownby and Mary Somers Heidhues (Armonk, N.Y.: M. E. Sharpe, 1993), 34–67; Jean Chesneaux, "Secret Societies in China's Historical Evolution," in *Popular Movements and Secret Societies in China, 1840–1950*, ed. Jean Chesneaux (Stanford: Stanford University Press, 1972), 6–7. As David Ownby points out, many brotherhood organizations had names and they were not a secret to authorities and local communities. See Ownby, *Brotherhoods and Secret Societies*, 2–3.

118. Liu, "Xiangjun yu gelaohui"; Wu, "Kemin, youyong, yanxiao," 32–33.

119. The origin of Gelaohui remains debatable. For a sophisticated hypothesis, see Barend J. ter Haar, "The Gathering of Brothers and Elders (Ko-lao hui): A New View," in *Conflict and Accommodation in Early Modern East Asia: Essays in Honour of Erik Zürcher*, eds. Leonard Blussé and Harriet Zurndorfer (Leiden: E. J. Brill, 1993), 259–283.

120. For the organization of Gelaohui, see ter Haar, "Gathering of Brothers and Elders (Ko-lao hui)"; Youn Eunja 尹恩子, "Qingdai gelaohui shantang kao: shantang zuzhi de fazhan yu dengji jiegou de bianqian" 清代哥老會山堂考-山堂組織的發展與等級結構的變遷, *Qing shi yanjiu* 清史研究 2010, No. 1, 27–36.

121. *Dongfang Zazhi* 3:1 (1906): 1–5.

122. *Shen Bao* 6287, October 20, 1890, 1.

123. *Shen Bao* 1334, August 30, 1876, 2.

124. For instance, *Shen Bao* 115, September 11, 1872, 3–4; *Shen Bao* 296, April 17, 1873, 3–4; *Shen Bao* 735, September 19, 1874, 3–5; *Shen Bao* 780, November 11, 1874, 4–5; *Shen Bao* 901, April 4, 1875, 5–6.

125. *Shen Bao* 1334, August 30, 1876, 2.

126. Stephen Averill, "The Shed People and the Opening of the Yangzi Highlands," *Modern China* 9 (1983): 84–126; Anne Osborne, "Barren Mountains, Raging Rivers: The Ecological and Social Effects of Changing Landuse on the Lower Yangzi Periphery in Late Imperial China" (PhD diss., Columbia University, 1989), 66–70; Sow-Theng Leong, *Migration and Ethnicity in Chinese History: Hakkas, Pengmin, and Their Neighbors* (Stanford: Stanford University Press, 1997); Kenneth Pomeranz, "Re-thinking the Late Imperial Chinese Economy: Development, Disaggregation, and Decline, circa 1730–1930," *Itinerario* 24, nos. 3–4 (2000): 29–74; Wang I-Chiao, "Tianxia zhi huan wei renman: Qingchao Jia Dao Qian yilai de pengmin wenti, shiren yilun yu guanfang zhengce" 天下之患為人滿——清朝嘉、道、咸以來的棚民問題、士人議論與官方政策 (PhD diss., National Taiwan University, 2013).

127. Gu Lu 顧騄, *Guangxu Baihe xianzhi* 光緒白河縣志 (Taipei: Chengwen, 1969), 232.

128. Huang Tingjin 黃廷金, *Tongzhi Ruizhou fuzhi* 同治瑞州府志 (Taipei: Chengwen, 1970), 605.

129. See, for instance, Liu Xianshi 劉顯世, *Minguo Guizhou tongzhi* 民國貴州通志 (Chengdu: Bashu shushe, 2006), 4725–4726.

130. *Shen Bao* 3007, September 14, 1881, 1.

131. *Shen Bao* 5787, May 31, 1889, 1.

132. See, for instance, *Shen Bao* 942, May 25, 1875, 3–4.

133. See, for instance, Sheng Yun 升允, *Guangxu Gansu xin tongzhi* 光緒甘肅新通志 (Nanjing: Fenghuang, 2011), 5729–5730.

134. *Shen Bao* 3600, April 23, 1883, 1.

135. *Shen Bao* 5047, May 7, 1887, 1.

136. See, for instance, *Shen Bao* 1594, July 6, 1877, 2; *Shen Bao* 2312, October 7, 1879, 3; *Shen Bao* 4871, November 5, 1886, 2; *Shen Bao* 4878, November 12, 1886, 12; *Shen Bao* 5669, January 27, 1889, 2; *Shen Bao* 8535, January 18, 1897, 1; *Shen Bao* 6517, June 14, 1891, 2.

137. Wu Youru 吳友如 et al., *Dianshizhai huabao: Daketang ban* 點石齋畫報·大可堂版 (Shanghai: Shanghai huabao chubanshe, 2001), Vol. 7, 77.

138. Wu, *Dianshizhai huabao: Daketang ban*, Vol. 3, 182.

139. Ibid.

140. *Shen Bao* 4384, June 29, 1885, 2.

141. Di Fuwen 翟富文, *Minguo Laibin xianzhi* 民國來賓縣志 (Nanjing: Fenghuang, 2011), 567–568.

142. Regarding the rise of local elite activism during the late nineteenth and early twentieth centuries, see Keith R. Schoppa, *Chinese Elites and Political Change: Zhejiang in the Early Twentieth Century* (Cambridge: Harvard University Press, 1982); Mary Backus Rankin, *Elite Activism and Political Transformation in China: Zhejiang Province, 1865–1911* (Stanford: Stanford University Press, 1986); Xin Zhang, *Social Transformation in Modern China: The State and Local Elites in Henan, 1900–1937* (Cambridge: Cambridge University Press, 2000). For recent studies on the strategies of local elites and social groups in late Qing political transformation, see Xiaowei Zheng, "Political Culture, Protest Repertoires and Mass Nationalism in the 1911 Revolution in Sichuan" (PhD diss., University of California at San Diego, 2009); Shih-Chieh Lo, "The Order of Local Things: Popular Politics and Religion in Modern Wenzhou, 1840–1940" (PhD diss., Brown University, 2010).

143. On the formation of a culture of protest during the mid-Qing period, see Ho-fung Hung, *Protest with Chinese Characteristics: Demonstrations, Riots, and Petitions in the Mid-Qing Dynasty* (New York: Columbia University Press, 2011). For a historical comparison of Chinese and European politics of protest, see R. Bin Wong, *China Transformed: Historical Change and the Limits of European Experience* (Ithaca: Cornell University Press, 1997), Part III.

144. *Minguo Yin Xian zhi*, zhengjiao zhi, 579–580.

145. Again, dates here correspond to the lunar calendar: May 1, 1911 (the third year of Xuantong's reign) in the lunar calendar converts to May 28 in the Western calendar.

146. In its later report, *Shen Bao* referred to Fang Desheng as "Fang Dehai" (方得海) and put the shop's name as "Xinderun" (新德潤). See *Shen Bao* 13790, June 30, 1911, 10; *Shen Bao* 13760, June 1, 1911, 10–11.

147. *Fazheng zazhi* 5 (1911), 35–39; *Shen Bao* 13760, June 1, 1911, 10–11.

148. *Fazheng zazhi* 5 (1911), 35–39.

149. *Shen Bao* 12585, February 14, 1908, 18; *Shen Bao* 12587, February 16, 1908, 19.

150. *Fazheng zazhi* 5 (1911), 35–39.

151. In order to make this analogy, the court might have bent the story. *Shen Bao* stated that Bao Renbao (or Bao Shunbao 鮑順寶) ran after Fang for a while and was stabbed in front of Haishen Temple (海神廟). The verdict in the Fang Desheng case, however, asserted that Bao was stabbed at the entrance of the shop. See *Fazheng zazhi* 5 (1911), 35–39; *Shen Bao* 13760, June 1, 1911, 10–11. The narrowed distance between the stabbing

incident and the shop could help the judge justify his reasoning that Bao, a neighbor of the shop, could be analogous to "the owner of the lost belongings."

152. *Fazheng zazhi* 5 (1911), 35–39. Translation of the Qing statutes is taken from William C. Jones, trans., *The Great Qing Code* (Oxford: Clarendon Press, 1994), 249–250.

153. *Shen Bao* 13760, June 1, 1911, 10–11.

154. Ibid.; *Shen Bao* 13771, June 11, 1911, 10.

155. *Shen Bao* 11597, July 31, 1905, 10; *Shen Bao* 11895, May 31, 1906, 17; *Shen Bao* 11896, June 1, 1906, 9; *Shen Bao* 11902, June 6, 1906, 9; *Shen Bao* 11925, June 30, 1906, 9; *Shen Bao* 11980, August 25, 1906, 16.

156. *Shen Bao* 12177, March 18, 1907, 10; *Shen Bao* 12188, March 29, 1907, 12.

157. In addition to food riots in other provinces in the preceding years, a Hangzhou rice riot that exploded in April 8, 1911, which was only one month before the Ningbo riot, also made the Zhejiang provincial government alert to popular revolts. For the official reports and court rulings, see *Zhejiang guanbao*, 1911, No. 22.

158. *Fazheng zazhi* 5 (1911), 35–39.

159. *Shen Bao* 13760, June 1, 1911, 10–11; *Shen Bao* 13849, August 28, 1911, 11.

160. *Shen Bao* 13761, June 2, 1911, 10–11.

161. *Shen Bao* 13760, June 1, 1911, 10–11; *Fazheng zazhi* 5 (1911), 35–39.

162. *Shen Bao* 13760, June 1, 1911, 10–11.

163. Ibid.; *Shen Bao* 13771, June 11, 1911, 10.

164. *Shen Bao* 13761, June 2, 1911, 10–11; *Fazheng zazhi* 5 (1911), 35–39.

165. *Shen Bao* 13771, June 11, 1911, 10.

166. *Shen Bao* 13635, January 20, 1911, 11.

167. The order was based on the Commission on Studying Constitutional Government's reply to the Eastern Provinces' inquiry. See *Shen Bao* 13663, February 23, 1911, 11.

168. *Shen Bao* 13747, May 19, 1911, 11.

169. *Fazheng zazhi* 5 (1911), 35–39.

170. *Shen Bao* 13761, June 2, 1911, 10–11.

171. *Shen Bao* 13762, June 3, 1911, 10–11.

172. Ibid.

173. *Shen Bao* 13777, June 17, 1911, 11.

174. *Xuantong zhengji*, in *Da Qing lichao shilu*, 54: 971b; *Shen Bao* 13773, June 13, 1911, 11.

175. *Shen Bao* 13790, June 30, 1911, 10.

3   Banzai! And the Others Die—Collective Violence in the Rape of Nanking

FRANK JACOB

There has always been violence in human history, but there are specific events that are so shocking that ordinary people cannot understand why they were allowed to happen. Iris Chang underlined that fact with regard to the events in Nanking in 1937/38 when she stated, that "even by the standards of history's most destructive war, the Rape of Nanking represents one of the worst instances of mass extermination."[1] One would assume that there is no need to discuss the fact that the actions of the Japanese military at Nanking were a crime against humanity, but in Japan, China, and even the United States, interpretation of the Rape of Nanking has undergone "continuous redefinition and reinterpretation."[2] What is seen to be an "emblem of Japan's wartime aggression," especially in the Western world, went through different eras of ignorance after the Second World War, orchestration of interpretation during the Cold War, and finally discussion about its truth since the end of the Cold War.[3]

Despite the different viewpoints, the Rape of Nanking finally became the "symbol of Japanese evil,"[4] and it is seen as exceptional compared to other events in the history of human violence, because its history was ignored for a long time.[5] Now, there is much more attention paid to the event itself. Recently a draft by historians, survivors, and family members of former victims was submitted to the Standing Committee of the National People's Congress in China, requesting the establishment of a national holiday on December 13th to commemorate the fate of the many people who were killed and the many women who were raped by Japanese soldiers.[6] Furthermore, the Chinese government applied for a listing of documents related to the Rape of Nanking on the Memory of the World Register.[7] With regard to the research demand of the so-called memory studies for the evaluation of such sources in an increasingly positive way,[8] it is definitely desirable that as many sources as possible are conserved for a larger public, which should never forget what human beings were able to do to other people.

Regardless of the fact that it seems reasonable to do that, there is still an ongoing discussion with regard to the number of victims in Nanking. Arguably, numbers themselves dehumanize the victims, dehumanize their personal stories, and dehumanize their memory. However, there is still denial by some parts of Japanese society of the fact that the Rape of Nanking was a crime, and this leads to anti-Japanese feelings.[9] This is especially understandable from a Chinese perspective, which takes issue with the tendency of some Japanese authors to challenge the number of 350,000 victims. While Yamamoto counts a number of 15,000 to 50,000 victims,[10] and Western sources on the Rape of Nanking—e.g., diaries and letters from American missionaries—provide solely an estimation of 3,400 to 5,000 deaths,[11] Chinese historians tend to provide a number between 200,000 and 350,000 victims. This leads to a seemingly never-ending discussion,[12] which tends to forget the consequences for the ordinary people, who were suffering from the outcome of the Second Sino-Japanese War (1937–1945).

The Memorial Hall of the Victims in Nanking—the Nanking mausoleum is now "for the Chinese what Yad Vashem is for Israelis and Jews worldwide"[13]—gives a simple definition of the Rape: "The Nanjing Massacre refers to an exceedingly *horrible massacre of civilians* by the Japanese army during a six-week period from December 1937 to January 1938 after its occupation of Nanjing, then the capital of the Republic of China. In flagrant violation of international conventions and fundamental moral codes, the Japanese invaders stopped at nothing in committing atrocities in the form of slaughter, rape, plunder, arson, and destruction."[14]

That seems to be a suitable definition of the Rape of Nanking. The number of victims will not change the fact that a crime against humanity took place there. With regard to this issue, the Memorial Hall quotes the investigations of the Nanking War Crimes Tribunal after the Second World War, which stated that the Japanese troops killed 190,000 persons due to 28 mass slaughters and more than 150,000 Chinese citizens in 858 sporadic killings.[15]

When it comes to a close analysis of the events in Nanking one has to be careful. Certainly, the question of the reason for the massacre itself is a driving one, but to answer it simply by stating that Japan's samurai culture was responsible for the high grade of violence would be too simple. It is also not appropriate to use such prejudices as a claim for an anti-Japanese policy, as Chinese Americans like Ruby Tsao are arguably doing when they state that "[w]e must be alert on Japan's ambition to dominate in Asia again. Americans should not forget Pearl Harbor."[16] Such views of a general Japanese evilness even in our times were also provided by the "controversial international bestseller"[17] by Iris Chang, *The Rape of Nanking. The Forgotten Holocaust of World War II* (1997), which some academic reviewers asserted drew a picture of "half-baked history"[18] that established Chang as one of the leading "Japan-bashers,"[19] because "numerous historical facts are misconstrued."[20] Chang sought to condemn all Japanese people for not acknowledging the facts, although there are sectors of contemporary Japanese society that do understand the meaning of the Rape of Nanking and recognize it as a Japanese war crime. To state that "[t]he broad details of the Rape are, except among Japanese, not in dispute"[21] does not explain the exact situation of discussion in Japan at all. Even if many Japanese do not know sufficient facts of their own past,[22] there also have been Japanese attempts to atone for the past. However, due to the fact that these attempts are not recognized at their whole level, a "fruitful or even civil dialogue about it between the Chinese and Japanese" has been elusive.[23]

In Japan there is not one universal view with regard to the Second World War in general or the Rape of Nanking in particular. There are right-wingers, moderates, and leftists struggling over the correct interpretation of the Japanese past as well.[24] Despite the fact that some documents on the history of the Sino-Japanese War were published in the 1970s,[25] the official *Record of Middle China Operation*[26] contains no specific information about the events in Nanking. Furthermore, the available letters of Japanese soldiers do not mention the cruelties that took place either.[27] Therefore, the deniers of the Rape of Nanking typically come up with the argument that there is no evidence of the events themselves.[28] Their question is always the same: If there were such cruelties, why are there not more Japanese sources dealing with them? It seems to be natural that there were no Japanese official accounts dealing with any atrocity during the war, which led to the opinion that the Chinese accounts[29] seemed to be invented. Furthermore, "the Japanese people were not told about such incidents as the Nanjing Massacre for decades after the war,"[30] a time when large parts of Japanese society considered themselves to be the victims of the war, especially due to the atomic bombing of Hiroshima and Nagasaki. The return of the Nanking events into international consciousness was shocking for the Japanese, which is why the Rape of Nanking is "still filled with problems today,"[31] despite the fact that many sources and even photographic materials[32] have been published so far.

When it comes to Japanese historians, there are three different schools struggling to uncover the true story of the atrocities. While the Massacre School accepts the events as true, the Illusion School denies the Rape of

Nanking. The so-called Centrist School acknowledges the events, but not the high numbers, and tries to find a middle way between the other two schools.[33] Takashi Yoshida describes the difficulties one has to face when dealing with the deniers: "The Nanjing Massacre has been taught as one of the symbols of Japan's wartime evil in postwar Japan, and revisionists, responding to an impulse that they look upon as patriotic pride, feel obliged to liberate the Japanese from the illusion fabricated after the end of the war. They truly believe in their judgment, and their efforts to revise the story of Nanjing will never cease until they silence their opposition, a highly unlikely possibility."[34]

While public figures still tend to publicly deny the evils of the Japanese past with simple arguments of belief and disbelief,[35] the Japanese historians who deny the Rape of Nanking have developed several arguments to underline their position in answer to the arguments of those Japanese who acknowledge the cruel past.

The initiative to deal with it was made by the journalist Honda Katsuichi, who published *Chugoku no tabi* (Travels in China)[36] in 1972. He had conducted interviews with many survivors of the Rape of Nanking and published them after some of them had been published by *Asahi Shinbun* previously. His book was widely read, but Japanese conservatives were not willing to accept his perspective as truth. Suzuki Akira answered with his book *Nanjing dai-gyakusatsu no maboroshi* (The Illusion of the Nanjing Massacre),[37] which attempted to counter Honda's claims. Tanaka Masaaki, the former secretary of the Japanese commander at Nanking, Matsui Iwane, published another work of denial a decade later.[38] The argument that was made was simple, but unreasonable. The massacre could never have happened because Japanese people had never heard of it during the war years.[39] Furthermore, it seemed to be just impossible to kill so many people in such a short time span with bullets or bayonets.[40] In many cases, the Japanese deniers also tend to compare the Rape of Nanking with the atomic bombings, stating that "Hiroshima was a crime planned in cold blood. Nanking was the kind of thing that happens in any war."[41] At the beginning, the struggle about truth, in contrast to the German *Historikerstreit* in which Germans have come to grips with their nation's war crimes during World War II,[42] was led by nonhistorians. It was also burdened by the fact that Prince Asaka Yasuhiko, the uncle of the Shôwa emperor, had been in command of the Shanghai Expeditionary Force, which is why the conservatives of Japan were especially eager to completely deny the happenings.[43]

Despite Asian and international harsh reactions to the denial, Japanese historians like Higashinakano Shudo continue repudiating the past by claiming the Western and Chinese sources to be unreliable[44] and ask: "How do we explain a massacre with no witnesses?"[45] He also uses the already-known argument of deniers: "Accordingly, during the 11-year period spanning December 13, 1937, the day Nanking fell, to December 1948, when the Tokyo Trials ended, no one accused Japanese troops of having killed prisoners of war in violation of the aforementioned regulations. Confronted with these facts, how can anyone claim that the Japanese murdered prisoners of war?"[46] The 1938 account of Harold J. Timperley is simply called "a propaganda book issued by the Nationalist Ministry of Information."[47] In recent years, a number of other Japanese authors have published similar articles denying the Rape of Nanking.[48] However, there are also Japanese scholars who have been dealing with the Rape of Nanking in a rather reasonable sense.[49]

Comparable to the situation of Japanese historiography, there exist several different approaches in historical museums in Japan.[50] While the so-called "peace museums" are eager to face the past and to explain the level of atrocities with a broader past,[51] government-operated museums or those that are attached to Shintô shrines, like the *Yasukuni Jinja*, by contrast are trying to put an emphasis on Japanese suffering during the war while denying atrocities and crimes like the Rape of Nanking.[52] The Yasukuni museum, Yûshûkan, does not mention war crimes at all and tends to glorify war as well as State Shintô and the cult of the emperor and personal sacrifice for the home country.[53] Despite steady criticism, this policy has not changed. The same is somewhat true with regard to the Japanese textbook struggle.[54] When, in 2005, the Japanese government sanctioned a revisionist textbook that did not deal with the Rape of Nanking in an appropriate way, meaning it was not depicted as a crime against humanity at all, riots broke out in China.[55] The struggle with regard to this issue goes on and there are also Japanese activists who criticize the government for such a rigid policy.

Whatever the final outcome might be in Japan, the world has recognized the importance of the Rape of Nanking, and many artists have been influenced by the event and its history. In addition to novels based on the events[56] or poems that were inspired by photographs of Nanking victims,[57] movies like Luo Guanqun's *Tucheng xuezheng* (Massacre in Nanjing) (1987) did much to present the case of Nanking to a wider audience.[58] With regard to Western knowledge about the Rape of Nanking, Iris Chang's book, despite the above-mentioned criticism, had a great influence and led to the documentary *Nanking* (2007).[59] More and more people started to become informed about the so-called "Asian Holocaust."[60]

However, it is disputable whether this term is appropriate for the Rape of Nanking.[61] The use of the Holocaust as a framework of interpretation is not uncommon with regard to the Chinese event;[62] however, this specific framework could also be used to trivialize a crime against humanity by comparing it to one that is simply incomparable. The Rape of Nanking has to be seen as an important event of Chinese and Japanese history, and the efforts of the government of China to assemble researchers to deal with the massacre and to collect and preserve existing sources[63]—which is in contrast to the former Chinese policy for dealing with the Nanking issue[64]—will ensure that it will remain a part of the collective memory of China and hopefully Japan as well.[65]

This long introduction to the Rape of Nanking is needed because "[d]iscussions of the event often raise more issues than are settled"[66] and it seems to be only reasonable to provide that broad explanation for the following specific approach of this essay. Certainly, "historical research should attempt to determine why, how, and to what extent the Japanese committed the alleged atrocities";[67] however, this essay focuses on why and how the Japanese committed the uncountable atrocities in Nanking between December 1937 and February 1938. I start with a brief introduction to the events of the Rape of Nanking, which will be followed by a section that deals with theoretical approaches to the use of violence in a war setting, explaining why people tend to use specific kinds of violence in situations of war. Based on this theoretical discussion, I then explain why the Japanese soldiers, agents of the Japanese state, tended to use a form of violence during the Rape of Nanking that in some respects resembles acts of lynching, which is typically perpetrated by non-state actors.

The Rape of Nanking

What Iris Chang calls "six weeks of horror"[68] describes "the totality of atrocities committed by Japanese troops against Chinese soldiers and civilians during and after the attack on Nanking. These atrocities were illegal from the perspectives of both international law on combat behavior and international humanitarian law."[69] After occupying Nanking, the soldiers of the Japanese imperial army started a campaign that consisted not only of destruction, but also of the rape of women and the slaughter of civilians. Many of the victims died during mass executions, but some were also just buried alive or assailed with gasoline and burned to death.[70] The whole Rape of Nanking lasted more than six weeks, because order was not reestablished before the end of March, but the level and frequency of violence decreased after February 1938. During the events, male civilians were murdered in groups or as individuals in "so-called mopping-up operations,"[71] because it was assumed that they had been soldiers of the Chinese army. The women became victims of rape and gang-rape, and many of them were forced into prostitution for the Japanese army. They became "comfort women" and had to sexually please up to forty Japanese soldiers per day.[72] However, the Japanese soldiers were not just raging violently against the people; they also destroyed property, and more than 70 percent of the buildings in Nanking were looted by them.[73] The capital of China, which reflected elements of North American architecture and provided a modern urban space in Asia,[74] was almost totally destroyed. Yet it was not just that modern type of urbanism that made Nanking special. It was its symbolic status as the Chinese capital that caused the Japanese to destroy it, because they wanted to show their superior power that could not be prevented from destroying and killing.[75]

The outbreak of violence in those days was not simply an accident of human affect, because it lasted too long and thereby "created a living hell for those who were trapped within."[76] The Japanese became "loosened barbarians" and "human beasts"[77] who raped up to 80,000 women in the city, whose ages ranged from 10 to 70 years. What was created by the abandonment of the city by the Chinese troops was a sphere totally controlled by the Japanese soldiers, who were outraged and began to kill and slaughter people without any reason and without any conscience. The people who were not able to leave Nanking before the arrival of the Japanese army in mid-December 1937 seemed to be almost helpless. The only thing that was able to save their lives was the International Committee (IC).

Almost a week before the city fell, the leaders of the Red Swastika Society[78] discussed the establishment of an International Safety Zone with foreign missionaries and businessmen.[79] Finally, this zone was created and the International Committee was supposed to organize it and guarantee the safety of the people who could not flee from the city.[80] The ambassador of Japan in Shanghai was informed about the establishment of the zone and the IC and asked to prohibit Japanese access to it in case of military confrontation in the city. When the mayor of Nanking fled on December 8, 1937, the IC de facto took over the government and received $80,000 from the Chinese government to provide food to the people.[81] The foreign members of the IC were often successful in saving the lives of Chinese civilians, even if they sometimes had to risk their own in exchange. They also provided descriptions of the events of the Rape of Nanking, which were later approved by the International Military Tribunal for the Far East in Tokyo and by the previous Nanking Trial.[82]

The responsible Japanese officers, Lt. General Tani Hisao and General Matsui Iwane, were sentenced to death as Class B war criminals.[83] However, this could not heal the wounds of so many Chinese victims, especially women who had gone through a "historical situation in which, in fact, beauty was a curse rather than a blessing."[84] The Rape of Nanking also represented the helplessness of the civilians, which is why the Maoist era did not produce heroic literature about it. Despite this, the events finally became not only a symbol of victimization, but also of heroism, especially of those who survived and of those who resisted the Japanese violence.[85] The intervention of the foreigners in Nanking saved many lives, which ensured that these individuals from Germany, Britain, Denmark, and the United States are still highly respected in China, even if many of them never received wider international attention.[86] It was "those brave Europeans and Americans who risked their own lives to protect thousands of Chinese refugees who were trying to escape the mass killings, rape, torture and systematic brutality of the massacre,"[87] and it was they who provided reports of the cruelties that were happening in Nanking between December 13, 1937, and March 1938. Therefore, some of their descriptions should be presented here in detail, because they will provide a vivid impression of the crimes that were committed against humanity in general and Chinese civilians in particular.

Miner Searle Bates (1897–1978), who worked as a history professor at Nanking University from 1920 until 1950, stated that "the Japanese Army has lost much of its reputation, and has thrown away a remarkable opportunity to gain the respect of the Chinese inhabitants and of foreign opinion."[88] The soldiers did not reflect the image of civilized Japan the professor was hoping for. He noted that in just

> two days the whole outlook has been ruined by frequent murder, wholesale and semiregular looting and uncontrolled disturbance of private homes including offenses against the security of women. Foreigners who have traveled over the city report many civilians' bodies lying in the streets. In the central portion of Nanking they were counted yesterday as about one to the city block. A considerable percentage of the dead civilians were the victims of shooting or bayoneting in the afternoon and evening of the 13th, which was the time of Japanese entry into the city. Any person who ran in fear or excitement, and anyone who was caught in streets or alleys after dusk by roving patrols were likely to be killed on the spot. Most of this severity was beyond even theoretical excuse. It proceeded in the Safety Zones as well as elsewhere, and many cases are plainly witnessed by foreigners and by reputable Chinese. Some bayonet wounds were barbarously cruel.[89]

Another detailed description of the events is provided by the letters and diaries of Reverend James McCallum, who also stayed in Nanking at the time of the Rape, working in a hospital of the safety zone. He recognized the importance of the foreign protection of Chinese civilians, because he, like others, had to "be on duty 24 hours here at the hospital in order to deal with the Japanese visitors . . . often to protect women from soldiers."⁹⁰ He also described the city, which he said "presents a dismal appearance. At the time the Japanese Army entered the city little harm had been done to buildings. Since then stores have been stripped of their wares and most of them burned."⁹¹ However, it was not the destruction of the buildings that shocked the Reverend, who noted: "Far worse is what has been happening to the people. They have been in terror and no wonder. Many of them have nothing left now but a single garment around their shoulders. Helpless and unarmed, they have been at the mercy of the soldiers, who have been permitted to roam about at will wherever they pleased. There is no discipline whatever and many of them are drunk. By day they go into the buildings in our Safety Zone centers, looking for desirable women, then at night they return to get them."⁹²

For these women, resistance was fatal. One "woman six months pregnant, who resisted, came to us with 16 knife wounds in her face and body, one piercing the abdomen."⁹³ But men were granted no mercy either when they had to face the Japanese soldiers: "Men who gave themselves up to the mercy of the Japanese when they were promised their lives would be spared,—a very few of them returned to the Safety Zone in a sad way. One of them declared they were used for *bayonet practice* and his body certainly looked it. Another group was taken out [of the city]; one who somehow returned, lived long enough to tell the fate of that group. He claimed they threw *gasoline over their heads, and then set fire to them*. This man bore no other wounds but was burned so terribly around the neck and head that one could scarcely believe he was a human being."⁹⁴ Not all Japanese were like this; some treated the foreigners very kindly, but others hit them because "soldiers with a conscience are few and far between."⁹⁵

Especially courageous was the "living Goddess of Nanking"⁹⁶—the American missionary Minnie Vautrin (1886–1941)—who later committed suicide, thereby proving that the trauma of Nanking could destroy the peoples' minds as well.⁹⁷ Due to "her admirable courage, humanity and tenacity, she saved thousands of Chinese women and children from rape and other crimes by Japanese soldiers in the Safety Zone."⁹⁸ Vautrin recognized from the beginning of the Rape of Nanking that women were the main target of Japanese desires. In her diary, she noted on December 15, 1937: "From 8:30 this morning until 6 this evening, excepting for the noon meal, I have stood at the front gate while the refugees poured in. There is terror in the face of many women—last night was a terrible night in the city and many young women were taken from their homes by the Japanese soldiers."⁹⁹ She continued, further describing the horrors: "The Japanese have looted widely yesterday and today, have destroyed schools, have killed citizens, and raped women. One thousand disarmed Chinese soldiers, whom the International Committee hoped to save, were taken from them and by this time are probably shot or bayoneted."[100]

It seemed to be very clear that in Nanking there was "probably . . . no crime that has not been committed,"[101] as Vautrin reports that the sound of "occasional shots that we hear out on the hills, or on the street, make us realize the sad fate of some man."[102] The "stream of weary wild-eyed women"[103] never stopped and there was nobody "who had time to write the sad story of each person—especially that of the younger girls who had blackened their faces and cut their hair"[104] to escape rape.

Dr. Robert O. Wilson (1904–1967) also served in Nanking; as he was the only surgeon left in the city, he had to conduct up to ten operations per day.[105] He also described the situation in the former Chinese capital very clearly: "The slaughter of civilians is appalling. I could go on for pages telling of cases of rape and brutality almost beyond belief. Two bayoneted cases are the only survivors of seven street cleaners who were sitting in their headquarters when Japanese soldiers came in without warning or reason and killed five of their number and wounded the two that found their way to the hospital. I wonder when it will stop and we will be able to catch up with ourselves again."[106] The "modern Dante's Inferno," as he called the Rape of Nanking, was "written in huge letters with blood and rape."[107] Despite all these depictions of Japanese war crimes in Nanking, the Japanese deniers claim these sources to be unreliable, because they could be, for example, postwar American construction. But there were not only American eyewitnesses, but also a German Nazi, who described what happened in the city.

John Rabe came to Peking in 1908 and joined Nanking's Siemens branch in 1911. From 1931, he was the director there and joined the NSDAP in 1934.[108] He was elected as the chairman of the IC and also saved many Chinese civilians, especially because the Nazis were seen as some kind of Japanese ally.[109] Rabe, whose story was forgotten for a long time, became known as the "Oskar Schindler of China."[110] He often interfered when Japanese soldiers tried to rape Chinese women, even risking his own life, because some soldiers were also willing to attack foreigners,[111] whom they would usually just deprive of their belongings.[112] These stories were not able to reach the time during the Rape itself, when Nanking seemed to be totally isolated, but in the aftermath the American Consul in the city was able to send some reports about the situation there. "Situation here is far more difficult and abnormal than we had anticipated. Atrocities committed during first two weeks after occupation of city were of a nature and on a scale which are almost incredible. Conditions as regards military unruliness are slowly improving but isolated cases of murder and other barbarities continue."[113]

It was also reported that: "two separate and completely reliable reports from American missionaries at Nanking ... who remained at their posts when the Japanese entered these cities regarding atrocities committed by the Japanese army.... Reports quote approximately 100 authenticated cases of rape in American university buildings in Nanking in the first few days of occupation."[114] Despite all these descriptions and reports of violence and rape in Nanking in this short time period between December 1937 and March 1938, it is still hard to understand why and how this could happen. This question cannot be solved only by reading the sources; one also needs some kind of theoretical explanation of this uncontrolled outbreak of violence.

Violence and War—A Theoretical Approach

In general, violence is a physical action of a person against another person or a thing with a physical or psychological consequence.[115] History, which is mainly the history of wars,[116] is the history of violence organized by one set of people to kill other people.[117] Consequently, as Hannah Arendt argued, "[n]o one engaged in thought about history and politics can remain unaware of the enormous role violence has always played in human affairs; and it is at first glance rather surprising that violence has been singled out so seldom for special consideration."[118] In a specific way, violence is also responsible for the creation of religion and politics, because the former explains why people tend to use it, and politics is the attempt to contain violence by rule, which also needs violence to secure an internal peace.[119] Therefore, the questions related to war are in general related to humankind itself, because war is the collective attempt of people to kill other people. It is—like lynching as well—collective group violence, albeit unlike lynching, collective violence sponsored by the state.[120]

Due to the fact that "violence is a constitutive problem of social order,"[121] it is also able to destroy time frames, and the existence of violence is able to create a helix of death.[122] When it is used, people tend to create a specific legal norm to legitimize their actions, which could be based on race, religion, sex, and so forth.[123] An analysis of violence has therefore several tasks to solve; it has to focus on the violent actions of the perpetrator and the suffering of the victim but also on the feelings, emotions, and interrelationship between both parties.[124] Despite the fact that the decision to use force against another person is the responsibility of the perpetrator, it also needs to be legitimized from the perpetrator's perspective.[125] It can definitely be seen as a tool to achieve control of power, which is one of the arguments for the use of force by the Japanese troops in Nanking.[126] Following the demands with regard to a future model of a sociology of violence,[127] one needs to:

1. determine the conceptual frame of reference (who acts, in what kind of interrelationship, in which situation, using what kind of violence, creating what kind of consequences),
2. consider the factor of injury,
3. analyze inverse sense operations,
4. use different methods for the approach
5. develop a theoretical model.

With regard to the Rape of Nanking, such a model could be described in the following way:

1. Nanking, December 1937 until March 1938: Japanese soldiers, who conquered the city, used collective and individual or small-group violence to rape or kill Chinese civilians.
2. The injury was both physical and psychological.
3. While the victims were tortured, the Japanese soldiers developed a sense of power.
4. The methods used combined a historical as well as a sociological, even psychological, analysis of violence in war.
5. The theoretical model that could be provided showed that soldiers who develop some kind of paranoia with regard to soldiers in civilian clothes react with a higher grade of uncontrolled violence.

Therefore, the theoretical approach—which will be explained in more detail, underlining the different responsible factors for the eruption of violence—could also be used to explain the Massacre of My Lai in 1968[128] during which U.S. soldiers killed Vietnamese civilians.

One also has to discern between individual and collective violence, i.e., micro- and macro-violence:[129]

Table 3.1 Varieties of Individual and Collective Violence

	Micro-Violence	Macro-Violence
Phenomenology	Isolated and brief event, during which just a single person is threatened. This also includes rape or vandalism.	Violence as a part of an organized action, e.g., war, genocide, or mass destruction.
Kind of violence	Individual physical or psychological violence, normally in a direct use. Mainly apolitical and rather intentional.	Collective or state-organized violence, usually a direct or structural use. Mainly political and functional use.
Perpetrator	Individual or small group acting on their own.	State, army, or other form of organization.
Victim	Individual.	Designated group.

Source: Created from Peter Imbusch, *Moderne und Gewalt. Zivilisationstheoretische Perspektiven auf das 20. Jahrhundert* (Wiesbaden: VS Verlag für Sozialwissenschaften, 2005), 21.

Following these criteria, lynching is a form of micro-violence, in which a smaller group of people seeks to harm an individual in a physical way. The Rape of Nanking as a whole was part of the Sino-Japanese War, meaning that it was part of macro-violence. However, the specific events in which Japanese soldiers acted in uncontrolled small groups in the city were a form of micro-violence as well. These smaller groups wanted to victimize individual women, to rape them. Because they also feared Chinese guerilla warfare, individual men were killed. Next to this, the mass killings of larger groups of Chinese men were also a form of macro-violence, possibly motivated by the same reasons.

Despite these results, Nanking is a special case, because it was not just a place in which violence was used on an abnormal scale, but it was also a place of cruelty denying all civilization, because "[c]ruelty is a mirror of the living conditions and achievements of a society. It appears to be as old as humanity itself and crosses societal and cultural boundaries. No society can say that it does not allow cruelty to exist, even if societies differ to an extreme in the amount of space they give to cruelty and which forms are practiced in these particular spaces."[130] It is also "an empirical phenomenon [that] appears unable to avoid the cultural and historical relativity of good and evil, morality and immorality, and right and wrong."[131] Furthermore, cruelty is used intentionally and can be physical, psychological, social, or spiritual.[132] If cruelty becomes meaningless it will be a symbol of the perfection of power. Cruelty and its use could therefore be seen as evidence of human almightiness.[133] However, there is another level of cruelty: stimulation.[134] Some people enjoy torturing their victims to death, and especially in Nanking there must have been many soldiers who enjoyed the fact that they were able to practice bayoneting on a living human body. Finally, cruelty could be racially motivated, because it often appears due to colonial warfare, when self-appointed "superior rulers" encounter foreign people against whom practices could be used that would be deemed uncivilized in the environment in which the soldiers were born and acculturated.[135]

If we therefore want to explain why and how the Rape of Nanking was possible, we have to look at the specific situation of the Japanese soldiers who arrived there in December 1937.[136] There is no simple explanation based on Japanese evilness, because all people have the capacity to use violence, to become a perpetrator, a "lyncher." The perpetrators of Nanking might have had the impression that their use of violence was legitimized,[137] and, because the act and the experience of violence are attached to the historical event and geographical place,[138] we have to take a closer look at the soldiers in Nanking in 1937. Violence is broadly accepted only when it seems to be legitimate to use it.[139] Therefore, while wars loosen the legitimization for violence,[140] it seemed to be rational for many Japanese soldiers to kill their Chinese victims. So, why did ordinary Japanese men became "cruel barbarians" in the Nanking environment?[141]

Violence and Cruelty in Nanking

In general, no theory is universally able to explain reality.[142] However, the formulated theoretical approach is able to underline the fact that there must have been specific factors that were responsible for the high level of uncontrolled violence that was used by the Japanese soldiers during the weeks of the Rape of Nanking. While violence in warfare is usually functional and controlled,[143] because people believed in the idea of a just war,[144] especially in a colonial setting, violence became part of the daily life of the colonial rulers, as it became a usual part of daily life in war.[145] The specific sphere of warfare is also responsible for the level of violence, and especially the war against guerillas, meaning asymmetric warfare[146] in the so-called "new wars"[147] led to a higher grade of violence.[148] Just as lynching in the United States is bound to concepts of racism and colonialism,[149] the Japanese atrocities in Nanking were based on specific presumptions, stereotypes, prejudices, and paranoia.

Following Michael J. Pfeifer's argumentation with regard to American lynching,[150] I argue that the events of individual and semicollective violence during the Rape of Nanking had lynching-like qualities, even as that violence was performed not by non-state actors such as American lynch mobs but rather by agents of the Japanese state. What remains is the question for the driving forces or factors that led the Japanese soldiers to such rage, because "the tortures and atrocities of the Rape were so extreme they were unthinkable."[151]

The massacre itself can be divided into actions of mass killing and those of sporadic killing. While the number of victims reached up to 50,000 in the first case, the number of victims of sporadic killings counted somewhere between 3 to 8 people.[152] The individual acts included "splitting, gutting, slicing, piercing alive, and dog biting."[153] The Japanese soldiers also developed some kind of group dynamic, due to which the level of violence further increased.[154] They became de-individuated and created specific new norms of law, order, and morality for the specific situation in Nanking.[155] The normative order of the group was therefore responsible for the eruption of violence, and this order was a consequence of several different factors, which I will now analyze.

The first aspect is determined by the morale of the Japanese soldiers. The atrocities were definitely not a consequence of a lack of discipline[156] or the generalized "barbaric nature of Japanese militarism."[157] With regard to drill and existing hierarchies, the Japanese army could be seen as "inhumane,"[158] but more important is the fact that the soldiers adopted this behavior when they began to deal with the victims at Nanking, who resembled another kind of subordinate to the soldiers. The aggressive behavior was learned, remembered, and finally reproduced.[159] However, it would be going too far to state that "[t]he Japanese soldier was not simply hardened for battle in China; he was hardened for the task of murdering Chinese combatants and noncombatants alike,"[160] because the massacre did not last forever and did not repeat in other Chinese cities in the same way, with the same consequences or numbers of victims.

Even more important as a factor for the high level of violence that was used in Nanking was the increasingly aggressive potential of the Japanese army as a consequence of the enduring war in China. When the soldiers began their task on the Asian mainland in 1937, they dreamed of a fast, glorious, and easy victory against the Chinese troops. However, in Shanghai the Japanese had to face an enduring and harsh resistance during which the "campaign of slaughter that started in Shanghai, moved through Nanking, and proceeded inland."[161] The impulsive use of violence can therefore be seen as a consequence of a common Japanese frustration.[162] While the Japanese military staff had calculated on a fast victory and a small number of casualties, the "events at Shanghai shocked them"[163] and the death of more than 9,000 men and 30,000 wounded created a full-scale war out of a minor "incident." Consequently, violence became a major part of the Japanese advance and the "glory-hungry, frontline units lusted to be first in the enemy capital and staged a mad day for it. Thus the attack on Nanking, like that on Shanghai, was out of control from the start."[164] The Japanese soldiers wanted to end the war in the capital and they were willing "to use terrorist tactics to force China to submit."[165] The use of cruelty was intended to destroy the morale of the enemy, whose troops had not surrendered but had fled from the capital to continue the fight on another day.[166]

As important as this wish for a fast end to the war itself was the paranoia of the Japanese troops in fighting against Chinese guerilla troops in Nanking, which was also responsible for the slaughtering. Violence was the tool to break resistance,[167] but the lack of a visible enemy at Nanking[168] led to the assumption that only preventive violence could help to defend oneself and destroy the enemy.[169] The former capital was encircled in a classical military campaign,[170] but the Japanese could not find an enemy, so they assumed that the Chinese had begun another guerilla campaign. Therefore, and due to the experiences in Shanghai, the Japanese began to kill civilians, who were suspected of being hidden soldiers.[171] This specific paranoia was possibly strengthened by the fact that not all Chinese troops were able to get out of the city, and many Chinese soldiers had simply abandoned their uniforms in the streets.

Despite these explanatory factors, there were definitely soldiers who simply enjoyed the killings. Some of them laughed or even applauded when Chinese were tortured and killed. People were also decapitated to be paraded through the streets with their heads on Japanese bayonets.[172] Drunk on violence, the soldiers became cruel and in several cases simply enjoyed it; they enjoyed the excesses and "committed atrocities with a certain kind of pleasant sensation."[173] What made this development possible at all was the final factor: the lack of law and order. As a consequence of warfare itself and the lack of the usual borders of law and order, the Japanese soldiers had to develop their own legal norm. The Japanese did not feel guilty for their actions[174] as a consequence of their role identity[175] of Japanese soldiers who were fighting a war against the Chinese guerilla forces in Nanking. Due to the fact that they felt superior and had to win against a dehumanized enemy, they had no legal or moral borders for their actions. The sexual discrimination in the form of rape or gang rape also represented their role identity in that specific moment of almightiness. Furthermore, due to the patriarchal society in Japan, women were not seen by many Japanese soldiers as individuals with legal or personal rights.[176] Consequently, neither killing Chinese civilians nor raping Chinese women caused any trouble for the soldiers, who had created their own legal and moral norms in the environment of Nanking. This re-creation of an extralegal sphere or space is also a part of the legitimization of lynching.[177]

Conclusion

"Violence is for the human an antonym to freedom,"[178] and in Nanking the people were not only raped of their freedom, but they also lost their lives and human dignity. When it comes to war, people have just three options: to flee, to participate, or to suffer.[179] The Chinese who remained in Nanking were forced into the latter. Due to the fact that oral history has become an essential part of historical research during recent decades,[180] we can use individual memory, which overlaps with collective memory, to understand the sufferings of human beings who have been victimized by war.[181] We can better understand what it means to people to survive,[182] and the testimonies of survivors should always be honored and valued as a part of history.[183] The fate of the survivors of the Rape of Nanking was mainly "silent poverty, shame, or chronic physical and mental pain"[184] and only in the last two decades has there been an increased focus on this dark chapter of human history. The work is not yet done, because there are many aspects to deal with in the future. However, the previous section attempted to explain why and how the Rape of Nanking happened in the way it did. It should never be seen as an excuse for the crimes and cruelties that killed so many people and made whole generations suffer from its memory. But there is always the possibility of similar eruptions of violence, due to wars, genocides, and global forms of lynching. The analyzed factors that are seen to be responsible for the outrage of the Japanese soldiers during the period between December 1937 and March 1938 are not specifically Japanese; they are human factors and may be responsible for similar violence again in the future.

Especially due to this fact, historians are needed. They are needed to remember the fate of the past generations and to warn the future ones. Violence is always a part of human nature, so cruelty will always remain a possible outcome of prejudices, stereotyping, and cultural arrogance. Humanity itself should always be aware of this, and remembering the Rape of Nanking, next to the Holocaust and the Armenian and Rwandan genocides, as well as American lynchings, will make sure that we do not forget.

Notes

1. Iris Chang, *The Rape of Nanking. The Forgotten Holocaust of World War II* (New York: Basic Books, 2011), 5.

2. Takashi Yoshida, *The Making of the "Rape of Nanking": History and Memory in Japan, China, and the United States* (Oxford: Oxford University Press, 2006), 4.

3. Ibid., 129–179.

4. Ian Buruma, "The Nanking Massacre as a Historical Symbol," in *Nanking 1937. Memory and Healing*, ed. Fei Fei Li, Robert Sabella, and David Liu (Armonk, N.Y.: M. E. Sharpe, 2002), 8.

5. Even if Harold J. Timperley's *What War Means: The Japanese Terror in China* (London: Victor Gollancz, 1938) was published in 1938, the Rape of Nanking remained a marginal topic of historical research for a long time. See Masahiro Yamamoto, *Nanking. Anatomy of an Atrocity* (Westport, Conn.: Praeger, 2000), 1.

6. "Never Forget," *Beijing Review*, March 6, 2014.

7. "Massacre Heritage," *Beijing Review*, June 19, 2014, 4.

8. Sun Jiang, "The Unbearable Heaviness of Memory. Nanjing to Tao Baojin and His Descendants," *Chinese Studies in History* 47:1 (2013), 55.

9. "Announcement of the 1999 International Student Conference: Memories of Nanking (Nanjing): Toward a Global Consensus," Washington University St. Louis, Mo. (November 8–13, 1999), *Chinese American Forum* 15:3 (2000), 44.

10. Yamamoto, *Nanking*, 292. Japanese authors usually enumerate less than 15,000 victims.

11. David Askew, "Part of the Numbers Issue: Demography and Civilian Victims," in *The Nanking Atrocity, 1937–38. Complicating the Picture*, ed. Bob Tadashi Wakabayashi (New York: Berghahn Books, 2008), 112.

12. Lu Yan, "Nanjing Massacre as Transnational Event and Global Icon," *Harvard Asia Pacific Review* 9:2 (2008), 69.

13. Bob Tadashi Wakabayashi, "The Messiness of Historical Reality," in *The Nanking Atrocity, 1937–38. Complicating the Picture*, ed. Bob Tadashi Wakabayashi (New York: Berghahn Books, 2008), 8.

14. Ruby Tsao, "Reflections: Why Did the Massacre Happen?" *Chinese American Forum* 30:1 (2014), 27.

15. Ibid.

16. Ibid., 30.

17. Gayle K. Sato, "Witnessing Atrocity through Auto-bio-graphy: Wing Tek Lum's The Nanjing Massacre: Poems," *Inter-Asia Cultural Studies* 13:2 (2012), 212.

18. Roger B. Jeans, "Victims or Victimizers? Museums, Textbooks, and the War Debate in Contemporary Japan," *Journal of Military History* 69 (2005), 149. See also the reviews by Joshua A. Fogel, *Journal of Asian Studies* 57:3 (1998), 818–820, and Mark Eykholt, *China International Review* 6:1 (1999), 70–73.

19. Bob Tadashi Wakabayashi, "The Nanking 100-Man Killing Contest Debate, 1971–1975," in *The Nanking Atrocity, 1937–38. Complicating the Picture*, ed. Bob Tadashi Wakabayashi (New York: Berghahn Books, 2008), 145.

20. Kitamura Minoru, *The Politics of Nanjing: An Impartial Investigation* (Lanham, Md.: University Press of America, 2007), 11.

21. Chang, *Rape*, 4. For similar argument, see Kevin Ng, "The Great Denial: How Japan's Policies Regarding Its Actions during WWII Are Denying Both Its Own People and the World of Moral Betterment, Social Progress and Political Integration," *Chinese American Forum* 23:3 (2008), 34.

22. Ding Ying, "History in Japanese Eyes," *Beijing Review*, May 28, 2009, 18.

23. Wakabayashi, *Messiness*, 3.

24. Jeans, "Victims," 149.

25. Hora Tomio, ed., *Documents on the Sino-Japanese War: The Nanking-Incident* (Tokyo: Aoki shoten, 1973).

26. *Record of Middle China Operation*, Chapter 1: From Incident Outbreak until Nanjing Capture, The National Institute for Defense Studies, Ministry of Defense, Army Records, Shina (China), The China Incident (Second Sino-Japanese War), Shanghai, Nanjing, C11111991300.

27. Amano Saburo, "Letters from a Reserve Officer Conscripted to Nanking," in *The Nanking Atrocity, 1937–38. Complicating the Picture*, ed. Bob Tadashi Wakabayashi (New York: Berghahn Books, 2008), 188–191.

28. Takashi Yoshida, "Wartime Accounts of the Nanking Atrocity," in *The Nanking Atrocity, 1937–38. Complicating the Picture*, ed. Bob Tadashi Wakabayashi (New York: Berghahn Books, 2008), 248.

29. Ibid., 249–254. An exception to Japanese official silence on atrocities is an article in the *Tokyo Nichi Nichi Shinbun* about a decapitating contest between two Japanese officers in China. The *Japan Advertiser* reported the incidents on December 7 and 14, 1937. Two Japanese officers competed on the issue of which of them would be first to decapitate 100 Chinese. Even if it is cited as a historical fact in many works on the Nanking massacre, Bob Tadashi Wakabayashi doubts that it ever happened in the described form; see Wakabayashi, "Nanking," 142. For a detailed description of the contest, see Honda Katsuichi,

The Nanjing Massacre. A Japanese Journalist Confronts Japan's National Shame (Armonk, N.Y.: M. E. Sharpe, 1999), 123–137.

30. Ibid., xxv.
31. Kitamura, *Politics*, 3.
32. Shi Young and James Yin, *The Rape of Nanking. An Undeniable History in Photographs*, 2nd expanded edition (Chicago: Innovative Publishing Group, 1997).
33. Kitamura, 4–8.
34. Yoshida, *Making*, 180.
35. Chang, *Rape*, 201–205.
36. Honda Katsuichi, *Chugoku no tabi* (Tokyo: Asahishinbunsha, 1972).
37. Suzuki Akira, *Nanjing dai-gyakusatsu no maboroshi (The Illusion of the Nanjing Massacre)* (Tokyo: Bungei shunjūsha, 1973).
38. Tanaka Masaaki, *Nankin gyakusatsu no kyokō: Matsui taishō no nikki o megutte* (The Fabrication of the Nanjing Massacre: On General Matsui's Diary) (Tokyo: Nihon kyobunsha, 1984).
39. Buruma, "Nanking Massacre," 3.
40. Ibid., 4.
41. Ibid.
42. Richard J. Evans, *Im Schatten Hitlers? Historikerstreit und Vergangenheitsbewältigung in der Bundesrepublik* (Frankfurt am Main: Suhrkamp, 1991).
43. Wakabayashi, *Messiness*, 11.
44. Higashinakano Shudo, *The Nanking Massacre: Fact versus Fiction, a Historian's Quest for the Truth* (Tokyo: Sekai Shuppan, 2006). Review by Bob Tadashi Wakabayashi, *Pacific Affairs* 79:3 (2006), 526–527.
45. Ibid., iii.
46. Ibid., ii.
47. Ibid., iv; Timperley, *What War Means*.
48. To name just a few from recent years: Nakagaki Hideo, "Nankin jiken no shinsô (The Truth about the Nanking Incident), *Defense* 31:1 (2012), 232–257; "Nankin jiken kôkoku kyohi ha Chûnichi shinbun no jisatsu da (The Veto against Announcing the Nanking Incident Is the Suicide of the Chûnichi Newspaper), *Monthly Will* 91 (2012), 104–112; "'Nankin Jiken' no kyokō ha kantan ni setsumei dekiru (One Can Easily Explain the Fiction of the 'Nanking Incident')," *Monthly Will* 89 (2012), 76–81; "'Nankin Jiken' shôko shashin ha subete decchiage (The Photographic Proof of the 'Nanking Incident' Is Definitely Fiction)," *Monthly Will* 89 (2012), 82–89; Watanabe Hisashi, "Nankin jiken no gyakusha wo saikô suru (Reevaluating the Slaughterers of the Nanking Incident)," *Chôkiren: Sensô no shinjitsu wo kataritsugu* 16 (2012), 85–103.
49. Shinohara Takaaki, "Chûgakkô no jugyô rekishi yori yoi Nicchû kankei no arikata: Nankin jiken megutte (A Better Approach to the Japanese-Chinese Relations in Highschool History Teaching: With Regard to the Nanking Incident)," *Rekishi chiri kyôiku* 794 (2012), 48–51; Suzuki K. "Nankin jiken ni okeru Shidehara gaikô no henyô (The Diplomatic Change of Shidehara during the Nanking Incident)," *Nihon Rekishi* 780 (2013), 68–85.
50. Kerry Smith, "The Showa Hall: Memorializing Japan's War at Home," *Public Historian* 24:4 (2002), 35.
51. T. R. Reid, "Japan Marks Day of Defeat by Facing Up to the Truth," *International Herald Tribune*, August 15, 1994.

52. Jeans, *Victims*, 193.
53. Ibid., 152–157.
54. Ibid., 183–193.
55. Ying-Ying Chang, "Reflections on the Nanking Massacre. After 70 Years of Denial. In Memory of Our Daughter Iris Chang," *Harvard Asia Pacific Review*, 77.
56. Meira Chand, *A Choice of Evils* (London: Weidenfeld and Nicolson, 1996).
57. Noam Scheindlin, "Ignored Tragedy. The Moment before Tears Would Well Up," *Chinese American Forum*, 29:2 (2013), 22–23.
58. Michael Berry, "Cinematic Representations of the Rape of Nanking," *East Asia* (2001), 86.
59. Peter Furtado, "Nanking on Screen," *History Today* (2008), 7.
60. Ng, "Great Denial," 33.
61. Buruma, "Nanking Massacre," 7.
62. Vera Schwarcz, "The 'Black Milk' of Historical Consciousness: Thinking about the Nanking Massacre in Light of Jewish Memory," in *Nanking 1937: Memory and Healing*, ed. Fei Fei Li, Robert Sabella, and David Liu (Armonk, N.Y.: M. E. Sharpe, 2002), 183–204; Kevin Uhrich, "The Other Holo," *Los Angeles Readers*, July 1, 1994.
63. Yuki Miyamoto, "The Ethics of Commemoration: Religion and Politics in Nanking, Hiroshima, and Yasukuni," *Journal of the American Academy of Religion* 80:1 (2012), 45.
64. Mark Eykholt, "Aggression, Victimization, and Chinese Historiography of the Nanjing Massacre," in *The Nanjing Massacre in History and Historiography*, ed. Joshua A. Fogel (Berkeley: University of California Press, 2000), 11–69.
65. Miyamoto, "Ethics," 43–50.
66. Buruma, "Nanking Massacre," 3.
67. Yamamoto, *Nanking*, 5.
68. Chang, *Rape*, 81–104.
69. Kasahara Tokushi, "Remembering the Nanking Massacre," in *Nanking 1937: Memory and Healing*, ed. Fei Fei Li, Robert Sabella, and David Liu (Armonk, N.Y.: M. E. Sharpe, 2002), 75.
70. "The Painful Memory," *Beijing Review*, May 28, 2009, 18.
71. Kasahara, "Remembering," 76.
72. For the "comfort women," see Frank Jacob, "Comfort Women—The Story of Forced Prostitution in World War II," in *Prostitution—A Companion of Mankind*, ed. Frank Jacob (Frankfurt am Main: Peter Lang, 2015).
73. Kasahara, "Remembering," 76.
74. Jeffrey W. Cody, "American Planning in Republican China," *Planning Perspectives* 11 (1996), 339.
75. Lu, "Nanjing Massacre," 67.
76. Ibid.
77. Lee En-Han, "The Nanking Massacre Reassessed: A Study of the Sino-Japanese Controversy over the Factual Number of Massacred Victims," in *Nanking 1937: Memory and Healing*, ed. Fei Fei Li, Robert Sabella, and David Liu (Armonk, N.Y.: M. E. Sharpe, 2002), 50.
78. The Red Swastika Society could be simply described as a Chinese version of the Red Cross.
79. Sun, "Memory," 57.

80. David Askew, "Westerners in Occupied Nanking: December 1937 to February 1938," in *The Nanking Atrocity, 1937–38. Complicating the Picture*, ed. Bob Tadashi Wakabayashi (New York: Berghahn Books, 2008), 227.

81. Ibid., 228–229.

82. Kitamura, *Politics*, 2; Lee, "Nanking Massacre," 49; Zhu Wenqi, "On the Tokyo Trial and Nanjing Massacre," Zhengfa Luntan (Tribune of Political Science and Law), No. 5 (2007), 122–136. Review by LI Hongying, in *Chinese Journal of International Law* 7:2 (2008), 571. For the Judgment of the International Military Tribunal for the Far East, see Timothy Brook, ed., *Documents on the Rape of Nanking* (Ann Arbor: The University of Michigan Press, 1999), 257–267.

83. Richard Falk, "Redressing Grievances: Assessing the Nanking Massacre," in *Nanking 1937. Memory and Healing*, ed. Fei Fei Li, Robert Sabella, and David Liu (Armonk, N.Y.: M. E. Sharpe, 2002), 11; Kitamura, *Politics*, 2–3.

84. Qinna Shen, "Revisiting the Wound of a Nation: The 'Good Nazi' John Rabe and the Nanking Massacre," *seminar* 47:5 (2011), 670.

85. "Never Forget," *Beijing Review*, March 6, 2014, 5; Qinna, "Revisiting," 672.

86. Lu, "Nanjing Massacre," 67. For a detailed list of these foreigners, see Suping Lu, *They Were in Nanjing: The Nanjing Massacre Witnessed by American and British Nationals* (Hong Kong: Hong Kong University Press, 2004), 283–285.

87. Ying-Ying Chang, "Reflections," 76.

88. Zhang Kaiyuan, ed., *Eyewitnesses to Massacre. American Missionaries Bear Witness to Japanese Atrocities in Nanjing* (Armonk, N.Y.: M. E. Sharpe, 2001), 4.

89. Ibid.

90. Andrew Carroll, "An American Missionary Describes 'Beastly' Atrocities in Nanking," *World War II* (July/August 2012), 25.

91. Ibid.

92. Ibid.

93. Ibid., 27.

94. Ibid.

95. Ibid.

96. Qinna, "Revisiting," 670.

97. Hu, Hua-ling, *American Goddess at the Rape of Nanking: The Courage of Minnie Vautrin* (Carbondale: Southern Illinois UP, 2000).

98. Ying-Ying Chang, "Reflections," 76.

99. Hua-ling Hu and Zhang Lian-hong, eds., *The Undaunted Women of Nanking. The Wartime Diaries of Minnie Vautrin and Tsen Shui-Fang* (Carbondale: Southern Illinois University Press, 2010), 38.

100. Ibid.

101. Ibid., 40.

102. Ibid.

103. Ibid., 43.

104. Ibid.

105. Brook, "Documents," 213.

106. Ibid., 214.

107. Ibid.

108. Qinna, "Revisiting," 663.
109. Ibid., 664.
110. Ibid., 661.
111. John Rabe, *John Rabe: Der gute Deutsche von Nanking*, ed. Erwin Wickert (Munich: Pantheon, 2008), 145.
112. Suping Lu, ed., *A Mission under Duress. The Nanjing Massacre and Post-Massacre Social Conditions Documented by American Diplomats* (Lanham, Md.: University Press of America, 2010), 3.
113. Suping Lu, ed., *A Dark Page in History. The Nanjing Massacre and Post-Massacre Social Conditions Recorded in British Diplomatic Dispatches, Admiralty Documents, and U.S. Naval Intelligence Reports* (Lanham, Md.: University Press of America, 2012), 18.
114. Ibid., 20.
115. Peter Imbusch, *Moderne und Gewalt. Zivilisationstheoretische Perspektiven auf das 20. Jahrhundert* (Wiesbaden: VS Verlag für Sozialwissenschaften, 2005), 21.
116. John Keegan, *Die Kultur des Krieges* (Berlin: Rowohlt Verlag, 1995), 545.
117. Michael Geyer, "Eine Kriegsgeschichte, die vom Tod spricht," in *Physische Gewalt. Studien zur Geschichte der Neuzeit*, ed. Thomas Lindenberger and Alf Lüdtke (Frankfurt: Suhrkamp, 1995), 136.
118. Hannah Ahrendt, *On Violence* (1970), xx, quoted in Trutz von Trotha, "Zur Soziologie der Gewalt," in *Soziologie der Gewalt, Kölner Zeitschrift für Soziologie und Sozialpsychologie*, Sonderheft 37 (1997), ed. Trutz von Trotha (Opladen: Westdeutscher Verlag, 1997), 59.
119. Karl Heinz Metz, *Geschichte der Gewalt. Krieg-Revolution-Terror* (Darmstadt: WBG, 2010), 7.
120. Ibid., 299.
121. Trotha, *Soziologie der Gewalt*, 10.
122. Wolfgang Sofsky, "Gewaltzeit," in *Soziologie der Gewalt, Kölner Zeitschrift für Soziologie und Sozialpsychologie*, Sonderheft 37 (1997), ed. Trutz von Trotha (Opladen: Westdeutscher Verlag, 1997), 102–103.
123. Jost Dülffer, *Im Zeichen der Gewalt. Frieden und Krieg im 19. und 20. Jahrhundert* (Cologne: Böhlau Verlag, 2003), 2.
124. Trotha, *Soziologie der Gewalt*, 21.
125. Ibid., 31.
126. Birgitta Nedelmann, "Gewaltsoziologie am Scheideweg. Die Auseinandersetzung in der gegenwärtigen und Wege der künftigen Gewaltforschung," in *Soziologie der Gewalt, Kölner Zeitschrift für Soziologie und Sozialpsychologie*, Sonderheft 37 (1997), ed. Trutz von Trotha (Wiesbaden: Westdeutscher Verlag, 1997), 61.
127. Ibid., 72–83.
128. Michal R. Belknap, *The Vietnam War on Trial: The My Lai Massacre and the Court-Martial of Lieutenant Calley* (Lawrence: University Press of Kansas, 2002).
129. Imbusch, *Moderne und Gewalt*, 31–35.
130. Trutz von Trotha, "On Cruelty: Conceptual Considerations and the Summary of an Interdisciplinary Debate," in *On cruelty, Sur la cruauté, Über Grausamkeit*, ed. Jakob Rösel and Trutz von Trotha (Cologne: Rüdiger Köppe Verlag, 2011), 4.
131. Ibid., 5.

132. Ibid., 10.

133. Trutz von Trotha, "Dispositionen der Grausamkeit. Über die anthropologischen Grundlagen grausamen Handelns," in *On cruelty, Sur la cruauté, Über Grausamkeit*, ed. Jakob Rösel and Trutz von Trotha (Cologne: Rüdiger Köppe Verlag, 2011), 126–128.

134. Ibid., 135–136.

135. Matthias Häussler, "Grausamkeit und Kolonialismus. Zur Dynamik von Grausamkeit," in *On cruely, Sur la cruauté, Über Grausamkeit*, ed. Jakob Rösel and Trutz von Trotha (Cologne: Rüdiger Köppe Verlag, 2011), 511; Trutz von Trotha, "Gewalttätige Globalisierung, globalisierte Gewalt und Gewaltmarkt," in *Globalisierung der Gewalt. Weltweite Solidarität angesichts neuer Fronten globaler (Un-)Sicherheit*, ed. Matthias Kiefer and Johannes Müller (Stuttgart: Verlag W. Kohlhammer, 2005), 4.

136. Michael Bollig, Erwin Orywal, and Aparna Rao, eds., *Krieg und Kampf. Die Gewalt in unseren Köpfen* (Berlin: Dietrich Reimer Verlag, 1996), 10.

137. Susanne Kuß, *Deutsches Militär auf kolonialen Kriegsschauplätzen. Eskalation von Gewalt zu Beginn des 20. Jahrhunderts* (Berlin: Ch. Links Verlag, 2010), 12.

138. Thomas Lindenberger and Alf Lüdtke, "Einleitung: Physische Gewalt-eine Kontinuität der Moderne," in *Physische Gewalt. Studien zur Geschichte der Neuzeit*, ed. Thomas Lindenberger and Alf Lüdtke (Frankfurt: Suhrkamp, 1995), 7.

139. Volker Sellin, *Gewalt und Legitimität. Die europäische Monarchie im Zeitalter der Revolution* (Munich: Oldenbourg Verlag, 2011), 15.

140. James J. Sheehan, *Kontinent der Gewalt. Europas langer Weg zum Frieden* (Munich: Verlag C. H. Beck, 2008), 17.

141. Harald Welzer already attempted to answer this question in *Täter. Wie aus ganz normalen Menschen Massenmörder werden* (Frankfurt: S. Fischer, 2005). However, the author mainly focused on the German soldiers and the Holocaust.

142. Cody, "American Planning," 12.

143. Daniel Hohrath and Daniel Neitzel, "Entfesselter Kampf oder gezähmte Kriegführung? Gedanken zur regelwidrigen Gewalt im Krieg," in *Kriegsgreuel. Die Entgrenzung der Gewalt in kriegerischen Konflikten vom Mittelalter bis ins 20. Jahrhundert*, ed. Daniel Hohrath and Daniel Neitzel (Paderborn: Ferdinand Schöningh, 2008), 9.

144. Udo Fink, "Der Krieg und seine Regeln," in *Kriegsgreuel. Die Entgrenzung der Gewalt in kriegerischen Konflikten vom Mittelalter bis ins 20. Jahrhundert*, ed. Daniel Hohrath and Daniel Neitzel (Paderborn: Ferdinand Schöningh, 2008), 40.

145. Kuß, *Deutsches Militär*, 15, 32–34, 46–48.

146. On these kinds of wars see Beatrice Heuser, *Rebellen. Partisanen. Guerilleros. Asymmetrische Kriege von der Antike bis heute* (Paderborn: Ferdinand Schöningh, 2013).

147. The "new wars" were defined by Mary Kaldor, in *New and Old Wars. Organized Violence in a Global Era* (Cambridge: Polity Press, 2012) and Herfried Münkler, *Die neuen Kriege* (Hamburg: Rowohlt, 2002), but the concept was also criticized by Dieter Langewiesche, "Wie neu sind die 'Neuen Kriege'? Eine erfahrungsgeschichtliche Analyse," in *Kriegserfahrungen-Krieg und Gesellschaft in der Neuzeit. Neue Horizonte der Forschung*, ed. Georg Schild and Anton Schindling (Paderborn: Ferdinand Schöningh, 2009), 289–302.

148. Concentration camps, e.g., during the Boer War (1899–1902), could be seen as one consequence of this kind of warfare.

149. Amy Louise Wood and Susan V. Donaldson, "Lynching's Legacy in American Culture," *Mississippi Quarterly* 61:1–2 (2008), 5.

150. Michael J. Pfeifer, *Rough Justice: Lynching and American Society* (Urbana: University of Illinois Press, 2004).
151. "Never Forget," *Beijing Review*, March 6, 2014, 3.
152. Sun Zhaiwei, "Causes of the Nanking Massacre," in *Nanking 1937: Memory and Healing*, ed. Fei Fei Li, Robert Sabella, and David Liu (Armonk, N.Y.: M. E. Sharpe, 2002), 36.
153. Ibid., 37.
154. Amélie Mummendey, "Macht-Konflikt-Gewalt. Eine sozialpsychologische Betrachtung von Individuen und Gruppen," in *Krieg, Konflikt, Kommunikation. Der Traum von einer friedlichen Welt*, ed. Gerold Mikula and Manfred Prisching (Vienna: Passagen Verlag, 1991), 42.
155. Ibid., 42–43.
156. Yamamoto, "Nanking," 282.
157. Sun Zhaiwei, "Causes," 39.
158. Kasahara, "Remembering," 78.
159. Manfred Prisching, "Einleitung," in *Krieg, Konflikt, Kommunikation. Der Traum von einer friedlichen Welt*, ed. Gerold Mikula and Manfred Prisching (Vienna: Passagen Verlag, 1991), 13.
160. Chang, *Rape*, 55.
161. Ibid., 215.
162. Erwin Orywal, "Krieg und Frieden in den Wissenschaften," in *Krieg und Kampf. Die Gewalt in unseren Köpfen*, ed. Michael Bollig, Erwin Orywal, and Aparna Rao (Berlin: Dietrich Reimer Verlag, 1996), 15.
163. Fujiwara Akira, "The Nanking Atrocity: An Interpretive Overview," in *The Nanking Atrocity, 1937–38: Complicating the Picture*, ed. Bob Tadashi Wakabayashi (New York: Berghahn Books, 2008), 31.
164. Ibid., 33.
165. Sun Zhaiwei, "Causes," 44.
166. Jürg Helbing, "The Tactical Use of Cruelty in Tribal Warfare," in *On cruely, Sur la cruauté, Über Grausamkeit*, ed. Jakob Rösel and Trutz von Trotha (Cologne: Rüdiger Köppe Verlag, 2011), 151.
167. Heimo Hofmeister, *Der Wille zum Krieg oder die Ohnmacht der Politik. Ein philosophisch-politischer Traktat* (Göttingen: Vandenhoeck and Rupprecht, 2001), 26.
168. Georg Klute, "Kleinkrieg und Raum," in *Begegnungen und Auseinandersetzungen. Festschrift für Trutz von Trotha*, ed. Katharina Inhetveen and Georg Klute (Cologne: Rüdiger Koppe Verlag, 2009), 287.
169. Seyom Brown, *The Causes and Prevention of War* (New York: St. Martin's Press, 1994), 16.
170. Fujiwara, "Nanking Atrocity," 43.
171. Ibid., 43–50.
172. "The Painful Memory," *Beijing Review*, May 28, 2009, 19.
173. Kasahara, "Remembering," 77. On cruelty and excess, see Norbert S. J. Brieskorn, "Grausamkeit-Gewalt-Macht," in *Globalisierung der Gewalt. Weltweite Solidarität angesichts neuer Fronten globaler (Un-)Sicherheit*, ed. Matthias Kiefer and Johannes Müller (Stuttgart: Verlag W. Kohlhammer, 2005), 72–73.
174. Kasahara, "Remembering," 77.

175. Thomas Klatetzki, "Cruel Identities," in *On cruely, Sur la cruauté, Über Grausamkeit*, ed. Jakob Rösel and Trutz von Trotha (Cologne: Rüdiger Köppe Verlag, 2011), 197.

176. Kasahara, "Remembering," 78.

177. Pfeifer, *Rough Justice*, 38–66; Michael J. Pfeifer, *The Roots of Rough Justice* (Urbana: University of Illinois Press, 2011), esp. 4–5.

178. Hofmeister, *Der Wille zum Krieg*, 31.

179. Klaus Schlichte, "Krieg und bewaffneter Konflikt als sozialer Raum," in *Kriege als (Über)Lebenswelten. Schattenglobalisierung, Kriegsökonomien und Inseln der Zivilität*, ed. Sabine Kurtenbach and Peter Lock (Bonn: Dietz Verlag, 2004), 186.

180. Steven High and Edward Little, Introduction, in *Remembering Mass Violence. Orald History, New Media, and Performance*, ed. Steven High, Edward Little, and Thi Ry Duong (Toronto: University of Toronto Press, 2014), 4.

181. Ibid., 6.

182. Henry Greenspan, "Voices, Places, Spaces," in *Remembering Mass Violence. Oral History, New Media, and Performance*, ed. Steven High, Edward Little, and Thi Ry Duong (Toronto: University of Toronto Press, 2014), 37.

183. Ibid., 39.

184. Chang, *Rape*, 181.

4 Making Sense of Lynching in Medieval Nepal

YOGESH RAJ

Public castration of "witches," parading the blood- and soot-covered, semi-naked "corrupt" persons in the streets, displays of mutilated bodies of the "class enemies" and "informants," macabre celebration of "democracy," blind blows on the dismembered body parts of a "thief," intense hate-shows against a "marked" individual—these are some common instances of extreme collective cruelty. These extraordinary incidents often shake up societies from their collective slumber. They generate all sorts of archival trails in their frantic wake: news and analysis in public and social media, police and court cases, inquiry commission reports, and traumatic collective memories. The forms of these instances of enveloping collective rage and the nature of their documentation shape how we interpret and explain them.[1]

Lynching is extraordinary among the forms of collective cruelty. It shares some features with other forms such as riots, uprisings, communal killings, and wars. For example, it cannot necessarily be anticipated; it cannot be observed objectively; and once it occurs, one cannot possibly obtain complete and reliable accounts. All extreme forms of collective violence are devastating in that they disrupt existing social arrangements. But lynching surpasses all of them both in the intensity of the immediate effects on its participants and in the degree of coordination among them. Lynching is also unique for its extreme brevity, for the absolute inequality of power between its orchestrators and victims, for both the social and judicial anonymity of its perpetrators, and, of course, for the certain fatality of its victims. Lynching is an exceptionally ill-bounded social event. Its beginnings and ends are hazy; its locality is ever-shifting and unfolding and is entirely governed by the actors. Consequently, records on lynching are almost always fragmentary: they are episodic both in the public memory and police archives.

Sociohistorical approaches to lynching have long noticed the episodic nature of these events and their fragmentary documentation. Indeed, the rapturous character of the events and the brevity of their records pose certain methodological challenges to developing a credible account of these phenomena. They try to circumvent the issue of the ill-bounded nature of lynching by developing and working with Events Catalogues (Tilly 2002). They analyze the events as protests, collective violence, collective action, or contentious claim-makings, and consequently they pursue different explanations. Charles Tilly classifies lynching as a case of "violent rituals," which is itself a subset of collective violence (Tilly 2003; Kousis and Tilly 2005). Tilly's approach to collective violence is framed within his paradigm of contentious politics (Tilly and Tarrow 2006; Tilly 2008) There is much to be said on the inapplicability of the ideology of everyday contention to the sudden burst of unbelievable and unexpected brutality displayed in lynching and other extraordinary forms of collective cruelty. This chapter contends that Tilly's approach is methodologically problematic insofar as the historiography of lynching is concerned.

This chapter demonstrates that these sociohistorical accounts are deficient in developing any credible historical account primarily due to their narratological bias. In contrast, the chapter argues that the Event Catalogues, which have been used so far for statistical acrobatics and frustrating historical speculations, call instead for a radically different approach to historiography. Using medieval records of lynching from Nepal, this paper further argues for employing analogy and not argumentation to develop a deeper historical understanding of lynching and other episodic phenomena in South Asian societies.

Sociohistorical Approaches to Lynching

Existing sociological and historical approaches to collective violence in general, and to lynching in particular, have wrestled with the methodological and theoretical consequences of the episodic character of both the events and their evidence.[2] Classical studies have treated them like the incidences of plagues. One set of the classics on the subject has focused on the clinical examination of their internal structure and growth (Rude 1964 [2005]; Badiou 2012). The other set has pursued epidemiological quantitative analysis of the contexts and contours of their occurrence (Gurr 1970). These approaches have not been very productive. They have struggled to overcome the issues associated with the rupture and murky boundaries in such collective actions. For instance, their theories and analyses strongly depend on the definitions and samples. Their units of analysis vary (that is, should they consider locality, event, individuals or social structures?). They have relied on a diverse set of source materials (that is, descriptions of the events, accounts of the participants or both?). Consequently, they have employed a wide range of theoretical tools (namely, their objects of speculation, the time spans they cover, and the resulting arguments—all of which vary significantly).

Historically minded sociologists have therefore wisely abandoned the medical approaches to the social outbursts. Instead of seeking causal explanations (that is, who, how, and under what conditions do collective violence occur?), they have concentrated on providing rich and nuanced descriptive analyses of these phenomena (Tilly 1969). Nevertheless, these sociologists also had to confront the issues related to the ill-bounded character of the events and their fragmentary documentation. They circumvented the problems by developing Events Catalogues from their source documents. An *Event Catalogue* is "a set of descriptions of multiple social interactions [chosen] from a delimited set of sources according to relatively uniform procedures" (Tilly 2002: 249). The four steps employed during the cataloguing process increasingly narrow down the analysts' data. First, interactions are preferred as units of analysis over actions; second, only those interactions are singled out that have discontinuous claim-making; third, only collective and bounded interactions (contentions) are selected from these interactions; and fourth, only specific sorts of social engagements (repertoires of contention) are finally listed in the Catalogue (Tilly 1987). The Events Catalogue is a useful strategy of locating collective violence onto a space where participants contend each other with a shared repertoire of interactions. It helps locate all forms of collective violence onto a space where participants contend each other with a shared repertoire of interactions. It transforms all incidences of collective interactions into *routine* performances of contentious politics.

Yet, not all events of collective interactions are *routine* performances of contentious politics. Lynching actually reveals limits to all forms of contentious politics in a society as it is a collective action to render its victim utterly powerless, depriving her/him of even a right to contend. Indeed, lynching briefly suspends all possible expressions of contention and reinforces the existing power structure violently. Lynching regroups/reunites a dominant group to perpetuate collective and anonymous strategies of repression on what it perceives as a deviation in the social arrangements. Originating in a given political milieu, lynching soon turns into a bizarre dance of social control beyond contention. The proponents of the Events Catalogue in fact acknowledge the problem of lynching. They label lynching as *violent rituals*, consigning them into archaic, perhaps premodern enactments of collective rage that are empty of any political meaning (Wood 2009). The theory of contentious politics and contentious performances therefore poorly fit into the Events Catalogues. The proponents, in other words, have selected the comfort of the middle ground of contentious politics by refusing to navigate through the edges of collective violence.

There is another, more fundamental problem with the theory of contentious politics. That has to do with the analysis of the Events Catalogues. The proponents of the Catalogue have struggled to connect the extracted fragments in order to produce credible descriptions. Two reasons may be cited for the poor results. First, the analysts' diverse views about what the events describe have strongly skewed their analytical tools. Some thought they were examining protests and therefore squabbled about the meanings of these interactions. Others thought they were measuring collective violence and therefore pursued general indexes of comparison. Still others perceived the events as collective action or conflict and sought to locate a raison d'être in individual motives, strategic interaction, or some social processes beyond rationality. The last cluster of scholars understood the catalogued events as contentious claim-making and attended to the study of social settings, institutional changes, and interactive processes (for an overview, see Tilly 2002). Second, the analysts could not discover innovative tools of analysis. The most sophisticated among them used three parameters for comparison: aggregates, incidence, and internal regularity in the events. Aggregates refer to quantitative measures of intensity of the effects, such as fatalities and the size of the affected population. Incidence covers the contextual aspects while internal regularity is essentially about the structure and growth of the events. In short, advocates of Events Catalogues have rediscovered the medical approach in the 2000s they set out to criticize in the late 1960s. The sociohistorical study of collective violence vis-à-vis contentious politics and Events Catalogues has thus come to a full circle in terms of its methodology and (having treated method as inseparable from) theory in the four decades.

The spectacular failure of sociohistorical analyses (presuming that the Events Cataloguers would somehow accommodate extreme cases like lynching) can be primarily attributed to their uncritical approach to historiography. The Modern historiography (read: European historiography or the standard academic historiography practiced globally) can hardly deal with fragmentary episodes because of its narratological bias. It inevitably requires a narrative form (with associated features of trope, argument structure, and so forth) to interpret or explain the episodes. While linguistic forms, such as sentence structure, verbal semantics, and deictic constituents may help to typify and classify the events, one cannot possibly generate narratives out of the fragments except by imposing an overarching law of induction. Historical sociologists as cataloguers have imitated public health officials not only because they are often commissioned to develop ways to control collective maladies, but also because the dominant historiography, where their interests lie, cannot generate historical sense without narration, just as medical knowledge is known to have generated out of the cases (Hess and Mendelsohn 2010). Can there be a historical alternative to the medical approach, one in which historical understanding is entirely based on the episodic events and records and not on the ability to reconstruct narratives from them?

Making Sense of Fragments

One crucial aspect of the medieval Newari historiography (XIV–XVIII centuries) in Nepal takes the problem of analysis to an entirely different order.[3] The Newars in the medieval period viewed history as a concatenation of episodes. They preserved all memories of their past as lists of events. In other words, they conceived history in fragments. I have argued for the historiographical significance of these records elsewhere (Raj 2012). Suffice it to say that these records constitute what I have argued as an exemplar of a particular type of case historiography, and not the infrahistory specie called *chronicles*, as is usually supposed. Unlike the specimens of the modern academic historiography, where cases are embedded as illustration of a general argument, these histories (I have called them *Chātas*) present a list of episodes in their barest possible particulars. The histories are not strict on chronology. In fact, as an early *Chāta* history, *The Gopalarajavamsavali*, attests, chronology seems to be deliberately sabotaged closer to their writing present.[4] They do not provide any overarching narrative, nor do they exhibit tropes. They rarely possess thematic unity and explain the events. An example presents events (in the order) of years NS 741, 685, 741, 741, 744, 774, then 772.[5] As I will show later, records of lynching are strung in the middle of the accounts of other social and personal events and without any logical (temporal, thematic, or causal) order. To make sense out of these episodic accounts, one must abandon the narratological aim of the sociologist-historians, who have struggled to reconstruct an explanatory narrative from their abstracts of Events Catalogues. Instead, one should seek ways to generate historical or sociological understanding of the events without resorting to the reconstruction route. More specifically, the methodological challenge for the students of lynching in Nepali history is to rediscover the logic of episodic history.

Before discussing some of the medieval records of collective cruelty in general and of lynching in particular, it will be useful to mention two important caveats in the available specimens of the *Chāta* historiography. First, available histories do not cover much of the XV–XVI centuries. Much of the materials in *The Gopālarājavamsāvali* concentrates mostly on the preceding centuries in a typical genealogical tradition in Sanskrit and was compiled around the year 1389 (Vajracharya and Malla 1985; Witzel 1990). Other medieval Newari *Chāta* texts present events from the XVII century onward. Although the latter texts compiled much older accounts as well, they were essentially "live histories" in the sense that accounts of events, be they contemporary or the ones just rediscovered, would be added to the book as they happened (just as newspaper archives of our day do). This is evident in the page of a *Chāta* text, where an event of NS 810 is added on the upper margins while the main body records another episode of NS 918. The chronicling, combined with the loose chronological schema, results in a handy reference to the events without having to narrativize the past, i.e., without resorting to the historians' presentist insistence on exhibiting how all past events lead to the present. Thus, history (not the past, but its accounts) remains fragmented in the *Chāta* specimens.

This feature of the *Chāta* historiography is also indicated by evidence internal to the texts (Raj 2012). Entries reveal that the *Chāta* texts were used to publicly distinguish among contesting claims about ritual or procedural norms.[6] They were also consulted by the state at the times of crises to devise ways out.[7] Unprecedented happenings were labeled as something not recorded in the *Chātas*.[8] In other words, *Chātas* served as normative accounts for dictating the ways to conduct the present state of affairs. We will come back to this crucial feature later while discussing how analogy is the key to making sense of the episodes in the *Chātas*.

Second, records of lynching are relatively scarce among the extant *Chāta* histories. Out of 30 or so *Chātas* I have consulted, about two dozen such episodes could be culled, although the number would rise if one also included instances of collective cruelty in general. And, except one, all belong to the late XVII to mid–XVIII centuries.[9] *Chātas* plentifully record negative events, both of a religious and secular nature, precisely because of their normative function. Hence, an argument of deselection (i.e., *Chāta* historians were predisposed to censor illustrations of moral decrepitude in the past) does not hold. I will endorse the other possible reason, which assumes the rapturous character of the period, as I will demonstrate later. Historians faithfully recorded the contemporary events either without really comprehending their moral significance or took care in not omitting the fragments because of their sociohistorical significance.

Episodes of Medieval Lynching

A fragment of NS 810 (1689) documenting the lynching of Lakshminarayan of Madu is noted in a *Chāta* almost as an afterthought:

> On the 9th of the Bright half in the month of Dira, [an auspicious element] came off from [the body of the deity Aryavalokiteswar]. That led to the [daylight] murder of Lakshminarayan of Madu on the day of Cotha. (Shakya 1125 NS: 58)[10]

The same episode also appears in other *Chāta*s from which we may conjure up other interesting elements, such as that Lakshminarayan was trounced suddenly by a group of *Khas*es. *Khas*es were members of the Nepali language–speaking population, especially those hailing from the west of the medieval Kathmandu Valley. The Khases were involved in Kathmandu Valley politics and warfare from at least the XIII century onward. For instance, we were told:

> In Sam 810 (1689) Bhadrapada Sukla Pamcami, Svati Nakshatra, Thursday. On this day, Minister Lakshminarayan was caught by the *Khas*es in his own house and was attacked with swords. He managed to flee out of his house. But he was again seized near the Maju temple and cut into pieces. His hand was cut for the gold bracelets. Later, one of the *Khas*es who looted the gold bracelets was imprisoned. All jewelry he had worn was ransacked. They made it like the bounty in a war. His body was placed in a funeral bed and awaited the arrival of his wife from Khapva. The three kings of Bhaktapur stayed in [Kathmandu] for seven days. Mansingh was given the ministry. (Panta 2066 VS: 216)[11]

The entries do not indicate who the *Khas*es were and what their motivation was for the murder. Clearly, Lakshminarayan was carrying out his routine departure to the palace when he was attacked and he could not offer any resistance. The XIX-century Nepali chronicles had an unmistaken propensity for narrativization of the past. Hence, they inserted elements to make the event seem comprehensible. In these latter accounts, the *Khas*es are shown to attack Lakshminarayan in the pretext of seeking advice. He was depicted as the prime minister and a favorite to the queen, who lamented the loss by collecting "his spilled blood in a silver bowl" and arranged the dead body to be carried in a funeral bed to complete the last rites (Lamsal 2023 VS: 100; "Nepalko Itihas Rajbhogmala" 1970: 1). Lakshminarayan was shown to have a morally fallen character in order to rationalize his violent end: he was said to spend day and night in the palace, wore the King's attire, slept in the royal bed with the queen, and crucially "did not pursue wars" when Yela king had just attacked his country ("Nepal Desko Itihas" 1972: 2).

The *Vamshavali*s also noted Lakhsminarayan's cruelty toward Pratap Malla's chosen successor and his youngest son Mahipatendra Malla. In Samvat 806 (1685), Mahipatendra Malla escaped to Lalitpattana, fearing for his life. Within days, Lakshminarayan managed to send Khas Magars to kill the prince. They failed as the locals responded to the prince's desperate call to rescue him by hitting the invaders. The *Khas* leaders Kashiram Ale and Kalu Kathaiya "were beaten, pushed in the drains, and had their skulls broken."[12] Unable to protect himself, Mahipatendra Malla, who had been rendered disabled, took refuge with the ascetic Raghavananda Svami in Deopatan. Lakshminarayan's men caught the prince and tied him up with a rope. As they wrestled to get the prince out, Raghavanada came to apologize, but they pushed him down the stairs. Mahipatendra was mercilessly murdered. The *Vamshavali* then concluded: "Minister Lakshminarayan saw his severed head" to ensure that the prince was indeed dead.[13] In other words, the *Chāta* historiography and the *Vamshavali* tradition differed in structuring the episodes, in that historians of the former insisted on recording only the basic and publicly verifiable elements of the event, while those encoding the latter wanted to make the accounts intelligible for them and for posterity.

Modern historians have outpaced the explanatory framework of the *Vamshavali*s by linking Lakhsminarayan's fate to that of his predecessor Cikuti alias Devidas Bharo, whose sad end he is said to have masterminded (Tevari 2021 VS). Thus, Lakshminarayan is depicted as Cikuti's competitor: it was he who spread the rumor that Cikuti had poisoned King Parthivendra Malla, Pratap's second son. The angry crowd that had gathered in the royal courtyard then set upon Cikuti and his followers.

The Newari *Chāta*s do not contain this narrative, however. Fragments refer to Cikuti, alias Devidas, as Pratap Malla's powerful minister (*Praman*), and as a key player in bringing Kantipur and Yela together against Khapo.[14] In two years' time, he fell out of the king's favor.[15] In 794, Cikuti took refuge (*purdava*) in Yela. The Yela king was, however, more interested in altering the council of minister in Kathmandu than in restoring Cikuti's privilege. Soon, he handed over Cikuti to Kantipur, and the latter was kept under house arrest.[16] Within a few years, in NS 804 (1683), this officer, who ran the state affairs "without a thorn spoiling his path" (*niskantak*), had again run away with his entire family and Khas entourage first to Yela, and then to Budhasim, a village in the outskirts of the Valley.[17] Three years later, one *Chāta* mentions Cikuti's passing away like this:

> In 807 (1686) Asadh Sukla Sasthi. Tuesday . . . Cikuti and others were dead.[18]

Another shows that Cikuti's death resulted in a lynching. The episode was horrendous.

In 807 (1686), Asadha Sukla Sasti, Tuesday, on this day, citizens (*Praja*) gathered [in the royal courtyard] in multitude and insisted on knowing the murderers of the King. They said they would murder the murderers. No one could pacify them. Sri 2 King of Bhaktapur (*Khapva*) tried to console them. After he promised to find the culprit by the evening, they dispersed. In the afternoon, Bamsidhar was captured from the royal palace and was brought to the Hiticuka. Cikuti of Pasupati (*Goro*) was accused of poisoning [the late King of Kathmandu] and was flogged mercilessly. His head was bleeding. [Notwithstanding this] every passerby punched and kicked him. The *Khas*es accompanying him were killed. His family members, including the children, were pulled out of the house and maimed. His men escaped. Both Cikuti and Bamsidhar were imprisoned and killed in Patan (*Yala*).[19]

A latter-day *Vamshavali* records not only the conflicts (Nep. *manugye*) among the selfish ministers but also relates Cikuti's lynching to the death of King Nripendra Malla under suspicious circumstances. Hence, the death of the Kantipur king on NS 807 (1686) Asadh Sukla 3 Saturday drew Cikuti into the vortex of the violence. The minister Cikuti had by then gone to reside in Devpattana and was spending his days offering prayers to Sri Pashupatinath, listening to the Puranas, and giving away cows, grains, clothes, and so forth. Nevertheless, on the fourth day after the death of King Nripendra Malla:

> Cikuti was beaten, pulled by the tuft of his hair (*tupi*), and was brought to Kantipur from Devpattan. He lost consciousness at Dhobi Khola. Shresthas, Mahats, Khusals, and Podyas, people of all castes hit him. When he was brought thus, someone hit him with a rod. The head started bleeding. A man called Bamsidhar urged people to stop the bleeding by saying, "I would give seven thousand *mohar*s if someone could help, and the cost of this blood is seven thousands." Upon hearing this, people went mad. They picked urine and scat up, and force-fed him. Then, both Cikuti and Bamsidhar were beaten to death. Cikuti's family members were caught and beaten to death wherever they were found. Only those who could escape survived. Save Taudhika, who escaped to Patan, only womenfolk and very young ones survived.[20]

Unlike this narrative, the series of lynchings, first of Cikuti and then of Lakshminarayan, were rationally incomprehensible to the contemporaries. To make it comprehensible, they too imposed chronological order and causal structure on the events. They thus attributed the events to the transgression of a forbidden norm. The illegitimate heir of one Mahadev Ujha, Kantu Ujha, should not be allowed to enter into the country. Hence, a copper-plate inscription in the Kathmandu Mulchok reads:

> Kantu Ojha, the son of Mahadev Ujha . . . because of his machinations, Sri Sri Jaya Parthivendra Malla and Sri Sri Yognarendra Malla died. By nailing this

copper plate inscription in the Main Courtyard, it was known that the bad-son should not have been allowed to enter into the country. Despite knowing thus, Lakshminarayan trusted him. As a result, Sri Sri Parthivendra Malla died, Cikuti with his family perished, Sri Sri Mahipatendra Malla also died. Lakshminarayan, who misread this copperplate in the Main Courtyard, also died because of his *error*. (Vajracharya et al. 2019 VS: 283. Emphasis added)[21]

This shows that while the medieval minds worked in the same way as modern historians' vis-à-vis narratology, their histories were kept insulated from the fallacies of narration, as it were.

The *Vamshavali* historians, on the other hand, were more pronounced in their moral verdicts. This was evident in the way they structured the episode. Hence, some portrayed the ascendance of the XIV-century king, Jayasthiti Malla (in the XIX century!) as a return of a legitimate heir and his violent machinations leading to taking power as a logical necessity; others sought to justify it as a forceful correction by the people of a wrong conducted by selfish queens and princes.[22] The *Chāta* historian, however, did not explain or interpret these events.

In 1697, Govardhan and Sivanarayan of Bhayamare and Sasi Upadhya of Navakvatha were pulled out of the fort at Gutha. They were garlanded with pig entrails, made to climb on buffaloes, and were tortured. In Madu, they were beaten with the Corrahs. People punched and kicked them. Govardhan and Sasi died on the south bank of the River Tukhu. On the following day, Govardhan's wife immolated herself in her husband's pyre.[23]

The *Chāta* historian did not pursue the reason behind the event and *reported* simply that the perpetrators also killed two armed men, who were the men they believed orchestrated the lynching at the direction of the younger prince (*Mirimha juju*).

The *Vamshavali* historians did not notice this episode. Yet all fragments in their selection were made intelligible by rational narrativization. Hence, in the reign of Jayaprakash Malla, popular resentment against the "innocent" Tirhutiya Brahmins resulted in a major lynching event because the King favored these outsiders.[24]

Analogon in the *Chāta* Historiography

In the absence of two basic elements of rational historiography—narration and chronology—the episodes in the *Chāta*s generate historical sense by analogy. Standard epistemologies in human and natural sciences operate either by inductive (particular to universal) or deductive (universal to particular) logic. Analogy provides a third relationship among the particulars.

Making Sense of Lynching in Medieval Nepal 113

An episode in the *Chāta* exhibits a general proposition without requiring further generalization. An episode in these histories, in other words, is to be read as a paradigm. More crucially, the *Chāta* historiography employed paradigms to produce a sense of history without resorting to diachronic (comparative) or synchronic (contemporary) analyses, thus freeing the historical sense from the bondage of time. It became possible to write histories without narration or causality.

In order to clear some ground, a brief review of theories of paradigm is imperative. The Kuhnian paradigm is a set of values and norms shared by scientists that inform them what science normally is and how it is done. The methods and models that scientists internalized during their training (exemplars) help them reside within a disciplinary matrix and operate within a paradigm. A *paradigm* is a singular historical phenomenon (that is, panopticon, clinic, madhouse, and so forth) that stands equally for all others in a class and makes the classification intelligible.[25] Paradigms produce normal science. In Kuhnian sociology, paradigms (for example, the Copernican model, Newtonian mechanics, quantum theory, and so forth) provide the context of science. In contrast, for Foucault, *paradigm*—although he does not use the term—is an exemplar that generates a particular regime of power and language. He considered it as an epistemological figure, or the basic text of power/knowledge. The question as to how a paradigm frees itself from a specific instance and illuminates other instances in other periods is a key to understanding the *analogon* (i.e., how analogy operates) in the *Chātas*. The argument here is that contemporary readers of the medieval fragments employed the analogical logic to make sense of the lynching and did not follow the common and more familiar method of overlaying chronological narratives as illustrated in the *Vamshavalis*.

Each entry in the *Chāta*s is a paradigm, an example par excellence: It is an example that illustrates (Skt. *Udaharana*) and defines what it stands to exemplify (Skt. *Dristanta*). In other words, a paradigm is both an example and a model inseparably. As the former, it represents a verifiable historical phenomenon. As the latter, it sets the norms for the class of similar cases. Because of its dual (sensible and ideal) character, it is not often possible to derive rules from a paradigm. It exhibits the rule only in its exhibition and not otherwise. Put differently, the rule does not precede but stands *beside* (*para*) a paradigm. Since no abstraction is possible from paradigms, enumeration is the only strategy available. *Analogon* moves from one episode to another.

A paradigm generates meaning because of its three constituents: First, it is a sign: It stands for an affair in the world. The linguistic structure and style of an episode in the *Chāta* substitutes a historical event. Second, it represents similarity both to the event and to similar episodes occurring elsewhere and in other times. This makes it an example of a class. Third, it is conferred some sort of sanctification. It is used to serve as a model/norm for comprehending other examples of the class. It is employed as defining the class. The efficacy of a paradigm lies in the third constituent. An example begins to operate as a paradigm when it is endowed with moral signification (Agamben 2009). Just as sacred water is water and something more, a case in the *Chāta* histories is an episode and something more: a model of all similar events. A paradigm is a signature that adds meaning to the class of events it represents.

It is important to realize that the task of creating paradigms is at the core of all knowledge-producing activities. The *Chāta* historian is already at a juncture historians seek to be. All practicing historians know that they do not randomly choose the documents out of the endless mass of the archive, but follow, in Agamben's words, "the subtle and obscure thread of signatures that demand to be read here and now" (Agamben 2009: 73). They string together episodes as signatures so that readers decipher the other meanings not referred to. Paradigmatic episodes can thus yield sense even when freed from the immediate context of their reference.

Hence, the *Chāta*s were frequently consulted to understand the past, but more significantly, to seek what the norm is both for the ordinary and extraordinary in life. The paradigmatic evidence may be found within a *Chāta*, now preserved in the National Archives in Kathmandu. The *Chāta* historian gives his verdict on the auspicious days for celebrating the Indrajatra in NS 854 and then, perhaps responding to the critics, immediately inserts an episode of how a similar row had been settled in NS 669. The astrologers residing in the northern and southern quarters in the city had a dispute over the criteria for determining the auspicious day of Indrajatra celebrations. Both the parties were then called in the royal court to produce *Chāta*s in support of their arguments (इहाया छातिचोस्यं तया जानालपा). The public congregation was convinced of Kusumraj Bharo's evidence. Then the King said: "Concurring with your view, I order you write today's decision in the *Chāta* and show it [to the posterity] just as we consulted the old *Chāta*s." The decision was inscribed for future use (दोकालेयात सोयेयात). The episode proves both the argument for the past consultative use of the *Chāta*s, and the exemplification of how these histories are best read today.[26]

Priests in Kathmandu decided the structure of the expiatory ritual in the summer of 1816 by consulting XVI-century records so that the return of an epidemic could be pacified (Raj 2012: 92, fn. 35). In NS 835–836 (1714–1715); a decision not to perform a ritual was reached by reading the *Chāta* records.[27] In NS 998 (1877), a dispute ensued in Sankhu about the involvement of Kathmandu priests in the Vajrayogini temple rituals. Jinendra, a priest favoring such participation, won the public approval by challenging his opponent Jayendra with these words: "I can show you that *nhasapola* ritual has been performed by involving the Gubhajus of Yam. Let me see if you can show even a single episode in which they were not allowed in."[28] The word *Chāta* was the established standard, an authority for dictating the present. Thus, a new *Chāta* was said to be established by an unconventional practice.[29] In NS 802 (1681), the people in Bhaktapur, Kathmandu, Lalitpur, and Gorkha celebrated the Dashain festival in Kartik following the Bhaktapur astrologer, Shiva Joshi, who attested for such precedence.[30]

Lynching episodes in the *Chāta* histories and, by extension, the episodes in the Event Catalogues compiled by the social historians are therefore to be read as paradigms and not as mere representations. To seek comparison between two episodes, in terms either of their internal structure or of their sociopolitical and cultural contexts, is to make sense of them by narrativizing them. This involves actions such as appending the episodes to specific time and place, chronologizing them so as to enable causal relations, analyzing the threads and traces in the contexts that seem to bundle up in the lynching event, and adding motivations to the actors. This is the familiar route pursued by the *Vamshavali*s and, to a large extent, of the academic histories. The failure of these histories is not linked to inadequate reconstruction and, therefore, could not be remedied by further exploration of the contexts, more accurate analyses, or innovative psychological theories. To contrast, nonnarrative historiography in the world, as illustrated by the medieval *Chāta*s here, preserves the past as signatures. They are signs of the times. That raises questions specific to the period. Then they yield similarity with other events both contemporaneous and transcendent. That raises problems of classification and typology. Crucially, they provide models/norms so that their readers frequently refer to them and, by analogy, understand what makes events in the world in general, and lynching in particular, episodic and how to act when such episodes recur.

Making Sense of Lynching

The phrase "Making Sense" in the title of this chapter has two inflections. First, it means making sense of the episodic historiography that ensured reproduction of knowledge about lynching, which is an episode par excellence. This is the attempt I have made in this chapter. There is another closely related notion, which involves making these extreme episodes legible such that these events are explained or interpreted in terms of their social context. These would then perhaps be held as illustrations for a general rule so that their near-present recurrences could be rationalized or warned against. Clearly, the second task builds on the first. Hence, the sociohistorical approaches to lynching and collective violence are greatly significant for their promise of developing a theory of method that would help generate insights into these extreme collective events.

Tilly viewed the method of constructing Event Catalogues as involving theorizing. Methodology of the Catalogues demanded, in his opinion, a continuous revision of the core concepts that laid at the foundation of the method. He took Event Catalogues essentially as exhibiting theoretical problems in relation to the logic of the method. To contrast, this chapter begins with a premise that the *Chāta* historians have already solved the methodological problem by putting to use a feasible template for constructing an efficient Event Catalogue (*Chāta*s). The *Chāta*s are proven to be efficient because they allowed generations of readers to gain historical sense without requiring them to fall back to a narrative mode of logic, which compulsively drove both the *Vamshavali* writers and today's historians. Indeed, narrative histories are a mainstay of the conventional historical imagination, be it in the Vamshavalis or in today's academic histories. Event Catalogues demand an exploration into nonnarrative logic of history. This chapter therefore takes the problem of interpretation, and not the problem of method, as the key to episodic historiography, of which both Tilly's Event Catalogues and the Newari *Chāta*s provide sample specimens. Put differently, this chapter seeks to contribute toward solving the epistemological puzzle of history as episodes.

The *Chāta* historiography, with its liberal attitude toward the logic of temporal ordering (in contrast with the strong emphasis on a secure temporal hinge for each episode), almost nulls emphasis on explanation, causal or otherwise, relying on the standard set of verifiable bare particulars of the event and nothing else (that is, no mention of psychological attributes), and the loose typology, both thematically or otherwise, calls for a radically different way of making sense of the episodes. This chapter argues for abandoning conventional inquiries into the relations among particulars in both inductive (particular to universal) and deductive (universal to particular) mode. Instead, it proposes the analogical logic of fragments whereby each fragment is to be seen as a paradigm for the class of similar events.

The *Chāta* historians included the episodes on the lynching of Lakshminarayan and Cikuti not only because these were the only events that occurred in the period but also because they were merely representative of the series of such episodes. Beyond serving as a sign (a linguistic substitute for the real event) and a representative example (one among the similar many), they presented each episode as a paradigm. That often made mentioning of other examples redundant. Frequent referrals to the *Chāta*s for seeking norms during incomprehensible crises, be they of immense magnitude or of critical nature, also proves their paradigmatic nature. Paradigms illuminate our minds by flashing light on any present instance that otherwise cannot be explained or interpreted by the usual logic of induction or deduction. Paradigms are examples that also exemplify the class, and stand on their own. They are very well amenable to contextual inquiries, but they transcend contexts and serve to build understanding by ellipsis. If one finds a wife almost incomprehensibly faithful to her husband, she/he says "sati Savitri," and everyone breaks into smiles. If one discovers a maliciously charged atmosphere with immanent likelihood of collective vendetta, you whisper "Hyoju," and everyone in Bhaktapur will become silent.[31] Some may question the comparison, but no one will doubt what these paradigms stand for.

A thorough examination of the making of the paradigms, however, is still due. First, it may be argued that all kinds of knowledge-producing activities involve some efforts to create paradigms out of examples encountered during observation. Many consider physics as a paradigmatic science because it seems to establish paradigms out of the natural world. Historians/anthropologists may argue that they are engaged in the worthy activity of discovering the paradigms of the past/the other and analyzing society through these paradigms. What is involved in proving an example as a paradigm is a question to be further investigated: Do examples need certain features to gain the status of the paradigms? Or, are there specific contextual features that help the rise and reproduction, or alternately, the demise, of the paradigms? One possible line of inquiry would be to build upon Donald Black's *Moral Time* (2011), specifically its early innovative applications to the problem of collective violence in general and in lynching in particular (de la Roche 1996, 2001), and to see if reversion to paradigms occurs during rapid alterations in the relational times in a society. One could then imagine why mimetic influences of an episodic historiography in South Asia help both the actors and victims restage cases of lynching despite themselves.

Second is, of course, the other inflection of "Making Sense'" in the title of this chapter. Making sense of lynching and other episodes is in part about making them legible to rationalization. Such endeavor will be fruitfully undertaken by paying attention to the times and places when societies seek paradigms to understand their immediate problems. To say that these situations will be moments of ruptures is obvious enough (Raj 2013), for during ruptures, known structures both of the world and of the understanding about the world are thrown into disarray, and profound epistemological crises occur. Paradigms save the face of the usual logical interpretation by teaching societies to practice analogy. The question as to whether one can meaningfully trace this movement from dialectical to analogical understanding also has to be considered. This question is applicable to lynching and to all episodic events (some may argue that all events are episodic by definition). Thus, this chapter only solves the puzzle of generating (in the *Chāta* examples) sense from the fragments, and that too partially. Much of the challenge of the arguments in this chapter will be met while seeking to establish a paradigm of lynching—a task I will attempt next.

Notes

1. This chapter was written during the fellowship period 2014–2015 at Nepā School of Social Sciences and Humanities, Kathmandu, Nepal. I acknowledge the generous grant and congenial environment provided by the School. I thank Dean Dr. Rajendra Pradhan and Professor Sudhindra Sharma for the invitation. The preliminary findings of this chapter were also presented as a lecture under the Martin Chautari–Nepā School Seminar Series. I am grateful to the coordinators of the Series for the request and the participants for their questions and comments on the presentation. This chapter uses sources in three more languages other than English: Sanskrit, Nepali, and Newari, the latter two are spoken in Nepal. Newari is a language spoken by the Newars in the Kathmandu Valley and has a written tradition of over a millennium. I have not used diacritics to transliterate non-English words for the cleaner appearance of the page, except one word *Chāta*, a particular type of Newari historical texts from the Kathmandu Valley. I should caution readers not familiar with the languages that they will be pronouncing the non-English words rather inaccurately. For those who are more familiar with South Asian writings, I have rendered both Nepali and Newari source texts, chiefly in the form of quotations in the endnote, in the Devanagari Script, used for Sanskrit, Hindi, and some other Indo-Aryan languages in India.

2. I am aware of other institutional, economic, and cultural approaches as well, but my critique in this chapter is limited to sociohistorical approaches alone.

3. For the purpose of this chapter, I have used the following published and unpublished medieval histories. Among the unpublished are: *Suthan Chāta A* (The Sunthan Collection, Bhaktapur), *Santi-svasti Saphula* (The Royal Library, Copenhagen), *Mallakalik Thyasaphu* (The National Archives, Kathmandu), *Khvapajujupini Vamshavali* (The Asa Archives, Kathmandu), and *Ghatanavali* (The National Archives, Kathmandu). The published histories are Aryal 2060 VS; Kayastha 2058 VS; Kharbuja 2057 VS; Naraharinath 2013 VS; Panta 2066 VS; Panta 2067 VS; Panta 2069 VS; Raj 2056 VS.a; Raj 2056 VS.b; Raj 2057 VS; Raj (forthcoming); Rajvamsi 2020 VS; Regmi 1966; Shakya 1125 NS; Sharma 1104 NS; Shrestha 2000; Vajracharya 1107 NS; Vajracharya and Malla 1985; Vajracharya 2023 VS; Vajracharya 2025 VS; and Vajracharya and Shrestha 2035 VS. I am preparing a critical edition of all known medieval *Chāta*s.

4. Cecil Bendall, the first historian to publicize what is now known as *The Gopalarajavamsavali*, notes that [V3] "begins with N.S.379 and the history would not seem to be treated on a strictly chronological basis, as the irregularity of order in the dates notes noticed in V2 is here *more pronounced*" (Bendall 1905: 4, emphasis added).

5. The year mentioned here is otherwise known as *Nepal Samvat* (NS) or simply *Samvat*, which started in 879 AD.

6. "In Samvat 918, Sravan Sukla Pratipada, a claim was made that the royal priest should conduct the chief puja during the pacification ritual. Those representing the royal palace, the followers of Pramajuju, the Elder of the Country, and respectable men, all gathered. After consulting the old manuals, they decided to allow Cakrapatiju of Duganbahi deity to lead the ritual" (Shakya 1125 NS: 58). Similarly, "On the day of Marga Purnima, a fire ritual similar to that conducted in the *Ka Swaye* ceremony was performed to consecrate the foundation of the main pillar. The eldest manager of the ritual was Sri Bhim, the Chief of the Mint. On this day, Jayendra from Sako protested in front of Sri Bhim the Chief that the priests from the country of Yem had not been invited in any of the rituals of the Vajrayogini deity before. Jinendra and Jnanasidhhi from the Mul invited them. Consequently, a public meeting was called at the Monastery in Sako. Much debate ensued. Jinendra and Jayendra were made to argue against each other. Then Jinendra replied that he could prove that the priests from Yem had been previously invited (in the Vajrayogini ritual), let him see what evidence Jayendra had for not inviting them. Jayendra confessed that he did not have any document to show. The presiding elder and the public present in the meeting then criticized Jayendra, saying if he did not possess any proof why did he raise the issue. Jayendra could not speak a word and was thoroughly defeated" (Raj 2012: 92 fn. 34).

7. "From Jestha Sukla 12 in this year, 20–50 human beings died every day following an outbreak of the devastating disease. Pacifying sutras were recited in all 32 quarters in the city. A chandravimsati sacrifice was performed by Muni Gubhaju of Asan, Atiharsha Gubhaju of Kamilachi, and Vajraharsha Gubhaju of Kelatol. When another outbreak began to devour 30–50 men in a single day, pacification was done by referring to a ritual conducted during the reign of Mahindra Malla" (Raj 2012: 92 fn. 35).

8. "No precedence (*Chāta*) is found for returning the goods offered in the Agam. This day it was set" (Regmi 1966: Appendix III: 56).

9. The exception is a XIX-century reconstruction of a mid-XIV-century event occurring solely in a Nepali *Vamshavali* and is framed in mythic terms (Sharma 1968: 4).

10. The passage reads:
संवत् ८१० दरि गा नओमकिुन्हु . . . ङसे पोर ओ
र, थुरयि उपदर जुयाओ, मदुया, रक्ष्मीनाराय(ण) . . . पाराओ स्या
त, दनि एदा चोथाक कुन्हु . . .

My reconstruction is based on other entries in the same *Chāta*. This particular history belongs to a Vajrayan monastery in Kathmandu, and its modern compiler has rightly called the string of events (*ghatanavali*) a *Santisaphu* (a book of pacifying formulae).

11. See also, Vajracharya et al. (2019 VS: 277–278); Regmi 1966: Appendix III, 34. Panta's reading is by far the best. It reads:
सं ८१० भाद्रपद शुक्ल, पंचमी, स्वातनिक्षत्र, बृहस्पतिवार, थ्वकुह्नु चौतारा, लक्ष्मीनाराण खस्तो
जाङाव, थव छेस भुज्यालनि पाराव पब्रिवाड बसिय वर, माजुया देवर क्वस राडाओ,
पाराव स्याक, राहात धेङाव, लुचुल्या काव खस छह्म राक कुडाओ तव, चु
ल्या छपा मदु, हमस चोकों काव, रणस राडा थे सङ, (परमस थङ, खपव्या करात मबिसिय वङ)
थाना वने धक मुनकाव तव, स्याङाव
मडाओ, खपव्या राजा सवम्हं हनसह्नु तो चोङ, मानसजियात चौतारा बियाओ ताथु ॥ (2066 VS: 216).

12. संवत् ८०६ सालमा महिपितेन्द्र मल्ल भागि ललितपट्टनमा गया । . . . भोलिपल्ट चौकि रहयाका परमानहरू आफ्ना आफ्ना घर गया । यसतै बेलामा कांतिपूरका राजाका मानसिषस मगरहरू आइ महिपितेन्द्र मल्ल बस्याको घरलाई घे-या । जबरजसति गिरा धरभित्र पसि समातन जांदा महिपितेन्द्र मल्लले झयालबाट अंगुलि बिहिरि निकोलि सारै रोइ हे परजा मलाई मारन लाग्या ढोका षोलि कोठाभित्र आउनु लाग्या मेरो जिवि रक्षा गर भनि बिति गिर्दा परजाहरूले सरन आयाकालाई यहांसम्म भयापछै अब क्या हेरि रहेछौ लौ समात लौ मार भनि जम्मै भै राजाकन घेरन्याहरूकन समाइ कुटिमा-या । कतिका हात भांच्या कतिका गोरा भांच्या सरिरिबाट रगतका धारा बहया कतिलाई लातले हान्या कतिलाई कुलोमा षांद्या कतिलाई कपाल फो-या कति भागि गया तनिहरू सबका हतियार लुटि लिया लबेदा पटुका पगरि समेत उतारि लिया कासीराम आले कालु कठैया मुषयिाहरूकन कुटि सिक्यापछि राजकुलमा थुनि राष्या । (Nepalko Itihas Rajbhogmala 1969: 24).

13. यहा पछि लक्ष्मीनारायण जोसि मूल काजी भया पछ अघि पाटनका थुनी राष्याका काजीहरूकन छाडी पठाया । याहा पछि केही सामर्थ नभयाका महिपितेन्द्र मल्ल डराइ लुकि रह्याका राजपुत्रकन भादरपद शुक्ल ११ बुधबारका दनि राघवानंद स्वामीका घरमा लुकि रह्याका महिपितेन्द्र मल्लकन डोरिलि बांधी तानातान गर्दा राघवानन्द स्वामीजे माफ गर २ भनी बुझाइ बतिगिरन आउन्या स्वामीकन भ-यांडबाट षसालि दिया । महिपितेन्द्र मल्लकन अन्यायसति जीवहरण ग-या । म-या उपरांत सति काटी ल्याई लक्ष्मीनारायण काजीले हे-यो । (Sharma 1969: 24).

14. सं ७८७ आषाढकृष्ण परतिपिदाकुहुनु . . . चान्ह्स चकिुटिपिरमान यल व घरछ लिवि खपोंया श्रीश्रीश्रीजगत्प्रकाशमल्ल वव प्याखनस श्री २ नविसमल्ल नापलाक सतकिुन्हु तोङ कथनं पछिया जुरो शुभमस्तु ॥ थ्वकुन्हु निस्यं खपो याकात जुरो ॥ (Rajvamsi 2020 VS: 3).

15. सं. ७८९ ज्ञा श्रीपरतापमल्लजुया परमान वंकलया देवीदास नाम कुनाम चकिुटी कुङ ॥ स्व नगरया गाम नयाव चोडम्हा जुरा ॥ (Ibid.).

16. सं ७९४ वैशाखकृष्ण षष्ठी शुक्रवार . . . श्रीनिवासमल्लन चकिुटिपिरमानपन बेस वयाव चोड डारा तो ज्ञलस थ्वकुन्हु लवल्हाडा थव छेस . . . क जुरो ॥ (Ibid.: 6).

17. The phrase occurs in Cikuṭi's inscription in Naudeval, near Machindrabahal in Kathmandu (Tevari 2021: 14). Similarly,
सं ८०४ कार्त्तकि शुदधटि ज्ञया चकिुटिपिरमान ज्ञल बेसे वव थंक्वाथस पेन्हु चोडाव गन्देपाल बुधसविङ (Rajvamsi 2020 VS: 17).
दं ८०४ कार्त्तकि शुक्ल ॥ अष्टमी, बुधवार, थ्वकुहनुया रात्रीस, चकिुति भाजुपनभोच्छि बसिय वङ यरस, पेहनुकुहनु बुधसिधाया गामस चोन वन, खस्तो उमराव भक्विं नाप वङ ॥ (Panta 2066 VS: 209).

18. सं ८०७ आषाढशुक्ल षष्ठीकुहनु अंगारवार . . . ज्ञया परमान चकिुटिपिनि सिकल्य मोचकु जुरो ॥ (Rajvamsi 2020 VS: 19).

19. सं ८०७ आषाढ शुक्ल, षष्टी, अंगारवार थ्वकुहनु, देशया परजापन मिुडाओ ओयाव, राजा सुनान स्यात धकाओ पर्रजान हयत याडाओ चोडाओ जुजु स्याकहम जमिसियन स्याय धक चोडाओ, सुनानं बोध याय मफु, श्री २ खप्वया राजान बोध बरि, हनिर्याकाओ बयि धक वरस तुनि परर्जा छे छे वन ॥ थ्वकुहनुया बाहननिलि, रायकुरस चोड, वंशीधर जोडाओ हतिचिुकस नविर थ्वपनि वाश्र नकु धकाओ, गोरस चोड चकिुटि चुन दनक दायाओ, कपारन हि वयक, खडखडहमन दायाओ हव, नाप चोड खस्तों दायाओ स्याक, वया परविारं मुचातों दायाओ रुया हयाओ स्याक, भर जोको बसिय, वङ, ज्ञलस, चकिुटि विशीधर नहिम कुडाओ स्यात ॥ (Panta 2066 VS: 212).

20. संवत् ८०७ आषाढ शुक्ल त्रितियामा शनिश्चरवारका दनि कांतिपूरका राजा नृपेन्द्र मल्ल परलोक भया । राजा भूपालेन्द्र मल्ल (उमेर) कचा उमेर हुनाले मंत्रिहरूले मनुग्य गर्दा यहापछि चिकुिटी नाम परमान अरु परमानहरूसंग विरोध भै कांतिपूरका देवपट्टनमा आइ श्रीपशुपतिनाथकन दर्शन गरि पूरान सुनि गोदान अन्न

वस्त्रादि दान गरी रहन्या परमानकन राजा नृपेन्द्र मल्ल परलोक भयाको चार दिनिपछि चकुटीकन देवपट्टनदेष कुटि लुछी कांतिपुर लयाया । धोबिषोला पुग्दा चेष्टा हरायाको थियो । श्रेष्ठ महात षुसल पोढ्या सब जातले षांद्या । यसतै तरहसंग समाइ ल्याउँदा यक जनाले कपालमा लाठाले बजार्दा रगतका धारा बह्यो । यहाँपछि वंसधिर भन्याकाले एक रगत बह्याको थामदेउ सात हजार मोहर लेउ यो रगतको मोल ७ हजार मोहोर हो भंदा झन सारो वष्ठि मुत्र बाटामा रह्याको ली मुषमा जबरदस्ती गरी षांदि राखदिया । यहाँ पछि चीकुटि विधसयिर (वंशीधर) दुवैलाई गुत्क्कटघरमा मा-या । चीकुटिको परिवारलाई जहां २ पायो, तहां २ समाइ कुटि २ मा-या । तव त भाला भाताका छोराहरू भागी जान सकन्या मातर बाँच्यो । पाटनमा भागी जान्या तौडकि बाहीक परमेक बालकहरू सतरहिरू मातर बाच्या । (Nepal Desko Itihas Rajbhogmala 1969: 24).

21. Vajracharya et al. (2019 VS: 283). Emphasis added.

22. अस्य पुत्र अशोक मल्ल वर्ष १९ । . . . फेरी इ अशोक मल्ल ले इ कुमारी ठूला हुन भनी सेवा गरी रहंदा समयमा कौमारी संध बहियाका विग्मत मिन्मत संगम धाराले जगा फराक गरी छाडि उत्तरपट्ट जाइ बहँदा भया । इन राजादेष गिंगा बलाकुमारी परसन्न हुंदा इ राजाकन बडो ज्ञानी पुत्र जन्म गराइदिया । पुत्रका नाम जय स्थितिमल्ल वर्ष-४३ (Nepal Desko Itihas Rajbhogmala 1969: 10). अशोक मल्लका नेवार्नीतर्फका छोराहरूले ज्योतिषी पण्डितिहरूकन धेरै घूस ख्वाई साइत छैन भनी टारी राख्दा अशोक मल्ल शान्त भै गया र रानी सतिगयिन् । नेवार्नीका छोराहरूले राजपुत्रकन धपाई काजीहरू सबै वश्य गरी राजधानी चलाई राज चौतरिया भै रहँदा दाजुले मुलाढल कुलो भाइले एक पोखरी बनाया । पछि मिध्यमा देवालय बनाउनलाई परजाकन झारा उठाई काठ लनि पठायाका थिए । सो काठ बोकन पठायाका परजाहरू बडो हांसी खेल भनी बूढाबूढाहरूले भनेको सुनी परजाहरूले राजा कसका कमारा भनी बूढाहरूसँग सुध्याउँदा बूढाहरूले अर्थ बुझाइदिया । सो सुनी बूढाहरूका साथ सबै परजा मिली बनबाट स्याउला ली धपायाका राजपुत्रकन खोज्न जाँदा खान नपाई बनैपुरका पसलमा चउरा मागिरिहेका राजपुत्र हुन् भनी बूढाहरूले ठह-याई परजाहरूले बोकी भक्तपुरका दर्बारमा लगी नेवार्नीका दुवै छोराहरू स्याउलाले छोपी थिची मारी असली राजपुत्रकन गादीमा राख्या । (Sharma 1968: 4).

23. सं ८१८ आषाढ शुक्लः ॥ त्रयोदशी, आदित्यवार, थ्वकुहनु, भयमारेया गोवर्द्धन, शविनारायन, नवक्वाथ्या, शशि उपाध्या, थ्वपनि सवहम गुथक्वाथन पति हयाओ, फान कोखायकाओ, मेश गयकाओ, सासतया(क, मदुस चाबुकन दायकु, परजापन्सियन दायाव, तुखुचा यतिास, गोवर्द्धन, शशि निहम सकि, सतकिुहनु गोवर्द्धनया करातं भारतोवनापं सकि, मरिहम जुजु वोढाओ स्यातकर धकाओ, माहा निहम स्याक ॥ (Panta 2066 VS: 219).

24. यी राजाले मैथिली ब्रामहणहरू गुह्येश्वरीका ठूला सेवक हुन् भनी यी राजाले धेरै परीत गिर्दा खसहरूले नसही नरिपराधमा हुल उठी तिरिहुतिया ब्रामहणका घर लुटी धन संपत्ति सबै ल्याई खाइदिया । (Sharma 1969: 10).

25. On Kuhnian paradigms, see Kuhn, *Structure of Scientific Revolutions*, and Kuhn, "Second Thoughts on Paradigms," 459–482. See also Margolis, *Paradigms and Barriers*. For the link between the Kuhnian paradigm and analogical thinking, see Nickles, *Thomas Kuhn*, 142–177 and Bird, "Naturalizing Kuhn," 109–127. Foucault chose the word *épistème* (in the classical sense) to mean the same effect of the Kuhnian term *paradigm*. Foucault, *L'archéologie du savoir*. See also Maclean, "Foucault's Renaissance Episteme Reconsidered," 149–166. For a fuller analysis of Foucault's use of the épistème, see Gutting, *Michel Foucault's Archaeology*.

26. My reading of the text below differs (shown here in bold typeface) slightly from that of Panta:
स ८५४ भादरशुक्र एकादशी ६० सतकिुहनु घलछदित, **बुय घटि दिकुहनु एनकलि** सवातकाम सतकिुहनु सुनं चोड ॥ द्वादशी उदयस मत छोयका त्रयोदशी उदयश मारयात चतुरुद्दशी अनंतवरत बुहनसि पतिा, तृतीयान धुनका ॥ स ६६९ भादरशुक्र ए ५१ द्वा ५६ त्र ६० त्र १ च ३

पु ८ थथ्य वव तथिसि यंबु दशिसि सिकलसयं धाया द्वादशीस एन्द लृस्वाय उदय पुह्नसि तो यात पादुस लृय ॥ एगल सगतं यिदं बाकायस्यं धाया एकादशीस एन्द लृस्वाय धर्मम पनसि तो यात, उदय पुनसिसि लृय ॥ थथ्यं यंबु थंछुको युदिशि वो यंग्रस तविा दाड़ाव श्री २ जयनरेन्द्र मल्लदेवप्रभुठाकुलस्यं आदेश बसिसयं ह्याव व स्वदेशय युदिशि मुनकाव राजकुल कोथा क्वाथ हनोलचोक यंताचपडसि दैवज्ञ कुसुमराज भालो बाकायसके यंबुन शास्त्रर नों इहाया छाति चोस्यं तया जानालपा सगतनि शास्त्रर नों हलाय महाववचन सार्द्धन एकादशसि स्वाय धालं थथ्यं थथे ख डेड़ाव श्री २ परभुठाकुलस्यके कुसुमराज भालोन यनिापा यंबुन धाया द्वादशीसं एन्द लृस्वाय दंदु पुनशि तो यात पादुस लृय ॥ यंगल सगतनि धाया एकादशीस स्वाय धर्म पुनशि तो यात उदय पुनसिनि लृय थथ्य दोको धास्यं यनिाप याड़ाव श्री २ प्रभुठाकुलस्यं आदेश बलि देवया ख शास्त्रर नो इहाया छातिनों सोयाव भनिके परनि इह्जेल ... थेंपालयाव धकं कुसुमराज भालो आदेश बलि कुसुमराज भालोन पाल यात यंबुन धाया थ्वं द्वादशीकुह्नु एन्द लृस्वाय उदय पुनसिसि तो यात पादुस लृय धकं पाल यातं, सगतं युदिशि बाकाय परमुख मदन वकु श्री २ परभुठाकुलस्यं सगतं युदिशि च्यासुका न्ह्याय याङ तल्यं सेस्तलोकस्यन थ्व छपोल मतेव धकं धायाव श्री २ प्रभुठाकुलससके इनाप याङ श्री २ प्रभुठाकुलस्यं थ्व छपोलया सहलये आवल लिया छात्या याड़ाव इह्याया छाति थियं केनेमाल धकं आदेश बलि लथिय दोकालेयात सोययात परज्याय चोस्यं तया ॥ (Panta 2069 VS: 156).

27. ८३५ स दनिसं चक्रपूजा मड़ाओ खयार गाड़ाओ थ्व थेङ छात दु । (Suthan *Chāta* A: fol. 87).

28. जनिन्द्ररन जबा बलि थ्वलं इहापा ञया गुरबाजुपनि बोड़ा याड़ागु हनसपोल याय धुनगु परंपरा जनि केने फया, ञयापन बोने मदु धायागु छगु जक छंके सोय हकधिक धालं जयेन्द्ररन जंजिा परंपरा केने मफु धाल, ओले, सभा नं मुख्यानं केने मफयकं छाय खं हलाड़ा धकं फचकि न्वाक् । (Ibid.: fol. 6).

29. शुभ सम्बत् ९१९ मार्ग शिरि बदि ११ स थ्वगु दन महाबलिपाल लाक जनिन्दरया पाल थ्वगु दब, बाहील हीगु, हनपाया छात सेनकाओ ज्या तोपुहम हम्यायमचान बाहीया ख्वलाल हकिल छोत होंपुजास बलसिं चोत थकाल जिगदानंदजु जुलो मेवन सुनानं छुं मधाओ थ्वते हनुल छात यात जुलो । (Ibid.).

30. सं ८०२ मार्ग्गशिरि कृष्ण: ॥ ... थ्वगुलछिात, खप्वया, थछेया, शिव जोशनि छात बयिाव, कार्त्तकिन महनि याड़ा जुरो ॥ वाराणससिं, तरिहुतसिं, राजपुरस, पर्व्वत सकलभैंन, आश्वनिन महनि याकजु ॥ खप्वया, यँया, यँरया, गोरखाया, थ्वतेस जुको कार्त्तकिन महनि याड़ा जुरो । (Panta 2066 VS: 204).

31. (Karnaprasad) Hyoju was a former member of parliament lynched to his death by a crowd in broad daylight in Bhaktapur, Nepal, in 1988. The government accused a local party of orchestrating the murder and brought homicide charges against the party leaders and members, who in turn portray the death as a state conspiracy. The charge was withdrawn by the state after the political changes in 1989.

References

Agamben, Giorgio. 2009. *The Signature of All Things: On Method*. New York: Zone Books.
Aryal, Mukundaraj. 2060 VS. "Bhaktapurko Ek Aprakasit Thyasaphu (An Unpublished Folded Book from Bhaktapur)." *Khopring* 11: 31. In Nepali.
Badiou, Alan. 2012. *The Rebirth of History: Times of Riots and Uprisings*. London: Verso.
Bendall, C. 1905. "A Historical Introduction." In Mahamahopadhyaya Hara Prasad Sastri (ed.), *A Catalogue of Palm-Leaf and Selected Paper Mss. Belonging to the Durbar Library, Nepal*. Calcutta: Baptist Mission Press, 1–82.

Bird, A. 2005. "Naturalizing Kuhn," *Proceedings of the Aristotelian Society*. 105: 109–127.
Black, Donald. 2011. *Moral Time*. New York: Oxford University Press.
de la Roche, Roberta Senechal. 1996. "Collective Violence as Social Control." *Sociological Forum* 11(1): 97–128.
———. 2001. "Why Is Collective Violence Collective." *Sociological Forum* 19(2): 126–144.
Foucault, Michel. 1969. *L'archéologie du savoir*. Paris: Gallimard (*The Archaeology of Knowledge*, translated by Allan Sheridan, New York: Harper and Row, 1972).
Ghatanavali (A Chronicle). Ms. NGMMP Microfilm No. A0922/07. The National Archives, Kathmandu.
Gurr, Ted. 1970. *Why Men Rebel*. Princeton: Princeton University Press.
Gutting, Garry. 1989. *Michel Foucault's Archaeology of Scientific Reason*. Cambridge: Cambridge University Press.
Hess, Volker, and J. Andrew Mendelsohn. 2010. "Case and Series: Medical Knowledge and Paper Technology, 1600–1900." *History of Science* 48(161): 287–314.
Kayastha, Ramkrishna. 2058 VS. "Mallakalik Santi-svasti Ghatanavali" (A Pacifying Ritual Chronicle of the Malla Period). *Pasuka* 6(3): 4–6. In Newari.
Kharbuja, Suryalal. 2057 VS. "Bhaktapur Bisket Katrasamga Sambandhit Euta Aprakasit Thyasaphu" (An Unpublished Folded Book Related to the Bisket Festival in Bhaktapur). *Pasuka* 5(2): 3–9. In Nepali.
Khvapajujupini Vamshavali (A Genealogy of the Kings of Khvapa). Ms. Cat. No. 780. The Asa Archives, Kathmandu.
Kousis, Maria, and Charles Tilly (eds.). 2005. *Economic and Political Contention in Comparative Perspective*. London: Paradigm Publishers.
Kuhn, Thomas. 1962[1970]. *The Structure of Scientific Revolutions*. Chicago: University of Chicago Press. 1970, 2nd Edition, with a postscript.
———. 1974. "Second Thoughts on Paradigms." In F. Suppe (ed.), *The Structure of Scientific Theories*. Urbana: University of Illinois Press, 459–482.
Lamsal, Pt. Deviprasad (ed.). 2023 VS. *Bhasha Vamshavali: Dvitiya Bhag* (A Vernacular Genealogy—Part II). Place not mentioned: Nepal Rastriya Pustakalaya. In Nepali.
Maclean, Ian. 1998. "Foucault's Renaissance Episteme Reconsidered: An Aristotelian Counterblast." *Journal of the History of Ideas* 59(1): 149–166.
Mallakalin Thyasaphu (A Folded Book from the Malla Period). NGMPP Microfilm No. A301/12. The National Archives, Kathmandu.
Margolis, Howard. 1993. *Paradigms and Barriers: How Habits of Mind Govern Scientific Beliefs*. Chicago: University of Chicago Press.
Naraharinath, Yogi. 2013 VS. "Nepalabhaktapuranaresapurohitavamsadhar Dhanesvararajopadhyayaka Dainandi Smritipustikama Praptamiti" (Dates Obtained from a Diary Memorandum of the Royal Priest of Bhaktapur Dhanesvar Rajopadhyaya). *Itihasa-Prakasa* 2(3): 567–570. In Nepali.
"Nepal Desko Itihas" (A History of the Country of Nepal). 1972. *Ancient Nepal* 19: 1–23. In Nepali.
"Nepalko Itihas Rajbhogmala" (A Garland of Regnal Years in the History of Nepal). 1969. *Ancient Nepal* 9: 1–24. In Nepali.
"Nepalko Itihas Rajbhogmala" (A Garland of Regnal Years in the History of Nepal). 1970. *Ancient Nepal* 11: 1–17. In Nepali.

Nickles, Thomas (ed.). 2003. *Thomas Kuhn*. Cambridge: University of Cambridge Press, 142–177.

Panta, Mahesraj. 2066 VS. "Sabbhanda Pahile Pracarma Ayeko Thyasaphu: 2 Khanda" (The Earliest Popular Folded Book. Part II). *Purnima* 131: 193–225. In Nepali.

———. 2067 VS. "Sabbhanda Pahile Pracarma Ayeko Thyasaphu: 3 Khanda" (The Earliest Popular Folded Book. Part III). *Purnima* 132: 295–348. In Nepali.

———. 2069 VS. "Naya Thyasaphu" (A New Folded Book). *Purnima* 138: 129–174. In Nepali.

Raj, Yogesh. 2012. "Towards a Case Typology of Historiography: Reading Historical Texts from South Asia." *Studies in Nepali History and Society* 17(1): 63–105.

———. 2056 VS.a. "Bhaktapur Malla Rajparivarsamga Sambandha Rakhne Aitihasik Tipot" (A Historical Diary Related to the Royal Household of Bhaktapur). *Pasuka* 4(4): 9–11. In Nepali.

———. 2056 VS.b. "Ahilesamma Prakasma Naayeko Euta Aitihasik Ghatanavali" (An Unpublished Historical Chronicle). *Pasuka* 4(5): 3–8. In Nepali.

———. 2057 VS. "Kehi Aitihasik Tipot" (A Few Historical Notes). *Pasuka* 5(6): 25. In Nepali.

———. 2013. *Ruptures and Repairs in South Asia: Historical Perspectives*. Kathmandu: Martin Chautari.

———. Forthcoming. *Kathmandauko Euta Chāta* (A Chāta from Kathmandu). Bhaktapur: Suthan. In Nepali.

Rajvamsi, Sankarman. 2020 VS. "(*vi sam 1723 Dekhi 1748 Takko*) Aitihasik Ghatanavali" (A Historical Chronicle of 1723 VS to 1748 VS). Kathmandu: Vir Pustakalaya. In Nepali.

Regmi, D. R. 1966. *Medieval Nepal*. Volume III. Part 2. Calcutta: Firma KLM.

Rude, George. 1964 [2005]. *The Crowd in History: Study of Popular Disturbances in France and England, 1730–1848*. New York: Wiley.

Santi-svasti saphula (A Pacifying Book). Ms. Warner-Jacobson Collection, No. 135, The Royal Library, Copenhagen. Fols. 53.

Shakya, Raja. 1125 NS. *Janabaha:dya:ya Santisaphu (Ghatanavali)* (A Pacifying Book of Janabaha:dya:). Yem: Premdharma Pithana. In Newari.

Sharma, Aishvaryadhar. 1104 NS. *Aginmatha:ya Aitihasik Samagri* (The Historical Materials Relating to Agnimath). Kathmandu: Puspanjali-Prakashan-Gosthi. In Newari.

Sharma, Balchandra (ed.). 1968. Kathmandu Upatyakako Ek Rajvamsavali (A Royal Genealogy of the Kathmandu Valley). *Ancient Nepal* 5: 1–17. In Nepali.

——— (ed.). 1969. Kathmandu Upatyakako Ek Rajvamsavali (A Royal Genealogy of the Kathmandu Valley). *Ancient Nepal* 6: 1–29. In Nepali.

Shrestha, Purushottam Lochan. 2000. "Sri 3 Talejuske Thapujaya Vakya: Ek Aprakasit Thyasaphu" (Sentences Pertaining to the Thapuja of Sri 3 Taleju: An Unpublished Thyasaphu). *Rolamba: Millennium Issue*, 113–118. In Nepali.

Suthan Chata A. Ms. The Suthan Collection. Bhaktapur. Fols. 90.

Tevari, Ramji. 2021 VS. "Chautara Devidas ra Cikuti." *Purnima* 1: 13–19. In Nepali.

Tilly, Charles. 1969. "Methods for the Study of Collective Violence." In Ralph W. Conant and Molly Apple Levin (ed.), *Problems in Research in Community*. New York: Praeger, 15–43.

———. 1987. "The Analysis of Popular Collective Action." *European Journal of Operational Research* 30: 223–229.

———. 2002. "Event Catalogs as Theories." *Sociological Theory* 20(2): 248–254.

———. 2003. *The Politics of Collective Violence*. New York: Cambridge University Press.

———. 2008. *Contentious Performances*. New York: Cambridge University Press.

Tilly, Charles, and Sidney Tarrow. 2006. *Contentious Politics*. London: Paradigm Publishers.

Vajracharya, Chunda. 1107 NS. *Madhyakalya Chum Ghatanavali: Chagu Addhyayan* (A Study of Some Medieval Chronicles). Yem: Saphu Dhuku. In Newari.

Vajracharya, Dhanavajra, and Kamal P. Malla. 1985. *The Gopalarajavamsavali*. Wiesbaden: Franz Steiner Verlag.

Vajracharya, Dhanavajra, and Tek Bahadur Shrestha. 2035 VS. *Pancali Sasan Paddhitoko Aitihasik Vivechana* (A Historical Evaluation of the Pancali System). Kirtipur: Institute of Nepal and Asian Studies, 241–252. In Nepali.

Vajracharya, Dhanavajra et al. (eds.). 2019 VS. *Itihas-Samsodhanko Praman-Prameya*. Lalitpur: Jagadamba-Prakasan. In Nepali.

Vajracharya, Gautamvajra. 2023 VS. "Aprakasit Thyasaphu" (An Unpublished Folded Book). *Purnima* 12: 22–39. In Nepali.

———. 2025 VS. "Aitihasik Ghatanavali" (A Historical Chronicle). *Purnima* 19: 9–14. In Nepali.

Witzel, Michael. 1990. "On Indian Historical Writing: The Role of the Vamsavalis." *Journal of the Japanese Association of South Asian Studies* 2: 1–57.

Wood, Amy Louise. 2009. *Lynching and Spectacle: Witnessing Racial Violence in America, 1890–1940*. Chapel Hill: University of North Carolina Press.

5 Public Anger, Violence, and the Legacy of Decolonization in India

NANDANA DUTTA

On July 22, 2014, *The Hindu* Kolkata Edition carried a front-page story titled "Manipuri Man Beaten to Death." The incident took place in the early morning at Kotla Mubarakpur in South Delhi. The 29-year-old man, Akha Salouni, from the Northeastern state of Manipur, was returning with two others in an autorickshaw from a visit to a friend's house. They were attacked by five or six young men who came in a white Hyundai Verna. The two friends managed to get away but from a distance watched Akha being beaten to death. *The Hindu* reported that the attack was "unprovoked" and in a later report (July 24, 2014) added that there was an exchange of "heated words." It would be easy to find incidents of this nature on any day in any Indian newspaper (local newspapers in the Northeast reported it, as did news channels), whether because of a proactive media or because of the frequency with which they occur.

This chapter is interested in a particular form of public violence—lynching—that has become commonplace in contemporary India. Studying this violence requires, this chapter proposes, that it be located against the backdrop of forms of agency that emerged within India's understanding and perception of the rule of law and the preindependence form of self-rule known as *swaraj*.

India has demonstrated several of the worst forms of violence in its public life, but for obvious reasons the commonest and most widely reported in the media have been riot- and terrorism-related incidents. India's postindependence history is drenched in the blood of communal violence that has often taken the form of riots. The *Hindustan Times* archives lists among such incidents in recent history: the Ahmedabad riots (1969); the Delhi riots following the assassination of Indira Gandhi (1984), which lasted for fifteen days; Meerut riots (1987) lasting for two months; the one-month-long Bhagalpur riots (1989); the Mumbai riots (1992); and the Gujarat/Godhra violence of 2002.[1] The most horrific and unforgettable episode is, of course, the 1948 violence following the Partition of the subcontinent into India and Pakistan. And terrorist incidents have taken lives several times in recent memory. Individual instances of rape and murder, as in the 2012 gang rape of the young woman in Delhi, now known famously as the Nirbhaya case, have been rising. Other forms of violence have also emerged in postindependence India. These include the increasingly common mass suicides of farmers in the face of crop failures in several of India's states and the peculiar drama of public self-immolation or doing harm to oneself that comes out of the modes of protest of the Independence movement. Recent prominent cases of self-immolation include that of Rajiv Goswami over the Mandal commission decision on reservations to India's minorities (June 24, 1990) and that of Pranab Boro in the case of protests over the issue of land rights spearheaded by the Kisan Mukti Sangram Samiti (February 24, 2014). The latter died the same day from the burns sustained; the former died in 2004 at the age of 33 of complications resulting from severe burns. The dramatic nature of riots, the incidents of terrorist violence, and these other attention-grabbing episodes have created the frame for understanding violence and, alongside the assumptions about nonviolence as a feature of Indian society that has been a favorite if utterly erroneous interpretation, have served to blank out of the mindscape the more innocuous and interpersonal forms of violence. Other countries in South Asia have shown a similar turn to violence, though local factors may vary. News of lynching frequently comes from Pakistan (the infamous Sialkot lynching of two young men in full view of the police on August 15, 2010, reported widely);[2] there is a clear statement of lynching being the "order of the day" during the Civil War between Sinhalas and Tamils in Sri Lanka;[3] from Bangladesh, we have statistics claiming that between 2009 and 2013, there were 686 cases of public lynching.[4] These are all nations with strong indigenous sociocultural systems that have experienced colonial rule, and violence has often stemmed from notions of "honor" and from religious and ethnic divides that have become clearer as a result of colonial policies.

While this chapter is conscious of violence in these other South Asian nations, it examines a form of violence that has been comparably subterranean in Indian society and has only recently come to attention because of news-media focus. The media has begun to describe these episodes as *lynching*—a term that seems to have crept into its lexicon almost without notice and is now used widely and indiscriminately. These have involved the pursuit of and brutal beating or killing of individuals by groups of people all over the country—thieves caught in acts of stealing or robbing, women identified as morally guilty, men suspected of child molestation and sexual assault, and ethnically different people living in cities like Delhi and Bangalore regularly targeted by locals—in most cases with the media standing by to record and disseminate.

Incidents of rape, assault, kidnappings, and extortions have risen, but this form of violence is significantly different in being resorted to generally by ordinary middle-class people frustrated by the failure of the police and the judiciary to prevent or punish. An aggrieved populace has frequently taken the law into its hands and sought to mete out violent retribution for such crimes on perpetrators it has identified and "captured" in the act or often on mere suspicion. These are indeed problems of several countries in South Asia in the postindependence era where there is a divide between British notions of law and justice set in place during the era of imperial rule and embedded in the current legal system in the country and a nostalgic perception of the fairness of the British system by the middle class, undercut by the real experience of governance and administration against specific local situations in the postcolonial present.

Public violence in India might be understood in the backdrop of three crucial concerns stemming from the forms of agency that emerged in the peculiar understanding of issues of modernity, the rule of law, and the indigenous Gandhian form of self-rule, swaraj, during and after the independence movement. It points to the liberal use of the word *lynching*, not only with reference to the taking of a life by a mob or group, but also to occasions wherein the dynamics of the individual-mob/victim-perpetrator relationship are the same (as in the case of effigies but also apparent "disciplinary violence" against an "errant" individual), even if death is not the endpoint of the mob action. Violence of this kind often also occurs in the backdrop of movements for autonomy and identity in independent India because the conditions created by such movements regularly position people of different groups against one another, so that a member of one group may be isolated and lynched by members of another.

The salutary "lessons" that such incidents seem to tacitly communicate stem from the public need to maintain dominance of good over evil or right over wrong; the need to maintain social order through the punishment of those who disturb or violate it; and an amorphous response to the "golden" past and its loss in the present that is not necessarily traced to such aberrations but decidedly evoke outrage. Public anger against supposed wrongdoers may be traced to a disjunction in common perception between the law and justice but also to a cocktail of factors that are a legacy from India's recent past as complex sociocultural traditions are suddenly transplanted to an India where the gains of modernity have been uneven among its people, and where modernity and tradition continue in an often awkward partnership. It is also perhaps important to note that, given this set of factors and influences, the incidence of violent public action seems to be most common among sections of India's emerging middle class on whom the play of these factors is most complex and urgent. The middle class caught in the zone between vaulting aspirations and their deflation is particularly exercised by the failure of institutions to safeguard their interests. Indeed it is the middle class that is most vocally angered by aspects of India's public life—corruption, lack of access to services, uneven benefits of development—and the corresponding nostalgia for the rule of law. In passing, one might note that the very poor do not have the luxury of expressing anger against the systems that fail them, while the very rich can and often do bend these systems and institutions to suit them. (And yet given the complex layering of Indian societies in the cases of honor killings or witch burnings—two common instances of collective/public violence—such class distinctions are not possible to sustain. The first has taken place across economic divides, while the second has occurred across India's more backward regions as a result of superstitions that do not respect social distinctions but may often occur in a partnership with local animosities or discriminatory gender perceptions.)

In the face of these episodes and as a ground for the primary thrust of this chapter, which is an effort to account for the translation of the symbolic or legitimized form of agency (as in the effigy burning or through self-rule) into a very real public agency outside the frames of the law, it is useful to flag three issues:

- What is the result of the rendering of violence as a spectacle by the media, making visuals of violent acts freely available and adding to the actual witnesses of an act a large community of virtual witnesses?
- What compels people into committing such acts of violence—are these spontaneous, gut responses or cold-blooded, preplanned attacks?
- How have historical and contemporary factors bringing about changes in Indian society influenced the perpetration of violent acts?

Lynching and Media Representation

This section offers a survey of the media representation of public violence in India and its liberal and indiscriminate use of the term *lynching*. Faced with the uninhibited expression of anger, the media adopts a hysterical and hyperbolic mode of reporting that serves to heighten public outrage at brutality but also interestingly provides an exemplary response in the face of police apathy. By bringing such incidents close to the public through visual and linguistic excess, a numbing effect is achieved so that the public outbreak of private emotions becomes "normal" and "acceptable."

The impression of the rise of such incidents has also been created by the print and visual media, which have enthusiastically reported these instances of people's anger, with the visual media capturing "people in the act" and running these pictures over and over again, desensitizing viewers and creating the appetite for the next such incident. The print media on the other hand has had the important role of imprinting certain descriptors in the collective consciousness, creating the language with which to speak of such incidents. And yet it is this same media that has fudged distinctions among these situations of violence by branding all of them as lynching, erasing the politics that propels different acts.

The term *lynching* appears to have emerged in the Indian print media in the last few years, widely used to describe all instances of people taking the law into their hands, but also gradually pushing the word's borders and making it a metaphor for other forms of violence. The language of lynching used in all these cases seems to diffuse its sharpness—all situations of good/evil, right/wrong, morality/immorality with an overall assumption about the unwillingness or failure of the state are so described, but so also are criminal acts where individuals are raped, murdered, or hanged from trees.[5] The Indian media seems to have started using the term freely from around the last decade, though there have been earlier instances of more scrupulous usage, especially in journals like the *Economic and Political Weekly*. Around this time, not only current incidents but also crimes that had happened earlier and had not *then* been described as lynching came to be so termed. The ghastly killing of a family by caste Hindus at Khairlanji on September 29, 2006, was not initially described as lynching. It featured as murder in news reports at the time, while a recent article actually used the word "lynching"[6] and a later report in *The Hindu* (August 23, 2010) referred to it as "lynching of four members of a Dalit family."[7]

A random selection from the recent past given below shows the many situations that have come to be described as lynching:

1. "Haryana: Girl lynched, boy beheaded in honour killing"[8]
2. "Six arrested for lynching 14-year-old boy"[9]
3. "Youth lynched at Rukminigaon"[10]
4. "Phool Mohammad lynching case"[11]
5. "A legal lynching: Indian government executes Afzal Guru"[12]

Public Anger, Violence, and the Legacy of Decolonization in India 131

6. "Thief Lynched"[13]
7. "Ignoble deed: The lynching of Amartya Sen"[14]
8. "Leopard lynched in Golaghat"[15]

The term conveniently elides over the distinctions between overtly criminal acts and those expressive of "righteous anger," as evident in this list and it appears that in the span of a few years the media has taken to using the term indiscriminately and without any sense of its historical associations. While these examples, which demonstrate a somewhat hyperbolic use of the term, are from the Indian media, it appears that other countries reporting on India have adopted this terminology, as evident in the following reports:

1. "Indian woman, 20, tortured and lynched by her family"[16]
2. "India: 20 killed by train—train driver lynched"—"A train in India ran over a group of pilgrims crossing the tracks. . . . The angry mob that noticed the driver leaving the train unscathed surrounded him and began beating him. Quickly the event turned into a lynching that the driver did not survive."[17]
3. "Ten men beaten to death in India . . . the incident highlights the widespread problem of mob lynching in India."[18]
4. A June 13, 2014, article on Uttar Pradesh, in an online paper describes it as "The Rape and Lynching Capital of India."[19]

While these are accurate descriptions of lynching as the term has been historically used, in the case cited below the girls were actually strung from trees:

1. "Indian police arrest three over gang-rape and lynching of teen sisters."[20]

And on the same incident,

2. "Indian Girls' Lynching suspected honour killing"[21]

The episodes that express one or the other form of public violence (as distinguished from the incidents that are, strictly speaking, not public violence in the sense that this chapter discusses) are however worth examining in some detail.

In the Nido Taniam killing in 2013, reports about the number of perpetrators vary between three and seven men, all connected to the shopkeeper who was apparently approached by Nido for directions, who teased him about his blonde dyed hair and—when he broke a glass counter in anger—attacked him with rods and sticks, injuring him fatally. The news report said:

> A student from Arunachal Pradesh was lynched to death in the heart of South Delhi after an altercation with a shop owner who "joked" at the hair style of

the boy Nido Taniam.... The boy lost his life as he got beaten up by the shop owner and his friends who extracted rupees ten thousand too from the boy for "breaking" their glass in the shop.[22]

This episode highlights one of the most important sources of recent public violence, that directed against minorities, but specifically against those from the northeastern states of India where the racial stock has distinctly Mongoloid strains and lifestyles and food habits are different. This kind of violence has begun to take place in some Indian cities, with New Delhi being the biggest offender. Delhi's strongly conservative patriarchal population base drawn from the northern states of Uttar Pradesh, Haryana, and Punjab, especially among house owners and shopkeepers with whom the Northeastern students in the city come into closest contact, seems to frequently express moral outrage that results in violence and deaths. The problem is one of perception of one social group by another with the minority coming off worse. The Northeastern students who are tenants in the outlying areas and villages around Delhi are seen as given over to drinking, noisy parties, sexual promiscuity, improper and scanty dress, and funky hair styles, and above all having nonvegetarian ethnic cuisines, the flavors of which offend the sensibilities of landlords and neighbors. Such revulsion has been legitimized by the political and economic marginalization of the Northeastern states, the still unsolved problem of insurgency in the region, and the long history of framing by the mainstream under the label of violence. Most of these states consequently also have active autonomy movements and corresponding insurgent groups that feed the perception of the rest of India, not only of a troubled region but also a troublesome and different people who should be forced into the mainstream.

The report that is cited here claims that people in Delhi feel that the Northeastern boys and girls must be integrated into the mainstream; in other words, lose their distinctiveness of look, style, food, and dress and become more like their neighbors. The result of efforts to deal with the problem has been the circulation of guidelines by police authorities (the report notes that a police official hailing from the Northeast was asked to frame these) on how to dress and behave and what to cook and eat. The Nido Taniam incident is only one of many that have targeted young Northeastern students in Delhi resulting in attacks and sometimes in deaths. A report by the North East Support Centre and Helpline (NESCH) puts the number of incidents that had led to grievous injury, rape, and killing of students from the region from the year 2005 at 96.[23] The worst case in recent times was the violence directed at students and others from the region in major cities across India—Mumbai, Pune, Hyderabad, Bangalore, and Delhi—and the fleeing of some 6,000 Northeastern people from Bangalore—following a clash (from July 20, 2012, through August 2012) between Bodos (one of India's largest indigenous communities, now demanding a separate state) and migrant Muslims in Kokrajhar, Assam, that left a large number of Muslims dead or displaced.[24]

A variety of factors are at work here, including the traditional nature of societies and the heterogeneous composition of the cities, the inherent racism, the perception of majority–minority premised upon caste and race differences, and above all the feeling that the official institutions supposed to maintain law and order have failed in ensuring that the outsider conforms to the social norms prevalent in a given place. While the actual killing or violent reprisal is more-or-less accurately described as lynching, its undercurrent of social coercion—directed at bending deviance to a public will—is closer to the European and English practice of charivari where an entire neighborhood is galvanized against an errant individual.

My second case comes out of the politicization of the relationship between Hindus and Muslims . On June 2, 2014, a 28-year-old IT professional, Mohsin Shaikh, was set upon and killed by a mob when he was returning home from prayers at a mosque around 9 P.M. The reason cited was that he had made objectionable remarks on Facebook about Shivaji, Bal Thackeray, and B. R. Ambedkar, historical and contemporary figures—of whom the first two are important to the Hindu Right, while Ambedkar is a revered icon for Dalits (the so-called "untouchable" castes),[25]—and had uploaded morphed photos of Shivaji and Bal Thackeray, according to the *Milli Gazette*, which describes itself as the "Indian Muslims' Leading Newspaper."[26] The episode shows that public anger may not always be a sudden impulsive outbreak but can be a planned attack by organized elements of fundamentalist forces, which disguise their actions as the mood of a majority "justifiably" inflamed by an individual's actions against aspects of its culture that are considered sacrosanct. Such episodes of lynching have their root in the discourse of secularism that prevails in India—written into its Constitution and articulated among a section of its citizens—which claims that the religious sentiments of different groups should be respected. The victim was a young IT professional—a career choice common among India's growing middle class—and the discovery that he had aired his opinions on Facebook suggests that, if not the mob itself, at least those who had set the process of violent reprisal in motion must have had similar easy access. Other kinds of violence may be traced to the caste divides of Indian society[27] or to ingrained superstitions, as in a June 2013 report in *Shillong Times* of a man accused of "sorcery" being "lynched" by Adivasi villagers and his body buried near a temple.[28]

Another instance, apparently with communal overtones, is, however, deeply embedded in anger at the corruption and inaction of India's bureaucracy and police. It pits an "honest" police officer against a corrupt system that traps him into certain actions that are then given a communal color. The online newspaper *Gulail* did a detailed investigation into the incident. *Gulail* reporters Shaunak Sen and Soumik Mukherjee, in their story of the lynching of Phool Mohammad—who had taken charge as station officer at Surval, Sawai Madhopur, and was "diligent and honest"—almost repeat the popular Bollywood narrative of the cop-hero who takes on all the powerful local forces: the honest cop getting on the wrong side of a corrupt circle officer and being drawn into a series of actions that are misinterpreted by the villagers; the officer's secular credentials attested to by his installation of the abandoned Hanuman idol in the station and contributing to a puja; and generally showing himself as a man who respected local sentiments. *Circle officer* is a term used to denote a police or revenue official who is in charge of an area or circle. In the Phool Mohammad case, the circle officer was the victim's immediate superior and of the rank of a Deputy Superintendent, or an Assistant Commissioner of Police. The actual event happened when—while trying to save a man who had accidentally set himself on fire in the process of making a dramatic protest—Phool Mohammad was hit by a stone from the crowd, became unconscious, and was left in a jeep that was surrounded by a crowd and set on fire. He burned to death. The riot was actively abetted by the circle officer Mahendra Singh. According to *Gulail*, the media, which reported the incident widely, "pegged it predominantly as an incident where an angry mob lashed out at the local police because of the latter's putative inefficiency and corruption." At the same time, the convenient factors that are usually trotted out at the time of such incidents were again offered: tossing a Hanuman idol out with the rubbish, beating up the family of a victim of a tiger attack, and being overtly communal—rationalizing the gruesome nature of the reaction through the accusation of violating public sentiment. Phool Mohammad was burned alive on March 17, 2011.[29]

The *Assam Tribune*, in its online edition (Guwahati, Sunday, February 24, 2013), carried the story of the "Youth lynched at Rukminigaon." The staff reporter wrote: "A 14-year old boy was beaten to death by an irate public after they reportedly caught him red-handed while making a burglary attempt along with another teenager in a shop in Rukminigaon area in the wee hours today.... Police said that although the minor was rushed to the Gauhati Medical College and Hospital he succumbed to his injuries a few minutes later.... The incident occurred last night around 1 A.M. when a group of residents of Rukminigaon turned violent at spotting the two teenagers inside a shop owned by one Diganta Das and started beating him 'mercilessly.'"[30] Rukminigaon is a middle-class residential locality, and this kind of incident is a common occurrence when a middle-class public takes violent action against minor offenders.

The report said that the boy was living with Khagen Das of the same area and was being educated by him along with his children. The *Telegraph* (Guwahati, February 26, 2013) reported that Khagen Das was arrested and that the boy was employed by him as domestic help; the weapon used was an iron rod, and five persons were arrested for the killing.[31] The local television news channels in Assam where this incident occurred—*News Live*, *DY365*, recently *News Time*, and several other smaller ones—have in the last few years taken to reporting such incidents almost every day, sometimes, as in a story carried on July 29, 2014, by *DY365* in its 7 P.M. *News*, even retrieving visuals from the past, that are provided to them by the many individuals who photograph scenes of violent action by groups against individuals and "give" them to the channels (their participation in the lynching is a peculiar mix of revulsion and voyeuristic activism). It is possible to actually track the rise in public indignation that targets small time-wrongdoers through the repeated running of such visuals that these channels offer as their version of social responsibility. In the incidents that these television channels reported, it is often residents in middle-class neighborhoods like Rukminigaon who express outrage at aberrations—minor thievery, drinking, or sexual "misdemeanors"—that occur in "their" localities.

The collective impact of the two modes of information dissemination—the print and visual media—is the impression of a dramatic rise in the incidence of such occurrences and the general turn to anger of an entire society. The media has succeeded in giving unprecedented visibility to such incidents since often the only notice taken of such cases is in the media—the television report and the newspaper headline—and the effect on the viewer's/reader's mind is intense but short-lived, passing out of range as the report of the next incident takes over.

The media with its visually and linguistically arresting delivery of violent episodes right into the drawing room of the viewer/reader contributes to a wider "sentimentalization of the public sphere" with sentiments of rage, anxiety, or sorrow now pervading the public space more often. The public sphere in the work of thinkers like Habermas is a necessary aspect of modernity and democratic processes that come with it. It assumes a space where "public opinion is formed . . . a realm mediating between the larger society and the state, and allowing for potential democratic control of social and political institutions."[32] Boggs points to the development of the public sphere in America as a result of growing education and social movements (among other causes), providing a space for public debate, questioning, and critique of government and institutions.[33] The decline of the public sphere is traced to the incapacity to "forge collective identities, uphold some notion of the public good, and work toward empowerment and change."[34] The emergence of the public sphere in India is commonly traced to "the experience of British colonialism and the national movement."[35] Social movements themselves, organizing and directing public discontent, have created conditions for the violent expression of indignation and outrage. The spectacles of lynching and group violence now provided so readily seem to overturn the idea of a rational public sphere.

Explaining Public Violence

The term *lynching* has entered popular perception in India from fictional accounts of black Americans being lynched by whites or, as in *To Kill a Mockingbird*, under threat of lynching, and of the cattle thief or suspect pursued and lynched by a posse of outraged citizens in the ubiquitous American western novel and cinema. These were popular reading and viewing for a section of the English educated middle class whose members dominated the print media in the formative years of the Indian republic. The currency of the term in the English print media and on television news frames not only suggests this legacy but may also draw from the wider perception of racism, the lynching of blacks by whites and the familiarity with the U.S. Civil Rights Movement in India, especially in the context of Martin Luther King's association with Gandhian nonviolence.[36]

The American scholarship on lynching (which is predominant in the field) makes a systematic study of a historical phenomenon. It has set historical markers (from the mid-nineteenth century to the early twentieth century), identified the three regions of the Midwest, the West, and the South, and shown how U.S. lynching derived from "a larger cultural war over the nature of criminal justice waged between rural and working class supporters of 'rough justice' and middle-class due-process advocates."[37] Michael J. Pfeifer's work helps to explain the way in which a legal failure (or at least a contested state and contested legal authority, as opposed to a state able to exercise a monopoly over the use of violence) is at the heart of the turn to public anger and the propensity for people to take the law into their own hands that has analogously overtaken India. Pfeifer describes lynching as an aspect in "a process of legal change" and the failure of lynchers "to assimilate conceptions of an abstract, rational, detached, and antiseptic legal process that urban middle class reformers wrote into statutes."[38] This is an understanding of public violence that cuts across nations.

Manfred Berg and Simon Wendt in their study of the global nature of such violence locate it in Russia (*samosud*), Germany (*katzenmusik*), France (*charivari*), and England (*rough music*), as stretching from medieval times to the present, and occurring in situations like blood feuds or the punishment of horse thieves.[39] The narrow definition of the term *lynching* given by Berg and Wendt as "extralegal punishment usually entailing death or severe physical harm, perpetrated by groups claiming to represent the will of the larger community" usefully describes the phenomenon in transnational terms since, cutting across differences in situation and ethnic and cultural character is the shared perception of a gulf between legal systems and actual justice in societies across the world. Such transnational explanations include other issues such as the modern state, the "dislocation wrought by globalization,"[40] and "deterioration of political stability and legitimacy."[41] "They argue that "common to lynchings across the globe is the ideology of popular justice; that is, the argument that lynching represents a form of communal self-defence against crime that is unchecked by the state."[42] The identification of legal lacunae or failure is a kind of lowest common denominator accounting for violence. The recall of the rule of law—established by the British, written into the Indian Constitution and judicial process, and regularly violated in practice—easily exercises the Indian public, especially the middle-class public, which is deeply immersed in ideas about the right regulation of society, is morally outraged by aberrations, and would like action to be taken against erring individuals.

Collective violence has been described as "a moralistic response to deviant behaviour" often termed as "popular justice."[43] Roberta Senechal De La Roche distinguishes "collective violence as a form of protest, a quest for justice" from earlier characterization of it as "mass hysteria" or irrational behavior by "violent crowds."[44] De la Roche also sees collective violence as "an extreme form of self help" as well as a form of "social control."[45] It is assumed that a wrongdoer is identified and targeted by the collective, but her generalizations about "unknown offenders" being treated more harshly by a group "than those with whom they are acquainted"[46] or sparing "those who are indispensable to their well being"[47] are not borne out by the evidence from recent incidents in India, where neighbors have gone after one of their own for some violation of a tacit internal social code of behavior, or employers have brutally beaten up and sometimes killed young boys and girls who work as house servants and on whom they are otherwise dependent.

George Bryjak in a chapter on collective violence in India underscores the rise of internal dissatisfaction as a reason:

The preindependence cohesiveness and internal solidarity of many new nations is being re-placed by regional loyalties and identification at the ethnic, religious, and linguistic level. In a society as large and diverse as India, the results of this phenomenon can be devastating. Bridging the gap from the traditional to the modern world is problematic enough for a basically homogeneous society where there is general agreement on national goals and priorities. For a country as heterogeneous as India, this transition may be impossible.[48]

Bryjak also finds reasons for collective violence in India's "effort to modernize" and its failure to find answers to social problems and improve life for its people. Other reasons adduced are its huge population, low standard of living, heterogeneous society, and caste system.[49]

While the Berg and Wendt survey of global lynching seems to rule out the influence of traditional societies and their entrenched social and familial hierarchies as possible grounds for such violence, in India—with its many kinds of differences and imbalances of race, caste, wealth, and gender; the simultaneity of the modern and the traditional; and its complicated colonial memories—it is virtually impossible to sort out and arrive at a single unified explanation. As the examples cited in the list of media references to lynching show, caste has played a significant role in the raping and lynching of the two young girls from the Dalit community, as have age-old prejudices about honor. Alongside these factors have been trends that entered with large-scale illegal immigration from neighboring countries that has suddenly swelled the population of cities, increased the numbers of service providers, especially as domestic help who are both indispensable and the first suspects in petty crime and frequently feed the suspicions and fears of the middle class. The violence against outsiders and insiders that results in what social scientists distinguish as "classic lynching" and "communal lynching"[50] are also an aspect of what we see in India; the process of alienation is an important aspect in all cases, whether this is because the wrongdoer is actually an outsider to a society or community or whether she/he estranges her/himself by committing an error/crime. In fact one of the commonest conditions for such violence is the clash between groups making claims for the same lands and natural resources and the ensuing movements for autonomy raised by many linguistic and tribal groups.

These are elements that have seeped into the collective psyche, and specifically the middle-class psyche (since it is this class that seems to have bittersweet memories and assumptions about the rule of law) from the past, from images of retribution and collective action in traditional ritualistic practices, and from the popular culture where the ambivalence of good and evil is ironed out and presented as clear binaries. It is possible to see emerging in the blend of all of these the kind of mind-set that permits people to collect in groups to punish an offender. It is also interesting to see that the materiality of many of these engagements often disappears and is replaced by symbolic acts of retribution. The performance of a symbolic act provides a powerful occasion for rehearsal and subsequent socialization or habituation into violence, which serves as a prior condition or preparation to actually engage in the act of violence that ends with the taking of a life. Becoming inured to violence through exposure to images and reports of it as well as participation in the symbolic violent act are preconditions that often lead to the real violent act or lynching. Amy Louise Wood has suggested that the visual spectacle was accommodated within cultural horizons by white southerners in the United States who

> produced and received these most modern lynching representations through very personal and local terms. Through them, they rehearsed narratives of crime and punishment, of sin and retribution, that they already understood through the practices of public executions and from their religious traditions. Their racial fears about crime and the loss of white masculine dominance only made these narratives seem all the more pressing and relevant.[51]

Such circulation of historical and traditional memories helps flesh out the imagery of public violence that inhabits the collective psyche and is a ready reference point for contemporary violence in India. As the incidents discussed above and the issues they raise show, lynching gets represented in two ways: a) as public anger and retribution, i.e., as an extralegal form of action and justifiable agency; and b) as criminal acts (and therefore nonjustifiable agency). Such spectacles of public anger and public action or agency achieve a particular set of effects: a tacit justification of mobocracy as a part of democratic processes, an image of collective agency that the legal system itself does not offer, and a moral spectacle of the triumph of right (self professed) over wrong.

Lynching and the (Postcolonial) Cultural Psyche

Several cultural and historical factors that explain this turn to violence may be responsible, especially in combinations among themselves or with other factors. These are the rule of law, swaraj (with specific aspects drawn from evolution of the public sphere in India), and the cultural representation of righteous anger.

Rule of Law: Discourse and Performance

In an opposition that he characterized as a caricature, Richard Fallon distinguishes between the rule of law and the rule of men. He points to certain features that are essential to the former: easy to understand; obeyed by all; stable so that it can be anticipated; bringing within its purview officials, judges, and ordinary citizens; and enforced by the courts "through fair procedures."[52] This reading more-or-less sums up the understanding of the rule of law that has prevailed in India from colonial times.

India's colonial history has involved a complex response of resistance and appreciation of the institutions created by Britain and the values embodied in them. Certain stereotypes, especially pertaining to the "character" of the British that evolved as a result, remain in circulation, recalled especially in the face of the failure of institutions and individuals.

The rule of law came out of the interpretation of existing Indian laws that was made by the British in their project of ruling India effectively, while its specific articulation in the Indian Penal Code gave a set of guidelines for justice to all citizens. The "Introductory Report upon the Indian Penal Code" (1837) by Lord Thomas Babington Macaulay is a statement of British rule of law as superior to all others, where he begins by dismissing "the criminal law of the Hindoos" as the "last system of criminal law which an enlightened and humane government would be disposed to revive."[53] In effect, this is a dismissal of a multiplicity of laws: customary laws, the judicial system of the Mughals, and so forth. The concern is with evolving the right kind of document that will once and for all set the code: "the code will at once be a statute-book and a collection of decided cases."[54] He also speaks of the necessity of having a Law Commission, a single tribunal that could be referred to, that the legislature should not decide doubtful points, and the accused should have the benefit of doubt.[55] In cases of there being some doubt about the wording of the law, illustrations must be added that will "show in what sense the legislature intends the law to be understood" as well as "render it impossible that the same question, or any similar question, should ever again occasion difference of opinion."[56] What is obvious from all this is the systematic nature of the law and regulations, and the concern with uniformity, general applicability, fairness, precise delivery, and above all the law's authority.

The Penal Code being explicated by Macaulay is an example of what is meant by the rule of law since it clearly indicates the impersonality of the law as its most crucial characteristic, removing it from the whims and faulty perceptions of individual judges.[57] The expectations created by such an articulation of law and its violations during the British rule itself is comparable with the situation in the present when the rule of law is enshrined in the Constitution and the judiciary but is frequently deviated from or violated. This is a fact that somehow seems to have been deleted from memory, contributing to a stereotype of the "fairness" of the British. Macaulay addresses the possibility of violations through the question of exceptions, and, importantly in the light of concern with the privilege under law, he mentions the sovereign houses of India whom "we have not proposed to except from the operation of this code":

> We will only beg permission most respectfully to observe that every such exception is an evil; that it is an evil that any man should be above the law; that it is a still greater evil that the public should be taught to regard as a high and enviable distinction the privilege of being above the law; that the longer such privileges are suffered to last, the more difficult it is to take them away; that there can scarcely ever be a fairer opportunity for taking them away than at the time the government promulgates a new code binding alike on persons of different races and religions.... That a man of rank should be examined with particular ceremonies or in a particular place may, in the present state of Indian society, be highly expedient. But that a man of any rank should be allowed to commit crimes with impunity must in every state of society be most pernicious.[58]

This is an impressive statement of intent about rule of law that invited opposition from "non-officials" who "threatened to 'lynch' Thomas Macaulay for drafting legislation that subjected them to the jurisdiction of the ordinary civil courts."[59] But in the actual practice, colonial law left a lot of room for suspicion. As scholars have demonstrated, though "the empire in India governed a vast population of colonial subjects purportedly according to an equal and impartial rule of law.... legal practice and conventions placed most Europeans in India above the law and, in effect, tolerated and condoned widespread physical assault and abuse."[60] This compelled Bal Gangadhar Tilak to comment in 1907: "The goddess of British Justice, though blind, is able to distinguish unmistakably black from white."[61]

Elizabeth Kolsky notes the many instances of violation of the rule of law where white men were involved. She cites the statement made in 1850 by the Nizamut Adalat Judge J. Dunbar who compared the exceptionalism evident in the application of the rule of law to Britishers: "The obstinacy with which persons even of liberal education cling to the idea of an actual and indefeasible right to exemption appears to be little less surprising than that perversion of mind which leads the white race in the Southern States of America to claim a right of property in their unhappy slaves."[62] And as her examples show, educated Indians were perfectly conscious about this legal racism and often commented on it (for example, Tilak, mentioned above, Hurrish Chunder Mookherjee, and many others who wrote in newspapers of the time like the *Hindoo Patriot* and the *Sulabh Dainik*). One of the worst cases of the violation of the rule of law was in the tea gardens of Assam in India's Northeast where the guarantees of justice of colonial law were systematically set aside by the white planters.[63] These planters established an economy that has never shaken off these legal and social divisions, which find expression in the present in sporadic cases of lynching of tea garden managers and their families by the oppressed tea garden laborer, still suffering under uneven and unfair wage and work conditions that have continued from the colonial administration of the plantations. The *Telegraph*, Calcutta (Friday, June 13, 2003) reported one such story about the manager of the Sapoi tea estate who was lynched by irate laborers.

The impression created in the minds of educated Indians by the apparent fairness of the British legal system and the colonial concern with rooting out "evil" practices from Indian society is evident in the perception of the practice of *sati* (burning widows on the funeral pyres of their dead husbands) and the regulations banning it.

Lord Bentinck, British Governor-General in Madras from 1828–1835, in his "Minute on Sati" of November 9, 1829, described sati as "criminal." He also expressed the hope that the Hindus may be brought to a "purer morality" and a "more just conception of the will of God," through a "dissociation of religious belief and practice from blood and murder."[64] This interpretation is the backdrop to the Sati Regulation that he passed on December 4, 1829, where he repeatedly describes the practice as evil and criminal and one that encouraged atrocities, and therefore he decides that its abolition is the only way to put a stop to such "abuses." The Sati Regulation demonstrates the operation of the rule of law, especially in its expressed intent of making no exceptions no matter how long and respectable a tradition is represented. The regulation is vindicated by the approval of Raja Ram Mohun Roy, the eminent nineteenth-century reformer who thanked Bentinck in eloquent terms, while declaring the act as murder: "Relatives of widows have, in the burning of those infatuated females, almost invariably used to fasten them down on the pile, and heap over them large quantities of wood and other materials adequate to the prevention of their escape."[65] Roy's view of sati as murder watched and participated in by relatives ties it to the notion of spectacle, the witnessing of the act by large numbers, which habituates them to the violence of the proceedings, and while this is not developed in this chapter the play of the image of violent rituals like sati in the collective memory might be one of the sources for collective violence. Sir Frederick Halliday, who was Lieutenant Governor of the Bengal Presidency from 1854–1859, described the last suttee sati as a voluntary act by a mature woman but then went on to comment: "The prohibition of this horrible custom which had been a subject of grave apprehension to which the Government, until the time of Lord Bentinck, had always feared to apply itself, was effected without the smallest opposition or difficulty."[66]

If the rule of law found its exemplary site in the Regulations on Sati, the actual situation revealed the existence of Crown Courts (for Britons), Company Courts (for Indians and non-British Europeans) during the years of Company Rule, and subsequently in the disconnect between the "codified rule of law designed by colonial administrators" for British and Indian alike and its contradiction in "the institutionalization of racial distinctions in the statutory law and by the overt partiality of white police, judges and juries."[67] Already apparent here is the inevitable exploitation on the ground of the supposed impersonality and impartiality of the rule of law by privilege—in this case, that of the ruler—and the tacit racism in the operation of the system that was articulated by the ordinary British soldier or tea planter that would become habitual in postindependence India.[68]

The evocation of so many different kinds of catalysts and engines for public violence is an attempt to register the complexity and the strange twist by which certain factors have unexpected effects. The general feeling among the middle classes, who benefited from many of the colonial era's modernity drives, including institutions and modern schools that ran with a useful curriculum, was that British rule brought good governance. My mother, who was a student in a girls' school in preindependence Chittagong (now in Bangladesh) and whose father was a high official in the Indian Railways, spoke often of the school's discipline and of the curriculum, which included hygiene, sewing, cutting, and having to stitch men's shirts as a curricular requirement. She also spoke of the British inculcating punctuality in the Indian systems; the railways and their tardy and erratic schedules in modern India became an occasion for her to remember how punctual trains were in the British era. As part of how well the British treated their employees, she would cite the example of her father having two coaches reserved for him on any train he traveled in, having the services of a cook on his official tours, the huge bungalows they were given at the headquarters in Chittagong and their scenic location, and so on. Discipline, fair play, punctuality, and above all "impartial" treatment of employees are a set of stereotypes that evolved about the British. This also represents a nostalgia that many of the middle class of her generation expressed, comparing the mess independent India was making of her systems with the much better days of the British. They all spoke of the justice system, how wrongdoers were punished and how fair the rule of law was—constructing an image of imperial rule that was obviously a blend of actuality and nostalgic fictions. Since the public anger we have noted as a feature of the unsystematic violence visible in India today is most often a feature of the middle class, who turn their anger at others of their class but also at those below them in the social scale, it is significant that the construct of British rule, of which the rule of law was a part, came largely from this middle-class experience and construct of imperialism. The rule of law may have in reality been violated often by its own guardians, but this is a fact that was far from the experience of this middle class. They seem to have constructed their version of the operations of the rule of law and then assigned to it an inviolability that put it beyond the range of critical scrutiny, finding in it an effective counter to the present-day failures in the delivery of justice.

In a recent article that appeared in the Independence Day special issue of an Assamese weekly, a similar nostalgia appears; the writer recalls the colonial era and compares it to the present where everything seems to be going wrong. He writes of the quality of Raleigh bicycles and of the pure cement used for pillars in houses and for floors. He goes on to give an example to establish the difference between proactive imperial rule and the apathy of current Indian governance:

> About 12 or 14 years ago a letter was sent from a Department of the English Government to our Government. The letter stated that, "In the town of Mangaldai, a bridge over a certain river or nullah would have reached the end of its life. Had it been dismantled and replaced by a new one? If not it should be immediately attended to."

This sense of "responsibility of the erstwhile ruler who we had sent back" becomes the occasion to comment adversely on the irresponsibility of "our government whose newly built bridges collapse and kill people."[69]

So the imperial legacy came with the broad perception of fairness, and equality before law, and continued into postindependence India where it then became transformed into a system that was vulnerable to various forms of power. A scenario was created where on the one hand was the rule of law, and on the other the repeated and visible violation and compromising of it by politics, money, and muscle that began soon after independence and has continued into the present.[70]

A rhetoric of entitlement marks the democratic discourses in countries that in recent memory freed themselves from dominance by another power:

Independence struggles, wherever in the world they have been conducted, have this idea of seizing power—and of taking for themselves that which is "rightfully theirs." These two impulses find their legitimacy in the perceived failure of the state (as in the regular subversion of the rule of law) on the one hand and the invitation to agency on the other. Pratap Bhanu Mehta speaks of how "democracy came to be produced and legitimized through a complex series of negotiations among Hindus" and of liberal democracy taking root in a hierarchical society.[71] This is a way of trying to understand not only the manifestation of public anger, which is enmeshed in the operation and disruption of the rule of law, but also swaraj, which came to be interpreted in the common mind as a form of agency, and above all, the coming together of ideas of the rule of law and agency in a democratic polity that is at the same time deeply hierarchical.

Swaraj and Agency

Gandhi's key text for understanding swaraj is ostensibly *Hind Swaraj*, but in its connotations of self-control the spirit of swaraj pervades all his positions on the other important areas of his thought and practice, i.e., nonviolence/ahimsa, swadeshi, satyagraha, and, above all, the search for truth or *satya*. In using the word "swaraj" instead of simply "freedom," he takes advantage of its nuances to suggest both self-rule or self-control and self-government, the psychological/spiritual dimension nicely meshing with the idea of freedom from British rule. Rudolf C. Heredia writes that "essential to both meanings of swaraj was a sense of self-respect that is precisely Gandhi's answer to colonial rule." Freedom for Gandhi meant "freedom for self realisation" and it had to mean "freedom for all," for the privileged and the masses.[72] And it required focus on the "welfare of the whole people."[73]

While swaraj has these two connotations in Gandhi's interpretation of it, the idea of associating self-control with masculinity is a direction that *Hind Swaraj* underlines. While rejecting Western medicine and Western treatment, Gandhi says that to be subject to these systems is to be "deprived of self control" and to "have become effeminate."[74] Extending the implications of being a subject nation he declares: "It is contrary to our manhood if we obey laws repugnant to our conscience." And then "[I]f a man will only realize that it is unmanly to obey laws that are unjust, no man's tyranny will enslave him. This is the key to self-rule or home-rule."[75] The suggestion of masculinity in self-control as also in self-government has interesting repercussions: Certainly the idea of masculinity and the distinction made from effeminacy is a way of pointing to the need for action rather than passive acceptance of foreign rule.

But it extends to the public sphere in the violent/masculine action deemed necessary in the face of perceived aberrations, even as it regularly appears in the figure of the messianic savior in the genre of the Bollywood action movie. And behind such proactive positions is the kind of action signifying a mature self-control that Gandhi suggests is the necessary premise for all the aspects of his program for swaraj—ahimsa, satyagraha, swadeshi, and the work on the charkha—each demanding immense restraint and self-regulation.

In the meantime, the idea itself created ripples in the intellectual fraternity around Gandhi, and one serious engagement with it was that of Rabindranath Tagore, who corresponded with Gandhi on many issues. In an article in the *Modern Review* (September 1925), Tagore wrote of the necessity of having "the complete image of swaraj," which he interprets as "the responsibility of the country for achieving its own swaraj;—that is to say, its own welfare as a whole. . . . Health and work, reason, wisdom, and joy, must all be thrown into the crucible in order that the result may be fullness of welfare." Explaining this effect further, he writes, "We must re-awaken the faculty of regaining the motherland by creating it. . . . When acquaintance with, practice of, and pride in cooperative self-determination shall have spread in our land, then on such broad abiding foundation alone may swaraj become true. So long as we are wanting therein, both within and without and while such want is proving the root of all our other wants . . . want of food, of health, of wisdom,—it is past all belief that any programme of outward activity can rise superior to the poverty of spirit which has overcome our people. Success begets success; likewise swaraj alone can beget swaraj."[76] Tagore here extends the element of personal self-control and self-upliftment, which is seen by Gandhi as the fount of strength and "manliness" into a cooperative and collective exercise. But finally, he comes around to the expansion of the idea of swaraj from mere self-government to an all-round development that will raise the society and the country. What we see in this climate of opinion is a conviction that individuals have to raise themselves and work on themselves and their surroundings for swaraj to be effective and not expect to be able to rule their country without undergoing such transformation.

The encouragement to assume agency by the individual or the collective—especially to take responsibility—carries the tacit suggestion of conditions that require such action. So today, the autonomy movement might refer to it with as much conviction as might a social movement for land rights, both finding in swaraj the rationale to take action when denied by the state and its laws. The Kisan Mukti Sangram Samiti (KMSS) fighting for the land rights of the farmer and the landless in Assam is an example of seizing agency that can easily turn violent. Akhil Gogoi, the young social activist spearheading this movement, has been regularly protesting the building of big dams in the region and the displacement of the farmer, besides articulating people's discontent over political and administrative laxity and corruption. He led a group of KMSS activists who took over approximately 9.82 acres of farmland at Khetri in Assam at 4 A.M. on January 23, 2014, which they then went on to distribute among the farmers of the area. The land had been illegally occupied by a company called Topcem Cement. The process of distribution was elaborate. A committee of local villagers and KMSS members was formed to draw up a list of beneficiaries from among the farmers of the area. The KMSS would approve the list, and the land could not be sold or transferred by any of the recipients. The report made headlines in the local newspapers: "KMSS grabs 34 bighas of Farmland at Khetri." The word *grabs* was repeatedly used. The *Assam Tribune*, reporting from the KMSS press release, said that "several thousand people took part in the campaign to grab the plots of land and then to build houses on these plots" (January 24, 2014). The same evening, between 5–6 P.M., Akhil Gogoi, in an interview given to a local television news channel based in Guwahati, *DY365*, was asked if he thought that he had overstepped the law. He replied that he didn't think he had, that he had rightfully taken land that belonged to the indigenous people and given it back to them, implying that he had had to seize agency in the face of government inaction.

Cultures of Public Violence

If the television media voyeurizes public anger, it also takes recourse to a condemnatory rhetoric in its presentation. On the other hand, the more organized visual depiction of such violence is actually presented as lynching in popular and widely watched Hindi/Bollywood films, where, at the end of the film, retribution by people who have been oppressed by a criminal or underworld don or a corrupt politician and his henchmen is invariably presented within a frame of good versus evil. The films represent violence as a legitimate act of retribution in the face of illegal and oppressive action that is rarely punished by police and judiciary. A slew of movies presenting the "deeply satisfying" spectacle of evil being punished by the good is one of the ways in which public anger has been legitimized and has entered the Indian cultural landscape. Here, the moral evaluations of a society and the usual helplessness of the public to address and find solutions to the unfair systems that oppress them come together and are addressed in straightforward acts of taking the law into one's hands and meting out just punishment. The public institutions are usually seen to be at the mercy of the criminal who is often a corrupt politician, a businessman who uses his money to advance his business and kill off rivals, or a godman (a term used derogatively for a self-styled spiritual leader who abuses the faith people seem to have in his powers)—all three exploiting India's porous public institutions and appearing frequently as wrongdoers in films; but they are also all coming out of India's public life, its political scene, and especially electoral politics where they frequently come together.

The intense suffering of the poor and powerless is followed by the emergence of a messiah—that one young man (and very rarely a woman) who is able to seize agency and lead the people in their retaliatory programs. In the hero-centered Indian /Hindi (Bollywood) film industry, much of the groundwork to trap the villain, smoke out his cohorts, and bring them to justice is done by the hero. In *Gangajal* (Prakash Jha 2003) for instance, the scene of lynching is the climax of the film, with the policeman-hero hunting down the villain and throwing him to the mob.

It is salutary to note the trajectory of such violence in the movies: Pre-1960s, with faith still resting in the judicial institutions, the villain would be duly brought before the court and punished under the Indian Penal Code; in the 1970s and 1980s, the "angry young man films" usually made around the actor Amitabh Bachchan—who would singlehandedly take issue with all the wrongdoers and deal out summary justice—saw a shift to a large-scale loss of faith in the system. Now the degeneration has reached the point where the vicarious satisfaction offered to the public through the hero's punishment of the villain is no longer adequate and there is therefore a shift of agency to the nameless public who directly participate in the action. Public satisfaction is also ensured through the pinning of blame for the apathetic and corrupt government machinery on the criminal-politician-bureaucrat manipulator of the system who is conveniently available to be lynched by the public.

In recent years the film *Gangajal* has been scheduled repeatedly on television. It contains several elements of collective violence that are visible in modern India: the rape of a girl from an amorphous underprivileged group (the caste/tribe factors are usually suppressed in the popular Hindi movie) by a the son of a powerful mafia don turned politician against whom nobody dares to act; the honest upright police-officer hero; and the faceless ordinary public always trodden and crushed under the heel of brute muscle, money, and firepower. Films like these where agency-as-taking-the-law-into-one's-hands is presented approvingly contribute their bit to the assumption of real agency through violence in the public sphere. Another popular film, rerun frequently on television channels, is Rakeysh Mehra's *Rang de Basanti* (2006) where a group of young, mostly middle-class, boys and girls take on and publicly punish a corrupt political establishment.

A culture of violence is also apparent in the anger directed at the effigy of a minister, bureaucrat, or public figure who is perceived to be at the root of concerns like rising prices, corruption in government, or lack of action in a specific area. Setting fire to the effigy of the offender provides symbolic gratification to a public that is helpless in the face of political clout. The effigy is kicked, set on fire, its limbs torn apart, and spat on, the pent-up anger of the public finding expression in this moment of symbolic violence.

People who gather to burn an effigy in India also have the symbolism of the burning of the effigy of Ravana, the epic antihero of the Ramayana; every year at Dussehra, this carnivalesque occasion carries a symbolism of good versus evil and the victory of the good over evil. This acts as a powerful agent in the transfer of this religious-festive episode to the site of revolutionary protest. It appears to be a nonviolent act, but it produces, in the "perpetrators" and participants, the vicarious satisfaction of having acted against evil, even as it provides an outlet for the anger within.

Conclusion: Sentimentalization of the Public Sphere

In all these sites of collective violence and anger—the burning of effigies of politicians and institutional officials, participation in the annual ritual burning of the effigies of the epic antihero Ravana (symbolic of evil on a mammoth scale and therefore the repository of all kinds of discontents and angers), the watching of movies that represent lynching as appropriate retribution, and the participation in regular acts of violence against individual targets—a crucial aspect is the act of witnessing or "standing witness" and not merely watching passively. The depiction of violent action on television unites a wide and scattered viewership into a community that arrives at a moral assessment of the act, empathizing with the victim or the perpetrators. Several questions arise from these multiple sites of violence and viewing. How does a viewer respond? Do bystander-viewers identify with the victim or the perpetrator? There is a peculiar ambivalence observable in the incidents cited in this chapter concerning empathy for victim and perpetrator. Those who participate in the act of violence or stand by and watch are possibly not sympathetic to the victim. Those who watch it on television along with the opinion-forming commentary of the news channel would probably empathize with the victim of such violence.

Analyzing mob violence in the American South, Amy Louise Wood writes of witnessing as a process through which disparate spectacles are united and are transferred to the spectacle of lynching:

> The act of witnessing, in this respect, unites the disparate, if not competing, cultural spectacles of executions, religious rituals, photography, and motion pictures. These phenomena were anchored in similar conceptions of truth and

evidence, and they established comparable modes of spectatorship. Southerners transferred the notions of witnessing generated in these social practices to the lynching spectacle.[77]

A similar process is at work in India in the witnessing of these spectacles of violence, which then make the crossover into the perpetration of the act of violence by an outraged public.

Public violence and expressions of public anger in contemporary India are now occurring against discursive formations about rights and civic responsibility that are enshrined in political documents, the rule of law that is perceived to have been regularly violated by powerful groups and individuals, and the idea of swaraj or self-rule that has entered the psyche of the contemporary Indian in unanticipated ways. The volatile combination of ideas about the rule of law being available to all in the same ways and the rightness of action against violations that are unaddressed by police and legal institutions is entangled in the media's circulation of visuals of more and more people taking the law into their own hands and contributing to the formation of a discourse about the rationale for such actions. The influence of such a discourse is further strengthened by the cultural representation of proactive citizens.

The result is a sentimentalized public sphere,[78] which seems to have now become the site of salutary lessons taught by the citizens who have given up on the ability and willingness of police and judiciary to act appropriately and who now express their discontent and anger directly in the public domain. This kind of violence is the result of a tension in Indian public life with the colonial legacy of a particular kind of modernity, of which the rule of law is representative. Postcolonial agency now is the backlash against the homogenization by rule-of-law mechanisms against that kind of modernity that gives no scope to the expression of public emotion. Traditions like the effigy burning at Dussehra, on the other hand, did offer an outlet. The righteous public anger against evil, expressed symbolically as the effigy burning at Dussehra, is repeated with a difference in lynching. Agency in this sense is the retrieval of a tradition and its translation into a "modern" context. It is a kind of eruption of the symbolic (the tradition of effigy burning) into the real (the modern legal system) and thus the assertion first of symbolic agency (the right to burn the evildoer in the form of an effigy) and then of very real public agency outside the frames of the law. This assumption of agency owes something to the virtual participation of a large community of viewers of media representations of violence, the only medium through which they actually have a sense of how common is their anger. The sentimentalization

Public Anger, Violence, and the Legacy of Decolonization in India   151

of the public sphere is therefore a backlash against its rationalization through the rule of law.

Notes

I would like to thank Michael Pfeifer and Pramod Nayar for their keen interest in the chapter and the suggestions they made at various stages of its development.

1. "Chronology of Communal Violence in India" (New Delhi, PTI) New Delhi November 9, 2011, http://www.hindustantimes.com/news-feed/archives/chronology-of-communal-violence-in-india/article1—8038.aspx. Accessed 08.07.2014 15:23.

2. "Two Brothers Killed by Lynch Mob," http://www.liveleak.com/view?i=01d_1282455999. Accessed 23.08.2014 20:12. "Anti-Tamil Riots and the Political Crisis in Sri Lanka," *Bulletin of Concerned Asian Scholars*, Vol. 16, No. 1 (January 6, 1984), http://www.marxists.org/history/erol/sri-lanka/tamil-2.pdf. Accessed 22.08.2014 20:06.

3. "Anti-Tamil Riots and the Political Crisis in Sri Lanka," *Bulletin of Concerned Asian Scholars*, Vol. 16, No. 1 (January 6, 1984), http://www.marxists.org/history/erol/sri-lanka/tamil-2.pdf. Accessed 22.08.2014 20:06.

4. "Statistics on Public Lynching," http://odhikar.org/statistics/public-lynching/. Accessed 22.08.2014 20:45.

5. The global use of the term to describe similar instances is documented in the volume *Swift to Wrath: Lynching in Global Historical Perspective*. Eds. William D. Carrigan and Christopher Waldrep. Charlottesville: University of Virginia Press, 2013. More specifically, Scott Morschauser in the chapter "'Vengeance Is Mine': 'Lynching' in the Ancient Near East," describes forms of torture that are very similar to what is termed by the media in India as *lynching*.

6. S. M. Dahiwale, "Khairlanji: Insensitivity of Mahar Officers," *Economic and Political Weekly*, Vol. XLIV, No. 31 (August 1–7, 2009), 29–33, http://www.jstor.org/stable/25663388. Accessed 2.09.2014 7:00.

7. "Khairlanji: The Crime and the Punishment," http://www.thehindu.com/todays-paper/tp-opinion/khairlanji-the-crime-and-punishment/article588920.ece. Accessed 22.08.2014 20:57.

8. "Haryana: Girl Lynched, Boy Beheaded in Honour Killing," www.indianexpress.com/news/haryana-girl-lynched-boy . . . /1170955/. Accessed 20.07.2014 20:14.

9. "Six Arrested for Lynching 14-Year Old Boy," articles.timesofindia.indiatimes.com › Collections › Murder Case. Accessed 20.07.2014 19:30.

10. "Youth Lynched at Rukminigaon," http://www.assamtribune.com/scripts/detailsnew.asp?id=feb2413/city05. Accessed 20.07.2014 19:35.

11. "Phool Mohammad Lynching Case," http://www.timesofindia.indiatimes.com Topics. Accessed 20.07.2014 19:46. Also, "The Lynching of Phool Mohammad and Why the Riots Never Stop," http://gulail.com/the-lynching-of-phool-mohammad-and-why-the-riots-never-stop/. Accessed 23.07.2014 20:10.

12. "A Legal Lynching: Indian Government Executes Afzal Guru," http://www.wsws.org/en/articles/2013/02/12/afza-f12.html. Accessed 20.07.2014 20:00.

13. "Thief Lynched," http://www.ndtv.com. Topic Press Trust of India | Sunday, September 2, 2012. Accessed 20.07.2014 20:05.

14. "Ignoble Deed: The Lynching of Amartya Sen," http://firstbiz.firstpost.com/economy/ignoble-deed-the-lynching-of-amartya-sen-43732.html. Accessed 20.07.2014 20:07.

15. "Leopard Lynched in Golaghat," http://www.telegraphindia.com/1140113/jsp/ . . . /story_17780991.jsp. Accessed 20.07.2014 20:20.

16. "Indian Woman, 20, Tortured and Lynched by Her Family," http://www.dailymail.co.uk/ . . . /Indian-woman-20-tortured-lynched-family-boyfriend. Accessed 20.07.2014 20:22.

17. "India: 20 Killed by Train—Train Driver Lynched," http://www.jerusalemonline.com/news/india-20-killed-by-train-train-driver-lynched-1337. Accessed 20.07.2014 20:25.

18. "Ten Men Beaten to Death in India," news.bbc.co.uk/2/hi/south_asia/6992446.stm. Accessed 20.07.2014 20:30.

19. "Uttar Pradesh: The Rape and Lynching Capital of India," http://www.americanbazaaronline.com/2014/06/13/rape-lynching-capital-india-uttar-pradesh/. Accessed 20.07.2014 20:32.

20. "Indian Police Arrest Three over Gang-rape and Lynching of Three Sisters," http://www.thenational.ae/world/south-asia/indian-police-arrest-three-over-gang-rape-and-lynching-of-teen-sisters. Accessed 20.07.2014 20:35.

21. "Indian Girls Lynching Suspected Honour Killing," http://www.independent.ie/world-news/asia-pacific/india-girls-lynching-suspected-honour-killing-30338959.html. Accessed 20.07.2014 20:38.

22. Vidya Bhushan Rawat, "The Lynching of Nido Taniam," http://www.countercurrents.org/rawat050214.htm. Accessed 20.07.2014 20:42.

23. "North-East Residents in Delhi Facing Bias: Report," http://indiatoday.intoday.in/story/report-says-north-east-residents-in-delhi-face-humiliation/1/135561.html. Accessed 17.08.2014 20:25.

24. "Yeh hai India," *Bihardays* (August 16, 2012), http://www.bihardays.com/ye-hai-india-6000-from-northeast-flee-bangalore-after-kokrajhar-mumbai-clashes/. Accessed 17.08.2014 20:36.

25. Biranchi Narayan Acharya, "Pune Culprits Who Lynched an Indian Muslim Youth to Death Must Be Punished," http://www.merinews.com/article/pune-culprits-who-lynched-an-Indian-muslim-youth-to-death-must-be-punished. Accessed 23.7.2014 19:50.

26. Mazin Khan, "Young Techie Mohsin Shaikh Lynched in Pune," http://www.milligazette.com/news/10599-young-techie-mohsin-shaikh-lynched-in-pune. Accessed 23.7.2014 19:55.

27. Meena Radhakrishna, "Crime of Vigilante Justice," *Economic and Political Weekly*, Vol. XLII, No. 2 (January 12, 2008), 16–18, http://www.epw.in/commentary/crime-vigilante-justice.html. Accessed 28.08.2014 20:10.

28. "Assam Villager Lynched on Witch Hunting Charge," http://www.theshillongtimes.com/2013/06/08/assam-villager-lynched-on-witch-hunting-charge/. Accessed 23.07.2014 20:07.

29. Shaunak Sen and Shaumik Mukherjee, "The Lynching of Phool Mohammad and Why the Riots Never Stop," http://www.gulail.com/the-lynching-of-phoolmohammad-and-why-the-riots-never-stop. Accessed 23.07.2014 20:10.

30. "Youth Lynched at Rukminigaon," http://www.assamtribune.com/scripts/detailsnew.asp?id=feb2413/city05. Accessed 20.07.2014 19:35.

31. "Lynch Victim Employer Arrested," http://www.telegraphindia.com/1130226/jsp/northeast/story_16605399.jsp. Accessed 22.07.2014 20:08.

32. Carl Boggs, "The Great Retreat: Decline of the Public Sphere in Late Twentieth-Century America," *Theory and Society*, Vol. 26, No. 6 (December 1997), 742.

33. Ibid., 744–745.

34. Ibid., 747.

35. Amir Ali, "Evolution of Public Sphere in India," *Economic and Political Weekly*, Vol. 36, No. 26 (June 30–July 6, 2001), 2419, http://www.epw.in/special-articles/evolution-public-sphere-india.html. Accessed 15.06.2016 2419–2425; U. Kalpagam, "Colonial Governmentality and the Public Sphere in India," *Journal of Historical Sociology*, Vol. 14, Issue 4 (December 2001), 418–440; and Arvind Rajagopal, *The Indian Public Sphere*. New Delhi: Oxford University Press, 2009.

36. The many ways in which lynching may have entered the lexicon in India invite speculation about the widespread influence of American literature and culture. The influence of the Black Panthers on Dalit Movements or the replication of the ambience and storyline of the western film in the Hindi movie industry, beginning with Ramesh Sippy's *Sholay* (1975), are significant instances.

37. Michael J. Pfeifer, *Rough Justice: Lynching and American Society, 1874–1947*. Urbana: University of Illinois Press, 2006, 2–3.

38. Ibid., 2, 3.

39. Manfred Berg and Simon Wendt, "Introduction: Lynching from an International Perspective," in *Globalizing Lynching History: Vigilantism and Extralegal Punishment from an International Perspective*. Eds. Manfred Berg and Simon Wendt. New York: Palgrave Macmillan, 2011, 5.

40. Ibid., 4.

41. Ibid.

42. Ibid., 3.

43. Roberta Senechal de la Roche, "Collective Violence as Social Control," *Sociological Forum*, Vol. 11, No. 1 (March 1996), 97–128, 98, http://www.jstor.org/stable/684953. Accessed 11.01.2011 18:16.

44. Senechal de la Roche, "Collective Violence as Social Control," 98–100.

45. Ibid., 101, 103.

46. Ibid., 106.

47. Ibid., 111.

48. George Bryjak, "Collective Violence in India," *Asian Affairs*, Vol. 13, No. 2 (Summer 1986), 35–55, http://www.jstor.org/stable/30171906. Accessed 28.08.2014 20:40, 47–48.

49. Ibid., 46–47.

50. Roberta Senechal de la Roche, "Why Is Collective Violence Collective?" *Sociological Theory*, Vol. 19, No. 2 (July 2001), 126–144, http://www.jstor.org/stable/3108628. Accessed 26.06.2014 05:45, 129.

51. Amy Louise Wood, *Lynching and Spectacle: Witnessing Racial Violence in America, 1890–1940*. Chapel Hill: University of North Carolina Press, 2009, 13.

52. Richard H. Fallon, "'The Rule of Law'" as a Concept in Constitutional Discourse," *Columbia Law Review*, Vol. 97, No. 1 (January 1997), 1–56, http://www.jstor.org/stable/1123446. Accessed 10.07.2014 23:37, 8.

53. Lord Thomas Babington Macaulay, "Introductory Report upon the Indian Penal Code," (1837), *Archives of Empire. Volume I: From the East India Company to the Suez Canal.* Eds. Mia Carter with Barbara Harlow. Durham: Duke University Press, 2003, 268–281.

54. Ibid., 277.

55. Ibid., 278.

56. Ibid., 278.

57. S. S. Dhavan, who, in *The Indian Judicial System: A Historical Survey*, claims that the rule of law prevailed in ancient India, points out that Indian jurisprudence is based on a rule of law, whether derived from ancient India or from the British, http://www.allahabadhighcourt.in/event/TheIndianJudicialSystem_SSDhavan.pdf. Accessed 17.11.2014 18:10.

58. Macaulay, "Introductory Report upon the Indian Penal Code" (1837), 279.

59. Elizabeth Kolsky, *Colonial Justice in British India: White Violence and the Rule of Law.* New Delhi: Cambridge University Press, 2011, 19.

60. Ibid., 4.

61. Tilak cited in Ibid.

62. Ibid., 19.

63. Ibid., 142–184.

64. Lord William Bentinck, "Bentinck's Minute on Sati, 8 November 1829," *The Correspondence of Lord William Cavendish Bentinck, Vol I, 1828–1831*, ed. C. H. Philips (Oxford: Oxford University Press, 1977) in *Archives of Empire. Volume I: From the East India Company to the Suez Canal.* Ed. Mia Carter with Barbara Harlow. Durham: Duke University Press, 2003, 350–361.

65. Raja Ram Mohun Roy, "Address to Lord William Bentinck" (1830), *Archives of Empire. Volume I: From the East India Company to the Suez Canal.* Ed. Mia Carter with Barbara Harlow. Durham: Duke University Press, 2003. 370–372.

66. Sir Frederick Halliday, "A Suttee Anecdote—Appendix to Vol 1," in *Bengal under the Lieutenant-Governors Being a Narrative of the Principal Events and Public Measures during Their Periods of Office, from 1854 to 1898.* 2 Vols. Ed. C. E. Buckland, C.I.E. of the Indian Civil Service. Calcutta: Kedarnath Bose, 1902 (2nd edition), 161–162.

67. Kolsky, *Colonial Justice in British India*, 11–12.

68. Ibid.

69. Nagen Bhattacharyya, "Aami Baru Sabhya Jati Ne?" (Are We a Civilized Race?), *Sadin* (Assamese Language Weekly) August 15, 2014, 10 and 21.

70. There are many cases where the wrongdoer from the privileged classes has managed to get away either completely or with a mild sentence, while the victim or her/his family has had to fight losing battles against a process that has included disappearing or retracting witnesses and corrupt investigative mechanisms, and this has further contributed to the turn to violence of the ordinary citizen. Among recent cases where these factors were visible are, first, the Jessica Lal murder case. Jessica Lal was shot dead on May 28–29, 1999, at a party in South Delhi. The men involved in the shooting were, among others, Manu Sharma and Vikas Yadav, both sons of politicians, and they used all the clout at their disposal to stretch and delay the case by buying up witnesses. It was only in 2010 that Manu Sharma was finally given a life term (http://www.thehindu.com/news/national/jessica-lall-murder-case-chronology-of-events/article403202.ece;

accessed 23.07.2014 21:00). The second case was that of Nitish Katara, a young executive in Delhi, son of an Indian Civil Service (IAS) officer, who was in love with Bharti Yadav, the daughter of D. P. Yadav, a powerful politician. Her brother, Vikas Yaav, is believed to have murdered him because the Yadavs did not like the liaison. The case ran a similar course, with witnesses turning hostile and no convictions for a long time even as Mrs. Neelam Katara, Nitish's mother waged a battle in the courts (http://speakindia.wordpress.com/2008/05/28/nitish-katara-murder/; accessed 23.07.2014 21:10). Finally, the life term given in 2008 was upheld by the Delhi Court. In both cases, the involvement of powerful politicians has helped to make a travesty of justice. The public outrage that was expressed over these two incidents was effectively managed and presented by the television media, transforming the channels into forums for its expression.

71. Pratap Bhanu Mehta, "Hinduism and Self Rule," *Journal of Democracy*, Vol. 15, No. 3 (July 2004), 108–121. Project Muse DOI: 10.1353/jod.2004.0049 109–110.

72. Rudolf C. Heredia, "Interpreting Gandhi's *Hind Swaraj*," *Economic and Political Weekly*, Vol. 34, No. 24 (June 12–18, 1999), 1497–1502, http://www.jstor.org/stable/30171906. Accessed 22.07.2014 20:30 1498.

73. M. K. Gandhi, *Hind Swaraj or Indian Home Rule (1909)*. Ahmedabad: Navjivan Publishing House, 1938. EBook, http://gandhiashramsevagram.org/mkgandhi/ebks/hind_swaraj.pdf. Accessed 10.07.2014 20:31 64.

74. Ibid., 54.

75. Ibid., 75–76.

76. Rabindranath Tagore in *The Mahatma and the Poet: Letters and Debates between Gandhi and Tagore 1915–1941*. Compiled and Ed. Sabyasachi Bhattacharya. New Delhi: National Book Trust, 1999 (1st ed. 1997), 119, 120.

77. Wood, *Lynching and Spectacle*, 4.

78. In speaking of a sentimentalization of the public sphere, I am stretching ideas of state emotion and public feeling in the work of Lauren Berlant ("The Epistemology of State Emotion" in *Dissent in Dangerous Times*, Ed. Austin Sarat, Ann Arbor, University of Michigan Press, 2005, 46–80) and that of melodramatic political discourse in Elisabeth S. Anker (*Orgies of Feeling: Melodrama and the Politics of Freedom*, Durham, Duke University Press, 2014), especially the legitimizing effects of such public displays and sharing of emotion to read the kind of legitimation of violence focused on in this chapter.

6 New Situations Demand Old Magic

Necklacing in South Africa, Past and Present

NICHOLAS RUSH SMITH

South Africa's long history of vigilante violence made international headlines in the days following Nelson Mandela's funeral in late 2013 when it was revealed that the sign language interpreter for the event, Thamsanqa Jantjie, had participated in the lynching of two men in his neighborhood a decade earlier.[1] Given the interpreter's proximity to major world leaders, the revelations added a note of panic to what had been, until that point, merely an embarrassing situation for the government when it had earlier been revealed that the sign language interpreter did not know sign language at all. For his part, the interpreter was sanguine about his presence at the killings, telling the local *Sunday Times* newspaper, "It was a community thing, what you call mob justice, and I was also there."[2] The "community thing" he alluded to involved *necklacing* two men—placing gasoline-filled tires around their necks and setting them alight—for allegedly stealing a hot plate, a pair of shoes, and three eggs. Although he had been arrested for his alleged participation in the killings, he was let go after being declared unfit to stand trial.[3]

In their immediate wake, the revelations drew loud criticism of the African National Congress (ANC) government for supposedly putting world leaders at risk by having them on the stage next to Jantjie, who was employed by a politically well-connected firm that had been hired to handle the funeral arrangements. What was much less discussed was the nature of the violence Jantjie was accused of having committed. After all, it is not obvious why a crowd of people would perpetrate such gruesome violence against two petty thieves, especially because necklacing was first developed as a technique for punishing suspected collaborators with the apartheid regime.[4] Even if members of the crowd thought that thievery was a sufficiently serious crime deserving of death, it is not obvious why they would use a violent technique deployed against political threats under a racist authoritarian state to sanction small-time criminals under a multiracial democracy.

Nevertheless, the incident in which Jantjie participated was hardly unique in South Africa. Although it is difficult to quantify the frequency of necklace killings since the end of apartheid,[5] one need not look far beyond the Jantjie affair to find other instances. For example, just one month after the Jantjie controversy erupted, an official commission of inquiry into a series of at least eight necklace murders in Khayelitsha, a township outside of Cape Town, was due to begin.[6] Yet, despite its frequency, necklacing—as a specific repertoire of violence—has received relatively little attention in the growing scholarly literature on vigilantism in South Africa.[7]

That necklacing is practiced so frequently in the wake of South Africa's democratic transition is surprising because the country is often lauded for the scope of its political and legal reforms since the end of apartheid. For example, the country adopted one of the world's most celebrated constitutions and provided access to meaningful legal protections for the whole population for the first time.[8] And while crime rates remain unacceptably high and the police force is a troubled organization, it has been massively expanded to give all South Africans access to the state's protection in ways that were not available under apartheid.[9] In other words, while its legal apparatus still needs much improvement, South Africa has worked to create a democratic legal system that all South Africans can access without prejudice for the first time. Yet, despite these changes, necklacing is still practiced. Moreover, it is being practiced in a context far removed from its original creation—the violent sanctioning of political betrayal under a racist authoritarian regime. This chapter asks why. Why is necklacing practiced twenty years after the dawn of democracy to punish suspected criminals given that it was originally used as a tool in the struggle against apartheid to attack collaborators with the apartheid regime? And what enables a tool used to sanction one type of behavior to be used to sanction another, particularly when the two behaviors are of apparently different type and magnitude (for example, lethal political betrayal versus petty criminality)?

Understanding Necklace Violence

One explanation for why groups would use the necklace to punish criminals today is a repertory one. That is, one might argue that once the repertoire became available as a form of punishment during the apartheid era it could undergo an "object shift" and easily be appropriated to sanction other kinds of offenses like criminality.[10] One might hypothesize that once such an object shift occurred, necklacing, as is the tendency with other repertoires of violence, continued to be available as a form of punishment and persisted.[11] There is much truth to such a hypothesis, and we will see evidence of an object shift later in this chapter. Yet, such an account gives little sense of how an object shift occurs. Moreover, much theory on repertoires of violence holds that, when there has been a massive change in regime, repertoires are likely to change enormously along with the political context.[12] And, as I suggested earlier, there are arguably not many regimes in the late twentieth century that experienced more dramatic regime changes than South Africa. Thus, while we know that repertoires of violence undergo object shifts and persist across regimes, we still know relatively little about *how* they undergo an object shift or *why* they persist across regimes. And to understand the contemporary usage of necklacing we need to understand both of these processes.

A second explanation for why necklacing continues to be practiced despite radical shifts in object and circumstance is a strategic one. That is, the spectacular nature of necklace violence might communicate a warning to wrongdoers of the severe consequences they face, therefore reducing future malfeasance.[13] As Paul Richards writes of gruesome violence in a different context, violence is "supposed to unsettle its victims," and spectacular violence is "devilishly well calculated" to achieving such ends.[14] One might argue that necklacing, which so effectively warned against collaboration under apartheid through its over-the-top violence, has been appropriated to communicate a similar warning to criminals today. Undoubtedly, there is a good deal of truth in such arguments and perpetrators often explain their actions in these terms. However, rational explanations take us only so far toward understanding the persistence of necklacing because they take too narrow a view of spectacular violence's communicative potential. Specifically, spectacles cannot be only a way of sending a message to would-be wrongdoers because the majority audience at a necklacing is likely to be otherwise "upstanding" members of the community. In other words, strategic explanations have difficulty explaining what the message is for the perpetrators or witnesses of necklace violence—two groups that are as much audiences for its violence as collaborators or criminals.

That lynchings are communicative spectacles whose audience goes beyond would-be criminals has been established, for example, by the growing literature on Latin American lynching.[15] For scholars of Latin American lynching, the upsurge in lynch violence across much of the continent near the turn of the millennium can best be understood as a form of communication that transmits political discontent via the medium of spectacular violence.[16] For these scholars, while lynching does serve to intimidate criminals, such events are "also about being seen: calling attention to oneself or one's group by means of public display."[17] For these Latin Americanists, lynching dramatizes the lack of substantive law that disenfranchised communities experience and works as a protest to demand that law be provided by the state. In this sense, such scholarship rightly suggests that lynching's spectacular violence is "not *only* about crime" but also the social and political circumstances in which a crime takes place.[18] While this chapter agrees with this literature that lynching spectacles dramatize social and political concerns, it departs from the Latin American literature to argue that lynching does not merely mark a lack of substantive law. Rather, attention to South African necklacing suggests that communities have deployed the necklace both historically and contemporarily to challenge what the substance of the law should be in the first place.

Through analyzing the continuities in necklace violence past and present, this chapter argues that when South Africans deploy the necklace, intentionally or not, they challenge the terms upon which the legal apparatus is founded. Under apartheid, the necklace was used, in part, to contest the moral constitution of apartheid law, which embodied official state racism, and to resist the extension of the legal apparatus into the daily lives of South Africa's townships. Since the end of apartheid, the necklace has again been used to challenge the moral basis of the law. Ironically, however, contemporary necklacing challenges the legal rights regime that emerged out of the struggle against apartheid and upon which postapartheid law is based. For many South Africans sympathetic to vigilantism, the postapartheid legal system enables criminality (and by implication immorality) to proliferate as suspected criminals are released back into communities due to the rights they are afforded by the current legal dispensation. As evidence of this, we will see that the necklace has been deployed not only when the police fail to make arrests, but also when they succeed and suspects are released on bail. In this sense, contemporary South Africans attempt to create purified moral communities through violent techniques that are similar to vigilante violence from a previous era, albeit now in the context of a radically different legal system. Yet, in both eras the necklace has been used to challenge the ideological basis of the extant legal system and the way in which the legal system ostensibly prevents the creation of moral communities. Through its spectacular violence, both under apartheid and today, the necklace dramatized these critiques of the legal order. Thus, while necklace violence does serve a communicative function, it does not only communicate a warning about malfeasance. Instead, necklacing also communicates a set of moral codes to bystanders and communicates criticisms of the extant legal order to the state.[19]

To be sure, the argument that necklacing is a kind of moralizing communication is undoubtedly uncomfortable given that necklacing involves the gruesome extrajudicial murder of a person. To be clear, in calling necklacing a form of moralizing political action, my point is not to condone or validate necklacing or to claim that it is a moral act in the sense of a universal standard of ethical behavior. It is, however, to show the kinds of moral claims those engaging in necklacing make and how participants in the violence justify seeking redress for those claims outside of the institutions of the state through violent means. In other words, it is to show how participants could construct acts of spectacular violence as being moral in context, even if they appear morally abhorrent from the outside—an argument that has analytical advantages over other perspectives in explaining the "extralethal" nature of necklace violence, even as it raises troubling normative questions.[20]

For instance, emphasizing the morally expressive quality of necklace violence helps us to understand the apparent object shift of necklace violence over time—from its initial genesis as a weapon against collaborators with the apartheid state, to its transformation into a sanctioning mechanism for members of the liberation struggle, through its deployment against targets like witches and criminals during the latter years of apartheid and today. These seemingly disparate targets could become conjoined—and, indeed, often were conjoined even in the earliest acts of necklacing—because of their commonly being perceived as a threat to the moral purity of local communities. In important ways, the continued practice of necklacing during acts of vigilante violence in postapartheid South Africa is a continuation of the utopian project of community cleansing, which was started under apartheid and never completed. Thus, the repertoires of punishment developed during the late apartheid years bear a striking resemblance to the sorts of practices that are deployed today to punish suspected criminals who threaten the moral sanctity of the imagined township community.

Nevertheless, necklacing today is not a mere continuation of a previous practice for punishing criminals. Indeed, given the radical—arguably revolutionary—change in South Africa's political and legal institutions,[21] assuming that necklacing is still practiced as simply a received practice cannot account for its continuation. Instead, it is better to think of necklacing as a repertoire of violence that has been *repurposed* for a new political context—in this case as a practice used to challenge the substance of the law even though that substance has changed from one political context to the next.[22] Recognizing the continuities and discontinuities between necklace violence past and present also allows us to understand contradictions that characterize contemporary necklace violence, particularly the fact that the necklace continues to be deployed in a democratic era that it was ostensibly used to create.

To explicate the relationship between necklacing past and present, the chapter examines two episodes of necklace violence, one historical and one contemporary. The first, the case of Maki Skhosana's death in 1985, is particularly useful for understanding the dynamics of necklace violence for several reasons. It was the first widely publicized necklacing in apartheid South Africa and had dramatic effects on the spread of the practice. As a result, it has been widely documented through drawn-out court cases and Truth and Reconciliation Commission hearings (TRC), allowing rare insight on the emotional, social, and political context surrounding a necklacing.[23] And because part of it was recorded by news crews, it offers a rare (if also upsetting) opportunity to analyze (at least part of) the performance of a necklacing as it happened.[24] The second necklacing examined in the chapter was a 2013 event that made international headlines in which a crowd of four hundred people paraded through Khutsong, west of Johannesburg, and killed five alleged criminals and a traditional healer, necklacing several of them.[25] The violence in this case was particularly surprising because a number of the victims had recently been arrested by the police and were out on bail, which suggests that police "failure" cannot be a complete explanation for the violence as commentators argued in the wake of the event. Instead, we need to place this contemporary event in a broader historical arc of necklace violence as a technique to challenge the moral basis of the state's law. In order to understand these two events, however, we must first place necklacing in the broader history of the struggle against apartheid and the place of popular justice within it.

The Struggle against Apartheid as Political and Moral Revolution

The necklace—along with burning as a more general repertoire of violence—emerged during the latter decades of the struggle against apartheid. It is crucial to recognize at the outset that the struggle against apartheid, while always a struggle against an organized system of racial oppression, went beyond trying to bring about a new governing system. It was also a struggle to determine the moral and political grounds upon which local communities would be governed, especially in the latter decades of the struggle. The necklace grew out of this dual struggle and the profoundly moralizing politics inherent to it.[26]

Arguably, apartheid's collapse was precipitated by a key event: the 1976 Soweto Uprising. The response to it would also ultimately transform the practice of popular justice. The apartheid state's massacre of hundreds of unarmed, protesting students at Soweto radicalized youth across the country and sparked a mobilization that the state struggled to bring under control. The apartheid state's reaction to the Soweto Uprising was various—including widespread arrests and increasingly overt and covert violence against activists—but involved a crucial institutional shift: the establishment of Community Councils in 1977. The Councils provided a measure of self-governance to township residents, but they were also a mechanism for the apartheid state to abdicate responsibility for managing the townships. Notwithstanding the creation of the countrywide United Democratic Front,[27] the policy made the question of who would run day-to-day life in the townships increasingly central to antiapartheid politics.[28] These struggles over local governance during the latter decades of apartheid precipitated ideological and repertory innovations at the local level, which left indelible impacts on the practice of popular justice in its wake.

The first legacy of this period was a set of ideological innovations, which reimagined how communities should be run. Youth "became enmeshed in a web of social, economic and legal relationships" such that they saw themselves, more so than their parents, "as having rights to and claims on some kind of common society."[29] In this milieu, where visions of a common society were changing, communal life and how it should be lived came to the forefront of popular mobilization and of popular justice. Such moral rethinking increasingly "concerned itself with the daily lives of township dwellers, rather than simply opposition with the state."[30] At the center of these politics were radicalized youth who had "a transformative moral vision."[31] Especially during the insurrections of the mid-1980s, township youth worked to make the townships ungovernable such that they could actively create an imminent utopia "in which society would be purified. There would, at least some of the youth believed, be no crime, decay or alcohol, no oppression, no suffering."[32] In other words, this vision was powerfully local, powerfully moralizing, and predicated on beliefs about the creation of a harmonious communal life after the overcoming of apartheid.

Nonetheless, this imagined harmony was secured with a series of punishments that, at times, employed remarkable violence. Thus a second crucial innovation during this period was the emergence of new repertoires of violence to create an idealized form of communal moral cohesion. To be sure, some youth-led community justice initiatives tried to reconcile opposed parties.[33] But, at the same time, youth were also known to use techniques like *sjambok* (a stiff leather whip) beatings and forced evictions to "discipline," "re-educate," and "rehabilitate" offenders.³⁴ In some cases, when physical punishment was meted out, it was collectively administered "in order to stress that the offense was an injury to the community."³⁵ In this sense, community justice was a dramaturgical practice in which a set of ideologies about harmonious communal living was communicated to township residents³⁶ and a resource for youth activists for enforcing moral and political conformity, albeit through violence that could be brutal and terrifying.³⁷ And, as we shall see in the next section, the violent drama of communal justice was nowhere more visibly acted out than via the necklace.

The Genesis and Scope of Necklacing under Apartheid

Necklacing emerged out of this politically and morally charged struggle—one concerned as much with community-level governance as with national-level politics. In many ways, the necklace's dramaturgical violence was perfectly calibrated for displaying the complex and often contradictory political and moral messages of the antiapartheid struggle as they were being created in local neighborhoods. Necklacing spectacularly displayed the deeply moralizing politics and the locally oriented justice of the antiapartheid struggle along with all their attendant moral and political ambiguities.

We can see the degree to which the necklace was concerned with the confluence of local politics amid national repression by looking at its earliest performances. The first widely reported necklacing was on March 23, 1985, in the Eastern Cape township of KwaNobuhle, near the town of Uitenhage.³⁸ In the context of extraordinary tension about how the local community was being governed and about the role of the state's police in providing order, a group of Comrades (UDF-aligned youth) burned to death a local community councilor, Benjamin Kinikini.³⁹ The Comrades had demanded that councilors resign their posts, claiming that they were local agents of the apartheid regime, a call that Kinikini had staunchly refused. This hostility was heightened when police shot and killed twenty-one people during a memorial march for the Sharpeville Massacre in nearby Langa. Amid the tension, four UDF-aligned youth were abducted by a local vigilante group connected to the council.⁴⁰ A concerned crowd gathered as word of the abductions spread. After a frantic, unsuccessful search for the young men, the crowd grew both in size and anger. Members of the crowd began to *toyi-toyi* (a vibrant protest dance), while singing songs registering anger toward Kinikini and a close associate. Although the police managed to retrieve the young men from the grip of the vigilante group, they kept them under arrest and refused to return them home. Doubtful that the young men were actually safe and angry about the insecurity Kinikini perpetrated, a portion of the crowd sought him out. When the crowd found him, they stabbed him repeatedly before they made him drink gasoline, put a tire around him, and set him alight.[41] The crowd then killed three of his sons before attacking and burning the homes of every suspected police informer in the township.[42] Two men were subsequently tried and hung under the common-purpose doctrine for the murders.[43]

Despite the conviction and severe consequences meted out to the two men convicted of Kinikini's killing, the practice started to spread across South Africa. Although the exact numbers of necklace killings are difficult to know, the most complete data available (collected by South Africa's TRC) suggest a spike in necklacing and burnings in 1985 and particularly 1986.[44] These years coincided with a deepened focus on community-level politics by antiapartheid forces, the growth of people's courts, and increased counterrevolutionary mobilization by the apartheid state. Necklacing was both a response to and a driver of these political changes. Indeed, as we shall see below, it was Maki Skhosana's widely broadcast death that precipitated the state of emergency and ultimately contributed to the proliferation of the necklace across the country. Overall, between 1984 and 1990, when the state of emergency was lifted, the TRC estimates that between 400 and 700 people were necklaced, with hundreds more burned to death in other ways.[45] In other words, within the span of just a few years, necklacing had grown from an isolated practice into a major repertoire of violence—one connected intimately to the antiapartheid struggle and the state's reaction against it.

The raw numbers tell only part of the story, however. Just as important was how the necklace was used. The necklace was a particularly dramatic form of punishment whose ritualistic enactment was crucial to its effects. For instance, the TRC reported surprisingly few cases of crowd violence where an individual was stoned to death, despite its being a relatively "straightforward" method by which to kill someone.[46] Why would the crowd go through the trouble of necklacing a collaborator like Kinikini rather than using a more "direct" form of violence like stabbing or shooting him?

The ritualistic drama of the necklace and its "extralethal" nature provides a big part of the explanation.[47] Although always different in execution, some similar elements in the practice carried over from iteration to iteration. For example, there might be the repeated use of a central landmark in a given township as a site where multiple necklacings might take place. In Mlungisi in the Eastern Cape, to take one example, would-be necklace victims were often marched to a prominent light tower locally known as "the Golden" where they would be burned to death.[48] Outside of Fort Beaufort in the Eastern Cape, to take another example, a strip of land was used so frequently to burn people that it became known as "Necklace Valley."[49] Adding to the spectacle, the marches to these "necklacing sites" would be long and boisterous processions, often involving toyi-toying, singing struggle songs, and creating a festival-like atmosphere.[50] In other cases, necklacing would occur at emotionally charged events like funerals, and particularly funerals for young people involved in the struggle against apartheid.[51]

Like ritual dramas more generally, the violent dramaturgy of the necklace would also leave a lasting impression on the audience, albeit a traumatic one. As one witness to a necklace killing reported to researchers:

> That sight [a necklacing] will be with me forever. I saw the man burning until he stopped crying and the head burst. I will never forget the sight of the white area on his buttock which looked like fat. Even as I talk to you, I still hear a searing sound just like when one fries oil in a frying pan.[52]

The extralethal nature of this ritual violence is what produces such a long-lasting image—a potentially valuable political tool. Indeed, in some cases, Comrades were so intent on punishing collaborators with spectacular, horrifying violence that they refused to let victims be buried before their bodies had been burned.[53] In such cases, the extralethal violence simultaneously dramatized the moral and political revolution the Comrades were working to bring about and the moral and political betrayal to that cause that the necklace victims represented.

In this sense, who was necklaced was nearly as important as how many people were killed. The TRC report, as a kind of official history of the necklace, suggests that initially victims were killed almost exclusively for expressly political reasons, particularly suspected "collaborators" and "informers."[54] Chiefs and community councilors were early targets in this regard, as they were the most obvious symbols of collaboration with the apartheid state given their charge of implementing government policies and imposing taxes, all while being accused of putting their own economic well-being ahead of the liberation struggle. African police officers were quickly targeted in a similar fashion as they were thought to represent the violence of the apartheid state's oppressive machinery.[55] Eventually, township residents who had violated boycotts declared by Comrades against patronizing "white" stores and purchasing "white" goods were targeted with the effect that the range of victims of necklace violence was extended to average citizens who, through shopping at a "white" store, had become "sellouts."[56]

However, as the struggle intensified, the TRC suggests, "non-political" victims were targeted.[57] In particular, seemingly apolitical actors like suspected criminals and alleged witches came to increasingly be the focus of necklace violence. For example, Niehaus reports a gruesome incident from 1986 in which Comrades in Sekhukhuneland necklaced 43 accused witches, singing freedom songs while they did so.[58] Why would a group of youth whose goal was presumably bringing down the racist apartheid state devote so much attention to people who had no obvious relationship to the state and then perpetrate such seemingly exaggerated violence on them? Moreover, how did this transformation of the necklace from a tool to eliminate political traitors to one used to sanction seemingly nonpolitical, moral threats happen?

I would suggest that the answer to these questions is that "political" threats were always already moral threats and vice versa. In other words, *pace* the TRC, there was never a nonpolitical victim of necklace violence, because in many local communities the politics of the antiapartheid struggle were a form of moralizing politics seeking to create new forms of communal being. Similarly, struggles over the moral and legal constitution of communities, both during apartheid and today, have always been political struggles. We can see this, for example, in the fact that necklace killings began to increase again in 1990 even as the South African state was easing apartheid restrictions. The surge in violence could largely be attributed to a rash of witch killings across northern areas of the country in which Comrades necklaced or otherwise burned to death dozens of alleged witches.[59] Indeed, witches have always been seen as antisocial figures that survive and grow wealthy by feeding off of others—that is, they profit through deeply immoral means.[60] Therefore, as Peter Delius has argued, witches could be necklaced en masse even as apartheid was breaking down because few people "disputed that, if they could be eradicated, a new era of cohesion and harmony would dawn."[61] Thus, we can understand the rash of witch killings during apartheid's twilight as a form of moralizing politics preparing the way for a more morally cohesive postapartheid future. In other words, as we shall see in the next section through the case of Maki Skhosana, the goal of creating a state whose law would help foster newly cohesive moral communities following the downfall of the apartheid state was always bound up in the struggle against apartheid and, therefore, the practice of necklacing, regardless of how gruesome its violence. Moreover, we shall see later in the chapter through the Khutsong case that the necklace continues to be deployed against criminals and other "evildoers" in the hopes of achieving this imagined harmony—a hope that remains constantly beyond reach.

Maki Skhosana's Death and the Life of the Necklace

The 1985 death of a young woman named Maki Skhosana is arguably the most widely known instance of someone being necklaced in South African history. Not only did the Skhosana killing result in two contentious legal trials in the immediate wake of the killing, years later it was subject to fraught hearings at the country's postapartheid Truth and Reconciliation Commission, in the process standing in for much of the country's necklace violence. It also created the pattern for hundreds of subsequent acts of violence as necklacing and burning spread across the country in its wake.

Skhosana was killed in July 1985, in the wake of what eventually came to be known as Operation Zero Zero. Zero Zero was a plot devised by the apartheid security forces and executed by undercover policemen (*askaris*) to kill four youth plotting to attack local policemen in the East Rand township of Duduza. To apartheid's architects, attacks on black policemen were not only crimes against state law, they were also threats to the very viability of apartheid. "[W]e knew if we could not succeed in protecting our Black members," Security Branch General Johan Van Der Merwe told the TRC's Amnesty Commission, "the whole system would collapse and that we in no way would be able to defend ourselves against the onslaught."[62] Ruling out formal arrests for the young men on the belief that securing witnesses would be difficult, security branch officials concocted a plan to assassinate them.[63] Joe Mamasela, an undercover police officer who operated with a notorious hit squad called Vlakplaas, infiltrated the group by pretending to be a member of the liberation forces who could secure weapons. He supplied the activists with hand grenades and limpet mines that were rigged to explode immediately upon being activated. In effect this meant, as Van Der Merwe clinically put it in his TRC testimony, "any person throwing such a hand grenade at the home of a policemen [*sic*] would be affected first due to the shortened time-delay."[64] Eight people were killed and seven seriously injured when the group attempted to use the weapons to attack the homes of a policeman along with an electric power station.[65]

It was common after such killings for communities, supported by antiapartheid organizations, to hold mass funerals involving up to several thousand people to commemorate the dead. The same thing occurred in this case. However, the key difference between this funeral and many others was that rumors were circulating that the person who had sold out the youth to local police was in the crowd's midst: Maki Skhosana. Skhosana had been politically active and associated with many of those who had been killed.[66] However, she was also widely rumored to be dating a local policeman, Joel Msibi.[67] Although it would be revealed later at TRC hearings that Joe Mamasela had actually supplied the young men with the grenades, at the time residents suspected Msibi of having turned the young men's identities over to the security forces. Skhosana, in turn, was rumored to have disclosed the Comrades' identity to Msibi. In other words, Skhosana was being accused of being a traitor or sellout (*impimpi*), an accusation as we saw earlier that could be a death sentence.[68] Skhosana was aware of all this at the time that she died. Indeed, she knew she could potentially be targeted should she attend the funeral, telling her sister just before leaving the house, "If they kill me, they kill me, but I won't run and I won't leave my home or my community. I am innocent. I have done no wrong, I am not a police informer, I am not a traitor to my people."[69]

Typical of such events, the funeral at which Skhosana was killed was a raucous affair. Thousands of people marched in a procession down Serema Street from Duduza's stadium to a cemetery over a kilometer away carrying the coffins. As the crowd moved, people sang and danced.[70] Near the local graveyard someone recognized Skhosana at the rear of the procession and accused her of being the person who had sold out the young men to the police. Skhosana ran and a group of people gave chase, eventually capturing her and forcing her to the ground.[71] In the excitement of the chase, a larger group formed and surged toward the now prone Skhosana to see what was happening.[72]

Depending on when they arrived, witnesses might have seen Skhosana being beaten or kicked while lolling back and forth on her knees.[73] They might have seen Skhosana lying prone on the ground as someone stomped on top of her. They might have seen Skhosana struggling to get off the ground only to be kicked back down. They might have seen someone throwing bricks and rocks at her as she tried to struggle to her feet. They might have seen Skhosana on fire or watched her be beaten with sticks while she burned. They might have seen someone trying to fan the flames as her burning body threatened to extinguish itself as she rolled on the ground.

But witnesses would have seen more than just violence. For example, they would have seen an assailant making exaggerated, almost comical gestures mocking themselves after nearly being knocked off balance after stomping on Skhosana. Witnesses would have seen these attempts at humor being performed amid angry shouts, denunciations, and provocations. They would have heard commands like "*Mafiye inja*" ("Let the dog die") followed by the crowd giving a staccato ascent, "Hey, hey"—a common response to a speaker's call at protest events during a toyi-toyi.[74] In other words, witnesses would have seen a complicated and contradictory ritual performance—one that displayed anger and humor, violence and playfulness, individual acts of violence and expressions of communal and political solidarity.

Witnesses would have also heard references to Joel Msibi, Skhosana's alleged boyfriend. As she was being beaten and burned, members of the crowd sang, "Joel is a wizard."[75] As we saw above, many South Africans have long considered witches as those who tarry with evil through their usage of illicit occult powers, thus making the invocation of wizardry important—but also complex. It may have invoked the evil he represented in working for the apartheid state. But it also may have indexed the ill-gotten money that he received as salary from the state and which local residents would likely have seen as coming at the expense of their oppression.[76] Regardless of individuals' intentions in performing the song or in their reception of it, invoking wizardry evoked concerns over evil and its effects on the social and moral order. Joel, the policeman and alleged boyfriend, admitted as much on the witness stand during the subsequent murder trial, agreeing that for the crowd to associate him with witchcraft was to accuse him of being "a source of evil."[77] That informers were rumored to be paid by the police and that Skhosana was rumored to have acquired expensive new clothing around the time the young men were killed only heightened suspicions among activists that she had sold the young men out and become complicit with the evil that Joel represented, both as a wizard and an agent of the apartheid state.[78] Concern over the local moral community thus shadowed her death, the usage of the necklace in it, and the dissemination of the practice to other parts of the country.

Media members covering the funeral captured much of this contradictory ritual on video as they recorded Skhosana burning to death as a way to justify the apartheid state's own brutality in oppressing them.[79] Despite the complexity of the performance, apartheid state officials saw the performance as the result of the supposed immaturity, indiscipline, and brutality of the liberation forces. As a result, the apartheid state broadcast the recording on national television that night. The images hit the country like a bomb. The President, P. W. Botha, used the images to declare an immediate State of Emergency, which allowed the government to engage in a brutal crackdown on opponents of the state.

However, to some (particularly young) participants in the antiapartheid struggle, necklacing was understood as a symbol of the morally renewed future they wished to create and an effective technique through which to bring it about. As Mahmood Mamdani has argued, necklacing "seemed to give public evidence that the oppressed were capable of mustering a force to counter the growing tentacles of settler occupation."[80] As a result, it went on to become a key tool in the punitive repertoire of township youths, leading to a rapid increase in the number of necklacings across the country.

Necklacing at High and Low Levels

The increasing popularity of this new punitive repertoire placed leaders of the liberation struggle in a difficult position. Some leaders—particularly members of the clergy—immediately condemned the practice. "If you do this kind of thing," Desmond Tutu famously warned in the wake of the Skhosana killing, "I will find it difficult to speak for the cause of liberation. If the violence continues, I will pack my bags, collect my family and leave this beautiful country that I love so passionately and so deeply. . . . I say to you that I condemn in the strongest possible terms what happened in Duduza."[81] However, this condemnation was not universal. On the contrary, some leaders, responding to its growing popular usage, actively called for the necklace to be used more frequently by participants in the struggle. The populist firebrand, Winnie Mandela, was the most (in)famous person to champion its use as a key tool to fight apartheid, telling a crowd that "with our boxes of matches and necklaces, we will liberate this country."[82]

To be sure, Mandela was roundly criticized at the time for the comment by other ANC leaders. But the sentiment behind Mandela's call to action—that the necklacing could be a powerful weapon in the struggle against apartheid—found its way more subtly into the liberation struggle's messaging, placing many struggle leaders in, at best, an ambivalent relationship to necklacing.[83] For example, ANC President Oliver Tambo showed the difficulty of fully disavowing the necklace to an international community that was deeply critical of it, when he told a conference of nonaligned countries, "We are not happy with the necklace but we will not condemn people who have been driven to adopt such extremes."[84] What Tambo was suggesting was that it was the structural violence of apartheid that pushed local cadres to engage in such spectacular violence and that if the necklace were to end apartheid would have to end first. The effect, however, was to not condone the necklace while also not condemning it. In some instances, this ambivalence was heard at the community level as implicit approval of the practice, which only enabled its spread. For example, some people applying for amnesty in connection with necklace murders at the TRC went so far as to argue that "although not formally under orders of the ANC, they believed they were acting in accordance with ANC strategic objectives at the time."[85]

This ambiguity toward the necklace exposed a remarkable tension in liberation leaders' attempts to combat the apartheid state. On the one hand, collaborators represented such a danger to the liberation struggle that they needed to be "eliminated."[86] Yet, on the other hand, the brutality of the tactics that had been deployed up to that point—particularly the necklace—crossed some moral boundary that made it "unacceptable." The moral goals of the struggle had run up against the uncomfortable morality of the tactics being used to achieve them. In other words, there is an important discrepancy between what "moral authority" meant to liberation leaders and what it meant on the ground. For people acting as part of the "mob," it was the target of necklacing who was morally wrong and the necklace was a tool to make things right. As we saw with the Maki Skhosana case, instead of being seen as immoral, the necklace was associated with combating evil and creating moral order.

We shall see in the next section that this use of the necklace to combat evil and create moral order still structures the practice's deployment today. The moral ambiguity connected to the practice of the necklace, and the political ambivalence of liberation leaders, set the stage for future difficulties that the postapartheid state would have in stamping out the necklace—a technique that was nationally illegal and yet often considered locally licit.[87] The conflict between the emotional satisfaction of the necklace and the rational, organizational handling of justice is a tension that continues to characterize the use of the necklace in the context of slow, loping, and fallible legal procedures—something we will see in the next section through the remarkable account of a recent mass necklacing.

Necklacing at Khutsong

On the morning of November 3, 2013, a crowd gathered in a field in Khutsong, a sprawling township about sixty kilometers west of Johannesburg. Khutsong sits in the middle of the West Rand, a peri-urban area that hosts some of the most productive gold mines in the world. Yet, despite sitting atop enormous wealth, Khutsong is largely poor, serving as a bedroom community of small homes and shacks for underpaid mine laborers and their families. Gripped by ghastly rates of youth unemployment, Khutsong has become home to a number of youth gangs.[88] Fear and insecurity are rife among township residents, and the gangs are blamed for it. Amid an intensification of this insecurity precipitated by heightened gang violence, a flier was distributed throughout the township calling on concerned community members to skip Sunday church and meet in a central field instead.[89] About four hundred people responded to the call. Chief among the concerns discussed at the meeting were the Casanovas, a youth gang from an informal settlement adjacent to the formal township in which most of the crowd's members resided. Residents had grown fed up with the presence of the Casanovas in their lives and were determined to do something about it. Indeed, the flier instructed residents who planned to attend to bring weapons as they would be taking part in Operation Shapa Tsotsi ("Beat the Criminal") once the meeting was over.[90]

The crowd resolved to split into two groups to confront the gangsters and those who allegedly helped them. One group proceeded to the home of an elderly *sangoma* (traditional healer), James Magagula, who was accused of providing *muthi* (occult herbs and medicines) to the young men to help them evade arrest—a highly illicit practice in the local moral economy. The crowd broke into his home where they found him in the middle of a consultation with a patient as his pregnant sister bathed in the next room. Scared for their lives, the patient and the sister, still naked, fled the house and ran into the streets. As the sangoma begged for forgiveness, members of the crowd beat him before putting a tire around him and setting him alight. His body burning, the sangoma rushed from the house into the street before collapsing and dying. The crowd then burned down his home and the adjacent buildings in his yard.[91]

Meanwhile, the second group searched out the homes of alleged Casanovas, burning their shacks down if the gangsters were not home. Two unfortunate Casanovas out wandering the streets, however, were found by the crowd. Twenty-four-year-old Akhona Khumalo and his twenty-three-year-old friend, Mojalefa Maleho, had seen the crowd coming in their direction while loudly singing and brandishing weapons. They tried to take shelter in an adjacent home but were refused entry by the resident, who had locked herself inside at the sight of the approaching crowd. A second neighbor was either less afraid of the mob or more sympathetic toward the young men and allowed them to hide in her home. Despite the kindness, the two young men were found by the mob, dragged out into the street, and beaten while a member of the crowd was sent to buy paraffin. When the shopper returned, the accused criminals were doused with the accelerant, had tires placed around them, and were set alight.[92] The crowd was still not done, however. They soon came across twenty-one-year-old Samson Zulayo, a local barber who supposedly kept too close company with the gang. He was beaten and hacked to death before his body was set alight.[93] The crowd then chased two other alleged Casanovas several kilometers to the nearby town of Carletonville, where it eventually caught them and stoned them to death in the streets. In total, the two crowds killed six people, necklacing three of them and setting another alight posthumously.

Given that the necklace was originally developed during the struggle against apartheid to punish informers and collaborators, as we saw with the Maki Skhosana killing, why would a crowd use the technique against a group of alleged criminals almost twenty years after apartheid? What relationship might these postapartheid killings have to apartheid-era necklacing? Ignoring the practice's historical antecedents, commentators were quick to blame the killings on South Africa's failing police services, pointing to an ongoing series of scandals engulfing the organization's national leadership that had eroded the public's trust in it.[94] Yet even while the South African Police Service is a deeply troubled organization at the national level, a closer look at the events surrounding the killings and the police role in the events reveals a more complicated story than simple police failure. Instead, the events reveal a complex mixture of moral outrage, vengeance, and concerns that South Africa's strong rights regime perpetuates residents' insecurity. That is, as with the Skhosana killing, the crowd was using the necklace to challenge the substance of the law more than it was reacting to a lack of it. And they were doing so in the context of deep concern over what many perceived to be a moral collapse in the township.

Perhaps the best indications of the moral drama entailed in the necklacing are an examination of some of the actors in the vigilante play, their relationship to the victims, and the eventual circulation of the necklacing story within Khutsong. The necklacings happened amid not only a period of intense physical insecurity but of deepening moral insecurity. While participants had been instructed to bring weapons to the meeting that preceded the killings in anticipation of disciplining youth, as residents aired grievances their moral outrage and fear intensified. "Murders had been committed in Khutsong with no arrests," wrote two reporters of concerns participants expressed at the meeting. "People were being found dead near the river. Stabbings were witnessed in taverns. Girls were being abducted and held by gang members. The gangs were recruiting in schools. Crime became a daylight activity. 'These gangs, they draw their strength from blood,' yelled a woman."[95] The physical concerns explicit in her comments carry an implicit sense of a moral order that has been reversed—strength being generated by deeply immoral means, through drawing blood from others.

These moral concerns were heightened by the apparently occult nature of some of the Casanovas' killings. Residents were panicked that body parts had been removed from some of the gang's recent victims—an act often associated with supplying the *muthi* (occult herbs) trade. Residents had long suspected that the Casanovas were being supplied "no fear *muthi*" and *muthi* enabling them to avoid arrest by James Magagula, the sangoma who was necklaced. Thus, these violations likely made the crowd concerned that occult forces were at work amid the murders. In other words, as with the Maki Skhosana killing where rumors of wizardry circulated around her alleged boyfriend, the rumored occult aspects of the Khutsong killings only made the crimes more dangerous.[96] The concerns do not appear to be wholly unfounded. In fact, Magagula had been arrested in connection with the murder of a rival gang member whose body had been mutilated, only to be subsequently released by the police.[97]

This is not to suggest, however, that the necklacings actually resolved the moral concerns pervading the community. On the contrary, after the necklacings moral ambiguities proliferated, an outcome which is arguably no better illustrated than through the actions of Simon Khumalo. Khumalo was sufficiently enthusiastic about the possibilities that crowd violence could achieve that he not only chose to participate in the violence, he brought his son Desmond along with him. Little did Khumalo realize, however, that, as he and Desmond broke off to patrol with one group on the hunt for Casanovas, a separate group of patrollers were searching out one of his other sons, Akhona, whom they accused of being a gangster. The crowd necklaced Akhona and his friend Mojalefa, which the father, Simon, only learned about later. "If they trusted me, they would have told me that my child was on the list of people they were looking for. They did not even tell me they had killed him, I only arrived here to find ashes," he told reporters, noting that he was unlikely to participate in anticrime patrols in the future.[98] Although as a dramaturgical technique the necklace ostensibly displays moral purity, the Khumalo tragedy shows the impossibility of achieving it via such a violent means.

It was not only the heartbreak of a crime-fighting father discovering that his son had died at the hands of vigilantes that made for a contradictory morality play, however. Indeed, many in the crowd of anticrime patrollers were themselves members of youth gangs that had been in conflict with the Casanovas. Four gangs vied with the Casanovas for control of Khutsong: the Vandals, the Delta Force, the Creatures, and Marikana.[99] As opposed to the Casanovas, who were from Khutsong's informal settlements, these gangs reportedly hailed from the formal sections of the township and had been created by township youth for protection when the Casanovas started recruiting members in the township's schools.[100] Tensions among the gangs were high, particularly in the wake of the murder of a member of the Vandals gang, Calvin "Boy Boy" Mtombela, allegedly at the hands of the Casanovas. As a result, some people claimed the necklacings were revenge for Boy Boy's murder, something that the gangsters' participation in the crowd seemingly confirmed.[101] In other words, the line between a spectacular punishment conveying a moral message and its strategic deployment by opportunists was hopelessly blurred, as it had been under apartheid, albeit now in a very different context.

The most significant difference between apartheid-era necklacings and the Khutsong killings, of course, was the political context in which each occurred. Where apartheid police had a violently repressive relationship with township dwellers, the postapartheid police ostensibly provided a protective service for which residents were desperate. Indeed, in the month prior to the killings, township residents marched to the police several times demanding that they stop gang violence. To be sure, the police in the township could have vastly improved their responsiveness to the community, allegedly telling the concerned residents at one march, "We will get back to you."[102] However, while the police response to the events was troubling, the fact that community members engaged them through the classic structures of civil society indicates the sea change in the practice and meaning of policing from apartheid on through the democratic era. Instead of an oppressive force that residents actively tried to remove from the townships, the police had become a service they wanted to work for them.

Yet, even though township residents had been displeased with the police response, to suggest that the police were doing nothing about the gang violence would be incorrect. In fact, they had arrested three members of the Casanovas along with their alleged ally sangoma, James Magagula, for the murder of a rival gang member in the weeks prior to the mass necklacing.[103] Despite the arrests, the police released the Casanovas back into the community on bail. For many Khutsong residents, the release of the suspects on procedural grounds was confirmation of the police's failings. As one reporter wrote of the common sentiment in the lead-up to the vigilante attacks, "People felt the police weren't delivering justice, either not making arrests or arresting suspects and setting them free shortly afterward."[104] But there is an important distinction here that needs to be recognized: Releasing suspects after arrest is not necessarily a sign of police "failure." On the contrary, it might be taken as a sign of the "success" of police transformation, which enacted a model of policing dedicated to procedural justice in contrast to the often arbitrary nature of apartheid policing.[105] Arguably, what the arrests point to is the deep insecurity residents felt in Khutsong and a common sense that even if the state succeeds in arresting suspects, releasing them back into a community on bail (even where legally required) is ultimately a failure by the state's rights-based legal system to solve immediate problems of insecurity. The necklacings, in this sense, challenged the basis of postapartheid law, marking a demand (however implicit) for more forceful policing among residents.

This frustration is not only common among township residents; it is also common among police themselves who see the rights-based legal system as inhibiting their ability to keep the streets safe. Said one Khutsong policeman of the Casanovas whom they arrested and released:

> It is frustrating for us because mostly they are repeat offenders. They are called "children in conflict with the law." These boys are protected by the Child Justice Act, which says they should be released into the custody of their parents. They know the law says they should not be treated like adults. They even know that the law says they should not be placed in a marked police vehicle as it traumatizes them. That is the law, not me. I am not speaking only for myself, but for

all other detectives. In my case, I arrested a 17-year-old for murder, but he was released after appearing with one of his parents. I think the parents must tell the courts that they are unable to control these kids. It's a shit law, this Child Justice Act.[106]

The common concern residents and police officers have over the effects of South Africa's remarkably strong rights-based legal system leads to a common sympathy for popular justice. The same policeman suggested that while police don't condone mob justice, they see it as effective for controlling crime, pointing to a total absence of robbery, housebreaking, or theft in the area since the mass necklacings.[107] The ultimate effect of this spectacular violence, then, is to challenge the substance of the postapartheid legal system by challenging its procedural basis and how it affects how the police conduct their duties.

The circulation of images in the wake of the killings reinforced this challenge to the state's legal system by allowing residents to create a moral tale about the violence, similar to the ways the circulation of the Skhosana video allowed the creation of moral communities under apartheid that were premised on challenging the state. As morally ambiguous as the events were, the use of the necklace allowed township residents to narrate the attack as if it were a parable. For example, in the days following the necklacing, cell phone videos of the events were shared among Khutsong residents, creating the atmosphere for excited retellings of the killings. One reporter recounts being shown such a video by a woman who was present when two of the gangsters were killed:

> Somewhere in the background [of the video] music is pumping and a crowd of people is swaying and dancing to its rhythm and they are clapping and cheering. The video is 14 minutes long and records the horrific dousing in paraffin and incineration of two people accused of being gangsters. The hand holding the camera never shakes, only moving to wave with the pulse of the mob. The woman is jubilant. The police just searched her and everyone in her street for evidence, but they did so with little enthusiasm.

The woman's replaying of the video for the reporter gives her the opportunity to comment on the events leading up to the killings. "These creatures [gang members] went inside a church on a Sunday to rob people," she tells the reporter. "They had no fear."[108] Creatures is an ambiguous word here. It may refer to the local gang, the Creatures, or it may indicate the subhuman status often attributed to criminals in Khutsong. In either variant, however, it indexes the claimed righteousness of the crowd in acting to stop them even as they violated the young gang members' rights.

Conclusion

Although actively condemned by many,[109] necklacing is still alive in South Africa more than twenty years after the dawn of democracy. That this is the case is surprising given that the necklace was initially developed to punish collaborators with the apartheid regime and that there has been a revolutionary change in the functioning of the state's legal institutions. This chapter argues that we can understand this repurposing, in part, by understanding that the necklace is a technique that people use to challenge the substance of the legal system. Under apartheid, liberation forces used the necklace to challenge the state's racism and its cooptation of township residents to enforce the state's control. Today, township residents use the necklace to challenge the rights-based legal system that, ironically, emerged out of the struggle against apartheid. Connecting the use of the necklace during these two seemingly disparate eras are visions of a morally better future for local communities—visions that are communicated through the necklace's spectacular and horrifying violence.

Notes

Thank you to Jonathan Blake, Lee Ann Fujii, Mark Gross, Gary Kynoch, Jamie Miller, Michael Pfeifer, Gema Santamaria, and two anonymous reviewers for feedback on earlier versions of this chapter. All errors remain my own.

1. The title of this chapter references E. E. Evans-Pritchard's famous dictum: "New times demand new magic," which serves as an epigraph to Jean and John Comaroff's influential article on the resurgence of witchcraft and other forms of occult thinking in postapartheid South Africa. The title is intended to index, as should become clearer throughout the chapter, the ability of different moral economies to be flexibly adapted to new political situations despite radical institutional change and shape social action in the process. Jean Comaroff and John L. Comaroff, "Occult Economies and the Violence of Abstraction: Notes from the South African Postcolony," *American Ethnologist* 26, no. 2 (1999): 279–303.

2. Adam Withnall, "Nelson Mandela Sign Language Interpreter 'Helped Burn Two Men to Death,'" *Independent*, December 17, 2013, http://www.independent.co.uk/news/world/africa/nelson-mandela-sign-language-interpreter-helped-burn-two-men-to-death-9009935.html (accessed December 25, 2013).

3. Karyn Maughan, "Fake Interpreter's Murky Past," *eNCA*, January 7, 2014, http://www.enca.com/south-africa/exclusive-fake-interpreters-murky-past (accessed January 20, 2014).

4. Moreover, the gruesome nature of the violence arguably put the perpetrators at greater risk of imprisonment. Although Jantjie was set free after the incident, two others in the crowd were arrested and convicted of murder. Ibid.

5. The South Africa Police Service reports that approximately 5 percent of the murders in the country result from vigilante violence. However, they do not release detailed statistics about necklace killings as a specific subgenre of this 5 percent. SAPS, *Annual Report 2008–2009* (Pretoria: South African Police Service, 2009), 11.

6. Glynnis Underhill, "Khayelitsha Probe Fires Up Its Engines," *M&G Online*, November 15, 2013, http://mg.co.za/article/2013-11-14-khayelitsha-probe-fires-up-its-engines/ (accessed November 16, 2013). The Commission of Inquiry into Allegations of Police Inefficiency in Khayelitsha and a Breakdown in Relations between the Community and the Police in Khayelitsha ("The Khayelitsha Commission") has since concluded its final report, which examines broader relationships between the police and the township's residents. It is available here: http://www.khayelitshacommission.org.za/final-report.html (accessed September 10, 2015).

7. Although many studies of South African vigilantism discuss necklacing, its practice and repetition across time and space is rarely a major focus of the work. The only article-length study that I am aware of that devotes sustained attention to the actual practice of necklacing is Joana Ball, *The Ritual of the Necklace* (Johannesburg: Centre for the Study of Violence and Reconciliation, March 1994), http://www.csvr.org.za/index.php?option=com_content&view=article&id=1632:the-ritual-of-the-necklace&catid=138:publications&Itemid=2 (accessed December 19, 2011). Moosage examines the political difficulties that the necklace presented for leaders of the liberation struggle but does not explore the ritual itself. Riedwaan Moosage, "A Prose of Ambivalence: Liberation Struggle Discourse on Necklacing," *Kronos* 36, no. 1 (November 2010): 136–157. Two dissertations explore necklace violence, largely through a psychological lens, to understand the effects of committing violence on the psyche of the perpetrator—a different set of concerns than those in this chapter. See Pumla Phillipa Gobodo-Madikizela, "Legacies of Violence: An In-Depth Analysis of Two Case Studies Based on Interviews with Perpetrators of a 'Necklace' Murder and with Eugene de Kock" (PhD Diss., University of Cape Town, 2000); Sipho Mbuqe, "Political Violence in South Africa: A Case Study of 'Necklacing' in Colesberg" (PhD Diss., Duquesne University, 2010).

8. For example, on the constitution, see Drucilla Cornell, *Law and Revolution in South Africa: uBuntu, Dignity, and the Struggle for Constitutional Transformation* (New York: Fordham University Press, 2014). On the quality of the rule of law, see David Dyzenhaus, "The Pasts and Future of the Rule of Law in South Africa," in *After Apartheid: Reinventing South Africa?*, ed. Ian Shapiro and Kahreen Tebeau (Charlottesville: University of Virginia Press, 2011), 199–230.

9. On the stunning growth in the size and scope of South Africa's security services and prison population, see Tony Roshan Samara, *Cape Town after Apartheid: Crime and Governance in the Divided City* (Minneapolis: University of Minnesota Press, 2011), 36–39.

10. On object shift in contentious politics, see Doug McAdam, Sidney Tarrow, and Charles Tilly, *Dynamics of Contention* (Cambridge: Cambridge University Press, 2001), 144–145.

11. One could potentially see an analogue argument here with the literature on institutional persistence, seeing necklacing as a kind of learned social convention that has a tendency to naturally persist. See, for example, H. Peyton Young, *Individual Strategy and*

Social Structure: An Evolutionary Theory of Institutions (Princeton: Princeton University Press, 2001).

12. See, for example, Charles Tilly, *The Politics of Collective Violence* (New York: Cambridge University Press, 2003), 45–54.

13. Stathis N. Kalyvas, "Wanton and Senseless? The Logic of Massacres in Algeria," *Rationality and Society* 11, no. 3 (1999): 243–285. A corollary argument would be that institutional or economic constraints on groups and their leaders would be the primary deterrent for their carrying out such violence. For example, Scott Straus, "Retreating from the Brink: Theorizing Mass Violence and the Dynamics of Restraint," *Perspectives on Politics* 10, no. 2 (2012): 343–362, doi:10.1017/S1537592712000709.

14. Paul Richards, *Fighting for the Rain Forest: War, Youth and Resources in Sierra Leone* (Oxford: James Currey Ltd., 1996), xvi.

15. See especially Daniel M Goldstein, *The Spectacular City: Violence and Performance in Urban Bolivia* (Durham: Duke University Press, 2004); Angelina Snodgrass Godoy, *Popular Injustice: Violence, Community, and Law in Latin America* (Stanford: Stanford University Press, 2006).

16. For an important critique of this literature, see Christopher Krupa, "Histories in Red: Ways of Seeing Lynching in Ecuador," *American Ethnologist* 36, no. 1 (2009): 20–39, doi:10.1111/j.1548-1425.2008.01107.x.

17. Goldstein, *Spectacular City*, 17.

18. Godoy, *Popular Injustice*, 17, emphasis in original.

19. This argument that necklacing challenges the substantive constitution of the law resonates outside South Africa and particularly in the literature on the United States. See, for example, Jennet Kirkpatrick, *Uncivil Disobedience: Studies in Violence and Democratic Politics* (Princeton: Princeton University Press, 2008); Michael J. Pfeifer, *Rough Justice: Lynching and American Society 1874-1974* (Urbana: University of Illinois Press, 2006).

20. On extralethal violence, see Lee Ann Fujii, "The Puzzle of Extra-Lethal Violence," *Perspectives on Politics* 11, no. 2 (2013): 410–426.

21. See, e.g., Cornell, *Law and Revolution in South Africa*.

22. I thank Dan Slater for suggesting the term *repurposing* during a discussion about a much earlier version of this material.

23. The court records can be found in the University of Witswatersrand Historical Papers collection under the call number AK 2445. See *State v. Motaung and 10 Others* (Transvaal Provincial Court 1987). The Truth and Reconciliation Commission held hearings on the Skhosana necklacing on February 4, 1997, in Duduza, the township where she lived. See Nhlanhla John Buthelezi, *Case JB00266/01ERKWA* (Duduza: Truth and Reconciliation Commission, 1997), http://www.justice.gov.za/trc/hrvtrans/duduza/buthelez.htm (accessed March 10, 2011); Evelina Puleng Moloko, *Case JB0289/013ERKWA* (Duduza: Truth and Reconciliation Commission, 1997), http://www.justice.gov.za/trc/hrvtrans/duduza/moloko.htm (accessed March 10, 2011).

24. Part of the video of Skhosana's death is available for viewing as part of the South African Broadcasting Corporation program, "Truth Commission Special Report. It is available at *Truth Commission Special Report—Tape 7, Episode 7*, 1996, http://trc.law.yale.edu/video_episodes.htm (accessed March 28, 2014).

25. Thaphelo Lekgowa and Greg Nicolson, "Anatomy of the Khutsong Horror: When Rampant Crime Met Mob Justice," *Daily Maverick*, November 7, 2013, http://www.dailymaverick.co.za/article/2013-11-07-anatomy-of-the-khutsong-horror-when-rampant-crime-met-mob-justice/#.UnoeLeI4n-I (accessed November 8, 2011).

26. There had been burning previously as part of localized struggles against the apartheid state and its surrogate homeland governments, though it was not as widely spread as it would become after the Soweto Uprising. See, for example, Clifton Crais, "Of Men, Magic, and the Law: Popular Justice and the Political Imagination in South Africa," *Journal of Social History* 32, no. 1 (Fall 1998): 49–72.

27. Jeremy Seekings, *The UDF: A History of the United Democratic Front in South Africa, 1983–1991* (Athens: Ohio University Press, 2000).

28. As Martin Murray writes, militants during this period operated "sometimes with limited organizational links beyond a single township and often with tenuous ideological attachments to the broad urban-based political coalitions." Martin J. Murray, "The Popular Upsurge in South Africa, 1984–1986," *Critical Sociology* 16, no. 1 (April 1989): 56. See also Tom Lodge, *Black Politics in South Africa since 1945* (New York: Longman, 1983), 330.

29. Seekings, *UDF*, 13.

30. Belinda Bozzoli, *Theatres of Struggle and the End of Apartheid* (Athens: Ohio University Press, 2004), 2.

31. Ibid.

32. Ibid.

33. Sandra Burman and Wilfried Schärf, "Creating People's Justice: Street Committees and People's Courts in a South African City," *Law & Society Review* 24, no. 3 (January 1, 1990): 708ff.

34. Ibid., 714–715; Jeremy Seekings, "Social Ordering and Control in the African Townships of South Africa: An Historical Overview of Extra-State Initiatives from the 1940s to the 1990s," in *The Other Law: Non-State Ordering in South Africa*, ed. Wilfried Schärf and Daniel Nina (Cape Town: Juta, 2001), 71; Bozzoli, *Theatres of Struggle and the End of Apartheid*, 160.

35. Burman and Schärf, "Creating People's Justice," 725.

36. Wilfried Schärf, *Transforming Community Policing in Black Townships in the New South Africa*, Occasional Papers Series (Cape Town: Institute of Criminology, University of Cape Town, 1991); Bozzoli, *Theatres of Struggle and the End of Apartheid*. Though they were mostly urban phenomena, the courts were not without rural analogues. The primary difference was that in rural areas, the courts' legal dramas mocked the "customary" justice of collaborationist chiefs as much as that of the apartheid state. Crais, "Of Men, Magic, and the Law," 56.

37. Clive Glaser, "Whistles and Sjamboks: Crime and Policing in Soweto, 1960–1976," *South African Historical Journal* 52, no. 1 (2005): 139.

38. Whether or not Kinikini's death was actually the first necklacing is very difficult to say. For example, Ball cites reports of people—particularly suspected witches—being burnt with tires prior to Kinikini's death. What can be said with more certainty, however, is that Kinikini's death touched off a rash of necklacing in its wake. Ball, *Ritual of the Necklace*.

39. Though Kinikini's death is the first necklacing recorded in the TRC's database, it was not the first fatal burning committed by ANC- or UDF-aligned youth. The first fatal burning occurred in April 1983 at Crossroads, Cape Town. Truth and Reconciliation Commission, *Truth and Reconciliation Commission of South Africa Report*, Vol. 2 (Cape Town: Juta Books, 2003), 388.

40. The following account is drawn from Mark Swilling, "Urban Control and Changing Forms of Political Conflict in Uitenhage: 1977–1986," (PhD Diss., University of Warwick, 1994), 210–222.

41. Truth and Reconciliation Commission, *Truth and Reconciliation Commission of South Africa Report*, Vol. 3 (Cape Town: Juta Books, 2003), 108–109.

42. Truth and Reconciliation Commission, *Truth and Reconciliation Commission of South Africa Report*, 2003, Vol. 2:388.

43. Although the two men were convicted and killed by the apartheid state, the state could not conclusively prove that they actually participated in the assault on Kinikini, merely that they had been present in the crowd when he was killed. Nevertheless, their presence was sufficient grounds under apartheid law for the state to convict them of murder and kill them. Swilling, "Urban Control and Changing Forms of Political Conflict in Uitenhage," 208.

44. Truth and Reconciliation Commission, *Truth and Reconciliation Commission of South Africa Report*, 2003, Vol. 2:389.

45. Ibid.; Truth and Reconciliation Commission, *Truth and Reconciliation Commission of South Africa Report*, 2003, Vol. 3:23. It is also important to note that not all victims recorded in these estimates were killed by antiapartheid activists. It was also a convenient way for agents of apartheid to cover up murders they committed, including the well-known PEBCO Three and Cradock Four cases. Truth and Reconciliation Commission, *Truth and Reconciliation Commission of South Africa Report*, 2003, Vol. 2:389.

46. Truth and Reconciliation Commission, *Truth and Reconciliation Commission of South Africa Report*, 2003, Vol. 2:392.

47. Fujii, "Puzzle of Extra-Lethal Violence."

48. *State v. Gqeba and Others* (The Supreme Court of South Africa, Appellate Division 1986).

49. Truth and Reconciliation Commission, *Truth and Reconciliation Commission of South Africa Report*, 2003, Vol. 2:681.

50. Ball, *Ritual of the Necklace*.

51. See, for example, Ntuthu Nomoyi and Willem Schurink, "Ukunxityiswa Kwempimpi Itayari Njengotshaba Lomzabalazo: An Exploratory Study of Insider Accounts of Necklacing in Three Port Elizabeth Townships," in *Violence in South Africa: A Variety of Perspectives*, ed. Elirea Bornman, René Van Eeden, and Marie Wentzel (Pretoria: HSRC Press, 1998), 157–158.

52. Ibid., 158.

53. Truth and Reconciliation Commission, *Truth and Reconciliation Commission of South Africa Report*, 2003, Vol. 2:385, 388.

54. Ibid., Vol. 2:388.

55. Ibid., Vol. 2:389–390.

56. See, for example, Mbuqe, "Political Violence in South Africa."

57. Truth and Reconciliation Commission, *Truth and Reconciliation Commission of South Africa Report*, 2003, Vol. 2:391.

58. Isak Niehaus, *Magical Interpretations, Material Realities: Modernity, Witchcraft and the Occult in Postcolonial Africa*, ed. Henrietta L. Moore and Todd Sanders (London: Routledge, 2001), 184.

59. Ralushai Commission, *Report of the Commission of Inquiry into Witchcraft Violence and Ritual Murders in the Northern Province of the Republic of South Africa* (Northern Province, RSA: Ministry of Safety and Security, 1996).

60. Isaac Schapera, "The Crime of Sorcery," *Proceedings of the Royal Anthropological Institute of Great Britain and Ireland*, no. 1969 (1969): 15–23.

61. Peter Delius, *A Lion amongst the Cattle: Reconstruction and Resistance in the Northern Transvaal* (Portsmouth, N.H.: Heinemann, 1996), 194.

62. Truth and Reconciliation Commission, *Truth and Reconciliation Commission of South Africa Report*, 2003, Vol. 2:259.

63. Ibid.

64. Ibid., Vol. 2:260.

65. Ibid., Vol. 2:261.

66. Moloko, *Case JB0289/013ERKWA*.

67. *State v. Motaung and 10 Others* (Transvaal Provincial Court 1987), 1058.

68. Ibid., 1057.

69. Michael Parks, "Blacks Act on Informer Rumors: Rage over Apartheid—But Was Victim a Traitor?" *Los Angeles Times*, August 1, 1985, http://articles.latimes.com/1985-08-01/news/mn-4233_1_police-informer (accessed March 27, 2014).

70. *State v. Motaung and 10 Others* (Transvaal Provincial Court 1987), 103–108.

71. Ibid., 108.

72. Ibid., 1056–1057.

73. This account is drawn from portions of the video available for viewing in the South African Broadcasting Corporation program, "Truth Commission Special Report." The video is only partial and does not show the point at which Skhosana is necklaced, although accounts of the event always refer to it as such. See, for example, Truth and Reconciliation Commission, *Truth and Reconciliation Commission of South Africa Report*, 2003, Vol. 2:261. The video is available at http://trc.law.yale.edu/video_episodes.htm, *Truth Commission Special Report—Tape 7, Episode 7* (accessed June 21, 2016).

74. *State v. Motaung and 10 Others* (Transvaal Provincial Court 1987), 114.

75. Ibid., 592–595, 1091–1092.

76. On the antisocial nature of witches, see, for example, Comaroff and Comaroff, "Occult Economies and the Violence of Abstraction."

77. *State v. Motaung and 10 Others* (Transvaal Provincial Court 1987), 594.

78. Testifying in front of the TRC about Skhosana's death, her sister strongly denied that Skhosana had received any expensive clothing, and that the new clothing she was seen with during this period had been donated by a charity. Moloko, *Case JB0289/013ERKWA*.

79. Truth and Reconciliation Commission, *Truth and Reconciliation Commission of South Africa Report*, 2003, Vol. 3:667; See also Lars Buur and Steffen Jensen, "Introduc-

tion: Vigilantism and the Policing of Everyday Life in South Africa," *African Studies* 63, no. 2 (December 2004): 143.

80. Mahmood Mamdani, "Good Muslim, Bad Muslim: Post-Apartheid Perspectives on America and Israel," *PoLAR: Political and Legal Anthropology Review* 27, no. 1 (May 1, 2004): 5, doi:10.1525/pol.2004.27.1.1.

81. Quoted in Ball, *Ritual of the Necklace*.

82. Quoted in Moosage, "Prose of Ambivalence," 138.

83. Moosage, "Prose of Ambivalence."

84. Mamdani, "Good Muslim, Bad Muslim," 7.

85. Truth and Reconciliation Commission, *Truth and Reconciliation Commission of South Africa Report*, 2003, Vol. 2:339–340.

86. See, for example, "Notes of the Interview with Chris Hani and Steve Tshwete," June 3, 1988, AL 3041, South African History Archive, http://www.disa.ukzn.ac.za/index.php?option=com_displaydc&recordID=int19880603.043.049 (accessed March 3, 2014).

87. On the difference between legal/illegal and licit/illicit, see Janet Lee Roitman, *Fiscal Disobedience: An Anthropology of Economic Regulation in Central Africa* (Princeton: Princeton University Press, 2005).

88. Sipho Kings, "'We Have Made Our Point,' Say Khutsong Residents," *M&G Online*, November 8, 2013, http://mg.co.za/article/2013-11-07-we-have-made-our-point/ (accessed November 8, 2013).

89. The field was locally known as a central place for community members to gather, air grievances, and plan a community-based response to those grievances, some of which involved violence. For instance, the previous meeting in the field resulted in a series of violent protests to prevent Khutsong's incorporation into a different province from the one in which they were currently placed.

90. Rapule Tabane, "Khutsong: Brutality Prevails When Hope Is Lost," *M&G Online*, http://mg.co.za/article/2013-11-07-khutsong-brutality-prevails-when-hope-is-lost/ (accessed November 17, 2013).

91. This account is adapted primarily from Botho Molosankwe, Brendan Roane, and Lerato Mbangeni, "Khutsong Sangoma Beaten Then Necklaced," *Star*, November 4, 2013, http://www.iol.co.za/news/crime-courts/khutsong-sangoma-beaten-then-necklaced-1.1601758#.Uok_IuI4n-I (accessed November 17, 2013).

92. SAPA, "Khutsong Mob Necklaced Crime Fighter's Son," *eNCA News*, November 5, 2013, http://www.enca.com/south-africa/khutsong-mob-necklaced-crime-fighters-son (accessed November 17, 2013).

93. Lebogang Seale, "Khutsong Mob Justice Victim Buried," *Star*, November 11, 2013, http://www.iol.co.za/news/crime-courts/khutsong-mob-justice-victim-buried-1.1605266#.Uok-KeI4n-I (accessed November 17, 2013).

94. See, for example, Stephen Grootes, "Vigilante Killings: The Erosion of Public Trust in the Police and Criminal Justice System," *Daily Maverick*, November 7, 2013, http://www.dailymaverick.co.za/article/2013-11-07-vigilante-killings-the-erosion-of-public-trust-in-the-police-and-criminal-justice-system/#.UnoeHuI4n-I (accessed November 8, 2013).

95. Lekgowa and Nicolson, "Anatomy of the Khutsong Horror."

96. The consequences of the attack on the sangoma were also understood by some in occult terms. For example, the tabloid *Daily Sun* gleefully reported on its front page that

according to another local sangoma, the people who killed Magagula "would be cursed for the rest of their lives." *Daily Sun*, "'A Curse on Khutsong!'" *Politics Web*, November 6, 2013, http://www.politicsweb.co.za/politicsweb/view/politicsweb/en/page71627?oid=444547&sn=Detail&pid=71616 (accessed November 17, 2013).

97. Lekgowa and Nicolson, "Anatomy of the Khutsong Horror"; Molosankwe, Roane, and Mbangeni, "Khutsong Sangoma Beaten Then Necklaced."

98. SAPA, "Khutsong Mob Necklaced Crime Fighter's Son."

99. Seale, "Khutsong Mob Justice Victim Buried."

100. Ibid.

101. Molosankwe, Roane, and Mbangeni, "Khutsong Sangoma Beaten Then Necklaced."

102. At a subsequent meeting among community members to discuss the police inattention to their concerns, the Casanovas stormed the meeting wielding machetes and pangas, injuring twenty people. When the residents regrouped later that night to discuss how to respond, they "vowed to take on the gang." Lekgowa and Nicolson, "Anatomy of the Khutsong Horror."

103. Molosankwe, Roane, and Mbangeni, "Khutsong Sangoma Beaten Then Necklaced."

104. Lekgowa and Nicolson, "Anatomy of the Khutsong Horror."

105. Julia Hornberger, *Policing and Human Rights: The Meaning of Violence and Justice in the Everyday Policing of Johannesburg* (New York: Routledge, 2011).

106. Tabane, "Khutsong."

107. Ibid.

108. Kings, "'We Have Made Our Point,' Say Khutsong Residents."

109. For example, The Khayelitsha Commission (mentioned above) was initiated by a collection of local civil society organizations concerned about a spate of necklace violence in that township. Adam Armstrong, "GroundUp: Understanding the Khayelitsha Commission of Inquiry," *Daily Maverick*, January 21, 2014, http://www.dailymaverick.co.za/article/2014-01-21-groundup-understanding-the-khayelitsha-commission-of-inquiry/#.VXcCWEaCfYg (accessed January 22, 2014).

7   Sitting on the Volcano

Mob Violence and Lynching in the Zionist-Palestinian Conflict

SHAIEL BEN-EPHRAIM AND OR HONIG

The dynamics of violence in the Israeli-Palestinian conflict have been examined from many angles. There have been several studies of the causes and consequences of terrorism, sabotage, and vigilante activities between the Jews and the Arabs in Palestine. The studies examining Israel's use of counterterrorism have been numerous, and so have been the studies that examine the Palestinian Authority's suppression or encouragement of terrorism. Yet, there have been very few attempts to examine the lynching phenomenon in the conflict. This chapter seeks to fill this gap.

Examining the lynching phenomenon provides a unique prism for understanding the grassroots level of the interaction between the two societies that are locked in ethnic conflict. While political scientists have mainly paid attention to the strategic interactions between community elites, the lynching phenomenon speaks to the grassroots forces shaping the conflict: to what extent there is deep-seated hatred between the two societies, what are the notions of justice in each society, what is the strength of moderates in society and how great is their ability to act as a restraining force, what is the capacity of elites to mobilize, and finally to what degree each community is institutionalized.

We focus on lynching and mob violence in the conflict between Jews and Arabs in Palestine and will not investigate inter-Arab lynching attacks. We will also not investigate lynching attacks against Jewish communities in Arab states, even though they form an important part of the Arab-Israeli conflict.[1] Such a focus allows us to identify causal patterns, specify the functions that lynching attacks serve and assess their impact on the severity and development of the Zionist-Palestinian conflict specifically. Lynching attacks took place mainly during two stages of the intercommunal conflict: (1) during the years of the British control in Palestine until 1929 (1920–1929) and (2) since the first clashes between Israelis and Palestinians in the occupied territories in the late 1980s until today. The conclusion examines similarities and differences in the dynamics of mob violence and lynching within the two periods.

It is customary in popular culture to analyze crimes through the aspects of means, motive, and opportunity. These are useful metrics for generalizations on when and why lynching occurs in the Zionist-Palestinian conflict as well. Indeed, our main finding is that three elements increase the likelihood for lynching attacks to take place (the first two are necessary conditions). First, there must be an "opportunity" in the form of poor law enforcement and intercommunal interaction. Unlike terrorist attacks, which are planned and executed by motivated individuals focused on a political cause, lynching attacks are crimes of opportunity often committed by regular individuals who are not particularly committed to the cause. They are usually not trained to execute violent acts and often have a great deal to lose if arrested or hurt during the lynching attempt. Precisely because they are less resolute than terrorists or guerilla fighters, even a moderate presence of security forces can deter them. Sufficiently defended communities will face few lynching attacks due to the limited organization and capabilities of the perpetrators.

Second, there must be strong motivation. The motive element can be either tied to the goals of the national movements or to strong currents of racism or radicalization in society. The proximate cause or trigger can vary and may be an idiosyncratic event such as a brawl or a funeral. Third, the lynching mob must be the preferred tool given the strategic options available. In other words, if the ethnic community has sufficient institutional capacity to organize a guerilla or terror campaign, it will choose these options since they are much more lethal and generate less international condemnation. In this sense, we argue that lynching attacks are a tool for national liberation struggles lacking in nationalist institutions and are therefore mainly used when the community is easy to incite but lacks the sophistication or conditions that terrorism or guerilla warfare require.

Part I. The Lynching Phenomenon during the Years of the British Mandate

The Background to the Nebi Musa Riots

The Nebi Musa riots were the first instance of widespread political violence between Arabs and Zionist Jews in Palestine, and therefore their outbreak and immediate background bear careful scrutiny. They also marked the first significant instance of urban violence in several decades, after a period of intercommunal cooperation and coexistence. The fluid nature of the political climate at the time would seem to indicate that the motives behind the violence were rooted in nationalist motives rather than local ones. Jerusalem, the scene of the onset of the events, was decidedly mixed and intertwined.[2] Salim Tamri argues that during the Ottoman years Jerusalem was not typified by "the tolerant cohabitation of protected *dhimmi* minorities, but the positive engagement in the affairs of neighbors whose religion was coincidental to their wider urban heritage."[3]

With that in mind, the initial outbreak of spontaneous violence between Arabs and Jews in Palestine should be seen in the wider context of the difficult stilting attempt by the British to establish colonial rule in the Middle East. The British had raised the hopes of Arab nationalism in the Levant only to partially dash them by dividing the colonial spoils of the region with France. The corresponding unrest that hit the Middle East in the 1919–1921 period caught the British by surprise as they were demobilizing troops. The first riots in Palestine were part of this general pattern of unrest.[4]

The fate of Syria was a particularly sore spot for the Arabs of the region. In return for their assistance in the war against the Ottoman Empire, the British had promised the Hashemite family the right to rule Syria. One of the sons of the family, Faisal, had formed a government in Damascus based on this promise and laid claim to a Greater Syria, which included Palestine. Caught between the British and French colonial enterprises, Faisal's Greater Syria project presented the brightest hope of Arab independence at the time. In February 1920, the French announced that he would be removed in favor of a French Mandate in Syria. In a desperate gambit to retain power, Faisal pronounced himself king of Greater Syria.[5]

The claim resonated strongly in Palestine. Faisal's claim fell on fertile ground in a period during which identities in the Middle East were fluid and malleable. Identification with the idea of Ottomanism, previously popular among Palestinian Arabs, had been waning for years and had not been replaced by any clear formulation of national identity.[6] However, despite lacking a cohesive national identity, the time was ripe for political action. British policy, caught between Arab, French, and Zionist demands, seemed to be wavering. Palestine was still under military administration and a civil apparatus had yet to be created, and the form of governance that British colonial domination would take was still unclear.[7]

The Arab elite in Palestine sought a political program capable of addressing the twin threats of colonialism and Zionism. Incorporation into a greater Syria seemed like the most practical counter to the threat of Zionism and the most promising path to the abrogation of the Balfour Declaration.[8] The primary influence of pro-Syrian forces among Palestinian Arabs at this venture is expressed by the statement of the first Arab Congress of the Arabs in Palestine on January 1919 that "we consider Palestine as a part of Arab Syria as it has never been separated from it at any time."[9] The form of nationalism promoted by pro-Syrian groups was vehemently anti-Zionist in its goals.[10] A letter written by the head of the Arab Muslim-Christian Association (MCA) spelled out the attitude toward the local Jewish communities: "We declare that we cannot accept Jews in our country. Should they be permitted to do what they intend doing, we shall fight them till death . . . we declare that we do not accept the Jews neither as guests nor as neighbors in Palestine."[11]

The Zionist movement was not particularly powerful at that time and the demographic weight of Jews in Palestine was low, numbering around 10 percent of the population.[12] Furthermore, under the military administration, land sales were forbidden and land registers were closed, and Jewish immigration was relatively modest.[13] However, official British backing for the Balfour Declaration meant that the Zionist program could be implemented slowly but effectively. A quote that made a particular impression on Palestinian Arabs was Zionist leader Chaim Weizmann's quip that the goal of Zionism was that "Palestine become Jewish as England is English."[14] With British support, this goal seemed attainable.

Although there was no lack of impetus for political action, the nascent Palestinian national movement did not possess institutions suitable to promoting the nationalist cause. Notable families took on a mediating role between the authorities and the lower classes, utilizing patronage systems and family networks, while avoiding institutions of popular mobilization, which could erode their monopoly on political power.[15] The influence of the few existing nationalist organizations, such as the MCA, was limited to the young and educated sectors of society.[16] A further inhibition on collective political action was the lack of an agreed-upon political goal. The core of the emerging nationalist movement was the consensus on opposition to the Balfour Declaration. However, there was disagreement on all other significant points. Palestinian elites argued over whether to pursue a pro-British or pro-French orientation, a Palestinian or Syrian territorial focus, or whether the movement should speak for an Arab or an Islamic constituency.[17]

The Nebi Musa Riots

Nebi Musa is an annual Muslim festival held on Easter, which had never been marked by notable violence previous to 1920.[18] In 1920, the festival was held under the aforementioned tense and fluid political circumstances. Many of those gathered for the celebrations demanded unity with Syria and cried out "long live King Faisal."[19] The editor of the pro-Faisal newspaper, *Suria al-Janubia*, gave a speech on horseback, while the crowd chanted "Palestine is our land, the Jews are our dogs!"[20]

It was under these heated circumstances that on April 4th large Arab crowds attacked Jews in the old city of Jerusalem. Violence raged for three days and the authorities proved powerless to stop it. All told, the number of casualties in that first round of violence in Jerusalem was 5 Jews killed, 211 wounded, and 4 Arabs killed and 21 wounded.[21] The court determined that most of the attacks were "made in customary mob fashion with sticks, stones and knives."[22] It was also determined that the British authorities were not the targets; rather, "the attack was entirely directed against Jews" and that "practically all the losses were experienced by the Jewish community."[23] Arab casualties were mostly the result of attempts by the British authorities to control the rioting.[24] Violence started outside the Jaffa Gate, where looting and stoning of Jewish shops took place. Several Jews were beaten, stoned, and stabbed, and at least one was shot immediately after the altercation broke out.[25] Areas that were more homogeneously Jewish managed to fend off attacks, but the areas where the Jewish population was mixed with the Arab population saw prolonged and often lethal violence.[26]

The Zionist Commission and Zionist historiography blamed Faisal for organizing the riots through proxies in Palestine.[27] The British court of inquiry also noted that several "Sherifian agents" were partially responsible for the agitation.[28] One pro-Syrian newspaper wrote, "if our verbal protests are not heard, we shall resort to active protests. Instead of the pen, we shall use knives, in place of ink, blood."[29] However, the report determined that there was "no evidence of any definite plan on the part of an organized body of rioters and the whole affair has the appearance of spontaneity."[30] There is no clear evidence that the attack was planned, but an atmosphere conducive to violence was fostered by pro-Syrian forces in Palestine.

The violence was facilitated by the lack of preparation on the part of the military administration. While Zionists accused the policemen of cooperating with the rioters, the Court of Inquiry lay the blame on a lack of police personnel.[31] Furthermore, the changing political environment was not taken into account. The authorities had focused on potential hostilities between different Christian sects, which had been more common in the past than altercations between Arabs and Jews.[32] With these failings in mind, many in the Yishuv (the Jewish community in pre-state Palestine during the Zionist era) blamed the administration for the attacks. Menachem Ussishkin and David Yellin wrote to the Chief Administrator of Palestine, regarding the Jewish community, that "if within two hours their safety is not completely assured and their protection fully guaranteed, they will find themselves forced to realize that they cannot leave their fate in the hands of others and will, as one man, rise to defend themselves and their brothers who are being mistreated and murdered before their eyes."[33]

However, the defensive capabilities of the urban Jewish community in Jerusalem at the time were limited. Zionist proto-military organizations had focused on agricultural settlements in the past and had limited urban defensive capabilities.[34] Ze'ev Jabotinsky, a former Lieutenant in the British army and a noted Zionist activist, commanded the embryonic Haganah (the newly formed military arm of the Yishuv) chapter in Jerusalem.[35] However, he made the mistake of organizing most defenses around the Jewish commercial centers outside the old city, leaving the communities inside the old city vulnerable. The police attempted to keep the Haganah from entering the old city, and the residents inside the walls were almost undefended.[36] Jabotinsky was arrested for possession of arms and incitement and sentenced to fifteen years imprisonment with hard labor. Though the sentence was later shortened, the sentencing provoked an uproar in the Yishuv, particularly since many of the perpetrators had not been caught. The general sense among most Zionists was that the British administration colluded with the rioters and prevented the defense of Jewish victims.[37]

To the Zionist leadership, the level of violence aimed at Jews and the perceived cooperation of the authorities recalled the pogroms in Russia and Eastern Europe that many among them had experienced in their formative years.[38] David Ben-Gurion said that "we who experienced the pogroms knew quite well that without the wish of the authorities and their open or clandestine backing, actively or passively, the task of the pogrom cannot succeed."[39] The riots were reminiscent of the pogroms in other ways as well. The ripping open of the quilts and pillows of victims was a traditional part of pogroms in Russia. To the horror of Zionists from Eastern Europe, these scenes accompanied the Nebi Musa riots as well.[40] Zvi Nadav, a member of the Jewish defense organization in Jerusalem recounted that "we saw Jewish feathers flying, feathers symbolizing the precariousness of Jewish existence, blown away by every soft wind."[41]

However, despite significant similarities, the pogrom analogy was misleading and fostered Zionist misperceptions. Rather than view the violence as a reaction to political developments, the Yishuv leadership preferred to see the events as manifestations of uncontrollable anti-Semitism manipulated and orchestrated by Arab elites and tacitly approved by the authorities. The source of the enmity, according to the standard Zionist interpretation, was not the political threat that Zionism presented to Arabs in Palestine. Rather it was the inherent weakness of Jewish existence as a small minority that inspired hatred and disdain, both in Eastern Europe and Palestine.[42]

This interpretation was reinforced by the socialist leanings of many Zionist leaders and was based on an analysis of Eastern European social structure wholly inappropriate to Palestine. The traditional Zionist outlook on the "Arab question" had been that Zionism could develop without disenfranchising the Arab agricultural workers, the *fellaheen*, and that the economic benefits brought about by Jewish settlement would create mutually beneficial relations.[43] Ben-Gurion, early in his political career, expressed the hope that "a covenant between the Hebrew and Arab workers will establish and preserve the covenant between the Jewish and Arab nations in the country."[44] According to this perception, relations were less than harmonious due to the cynical manipulation of the *effendi* land-owning class among the Arabs in Palestine. As one Zionist put it at the time, "the reason for the hatred against us is because we aid the fellaheen and therefore cause damage to the interests of the effendis."[45]

The British administration, with more experience in nationalist awakenings, had a better grasp on Arab politics. The British Court of Inquiry report determined that Arab unrest emerged primarily over the fear that "eventual dispossession of Arabs by Jews is inevitable" due to a "very real fear of superior Jewish brains and money."[46] The report concluded that a history of Muslim domination over Jews and a religious sense that the Jews had committed spiritual crimes and remained unrepentant, meant that it was "difficult for the native population to contemplate with equanimity even the most moderate aims of Zionism."[47] The Court of Inquiry lay the blame for the riots on the Balfour Declaration of 1917, saying that this "perverted way of looking at things has converted a friendly people into one which is declared to be at present day as to ninety percent of its numbers definitely hostile to the British administration."[48] The inquiry also pointed to the growing institutionalization of the Yishuv as cause of animosity and cited Zionist organization of courts, defense, intelligence, and public health as signs of concern.[49]

However, a crucial element missed by the commission and by most interpretations of the Nebi Musa events is the centrality of religion. It is no coincidence that the first incidence of widespread political violence between Palestinian Arabs and Jews erupted in the religiously symbolic city of Jerusalem during an Islamic festival. The early sense of nationalism among Palestinian Arabs centered on the special religious significance of Palestine.[50] Religious motives were a powerful mobilizer in a society in which nationalism was just emerging. Furthermore, for centuries Palestine had been a territory with no political autonomy, but one that enjoyed a great deal of religious significance. Rashid Khalidi wrote that "for most sectors of the population . . . religion has remained the most important single source of identification and community feeling."[51]

The Consequences of the Nebi Musa Riots and the Background for the Jaffa Riots

The Arab nationalist movement in Palestine altered its orientation from a Syrian pan-Arab focus to a territorially limited Palestinian focus in the aftermath of the Nebi Musa riots. The fall of Faisal and the creation of a civil government in Palestine dashed the dream of a "Greater Syria." The general principles of a political program coalesced around stable political demands. The nationalist elite called for a recognized Palestinian national government governed by an Arabic-speaking parliament, which would exclude the Zionists while remaining within the confines of the British Empire. The MCA demanded a halt to Jewish immigration and the transfer of lands to Jews. The movement became more cohesive and quite active in the early 1920s as the Congress continued to meet and local branches were created.[52] Although the Arab Congress declared that national concerns took precedence over familial, regional, or religious concerns, this had limited influence among most sectors of society. Aside from a young nationalist elite, subnational affiliations remained paramount.[53]

Significant changes had also occurred in the structure of British colonial rule in Palestine. The inability of the military regime to provide security during the Nebi Musa riots prompted the appointment of Herbert Samuel, a noted pro-Zionist, to the post of High Commissioner of Palestine. This had a significant calming effect on the Zionists. Chaim Weizmann, wrote to his wife that "our trials have come to an end."[54] In his inaugural assembly, Samuel outlined the steps necessary to establish a Jewish National Home. These included the renewal of land sales, opening Palestine to limited immigration.[55] This made the next series of attacks, occurring in 1921, all the more shocking to the Yishuv.

The Jaffa Riots

The catalyst for the second round of large-scale political violence was a Jewish political parade. A First of May demonstration by the Socialist Workers Party, a Communist Party, faced a demonstration by the new mainstream Labour Zionist Achdut Ha'avoda party in Tel Aviv. The two parties were bitter about the recent split in their shared movement of Poalei Zion, and therefore the outburst had a particularly bitter internecine character. The police tried to break up the scuffle, and Arabs from nearby Jaffa rushed in and joined the melee, looting Jewish-owned shops nearby.[56] This led to what the Commission of Inquiry called "a general hunting of the Jews."[57]

The circumstances surrounding the initial violence are obscure and seem disconnected from its deeper motives. The Haycraft Commission, appointed to investigate the riots, tied the onset of the violence to the spread of rumors that Bolshevik Jews were indiscriminately murdering Muslim women and children.[58] The commission reported that "with all their intelligence, the people are credulous to an incredible extent, provided that the rumors circulating are of a nature to excite an existing emotion."[59] However, the commission concluded that the deeper motive was the opposition of the rioters to the pursuit of the Balfour Declaration and the policy of a Jewish National Home. They wrote that the major fear for Palestinian Arabs was that "the Jews when they had sufficiently increased in numbers would become so highly organized and so well armed as to be able to overcome the Arabs, and rule over and oppress them."[60] As a result, the Arabs "were the first to turn the quarrel into a race conflict" and "behaved with a savagery that cannot be condoned."[61]

This analysis was corroborated by the location of the most vicious attacks in Jaffa. The worst of the violence occurred in the Zionist-run immigrants' hostel in the Ajami neighborhood of Jaffa. The building had been used for housing new immigrants by the Zionist commission before employment and permanent housing had been obtained.[62] Herbert Samuel remarked later that violence had emerged in Jaffa, since that is where Jewish immigrants mostly came to shore and anger is greatest where "the irritant which causes it is most in evidence."[63]

Violence spread to different locations in Palestine, particularly in Jerusalem, Jaffa, Rehovot, Petah Tikva, Kfar Saba, and Hadera.[64] One of the most gruesome episodes in the "Jaffa riots" took place in the Jewish Quarter of Jerusalem in November 1921. A crowd attacked Jewish residents with edged weapons, as Martin van Creveld wrote, "though the assailants possessed hardly any firearms, they compensated with edged weapons; eyes were gouged out, breasts and testicles cut off, and the like."[65] It was noted that many of the corpses had been found with signs of particularly brutal attacks, including multiple broken skulls and dozens of wounds, which would seem to indicate the extreme anger of the perpetrators.[66] There was no differentiation between victims, whether Zionist or non-Zionist, Arab-speaking or European, religious or secular. Victims were selected based only on their Judaism.[67]

The casualties of the violence included Yosef Haim Brenner, a literary luminary and a Yishuv celebrity. Unlike many Zionists of his generation, who underestimated Arab nationalism and analyzed relations with local Arabs through the prism of class, Brenner was fearful of the level of nationalist Arab enmity. Brenner wrote, "there is already hatred between us—there must be and will be."[68] He viewed the nationalist sentiment of the Arab majority in Palestine as a "volcano," which threatened to explode and bury the Zionist enterprise at any moment.[69] Brenner was a boarder in the "red house' in Abu Kabir, not far from Jaffa. When the riots began, the residents of the house had locked themselves in but then decided to risk making their way to Tel Aviv when they happened upon a funeral of an Arab boy killed in the violence the day before. Brenner and all five of his companions were brutally murdered and their bodies mutilated.[70]

Despite the widespread violence, there does not seem to have been a clear guiding hand behind the events. Yehoshua Porath wrote that the spread of violence around the country was made possible "not so much by nationalist slogans as by the spreading of false rumors that the Jews were slaughtering Arabs."[71] Riots heavily associated with rumors tend to be disorganized affairs that originate in the lower levels of society. It appears that the Jaffa riots were no exception.[72] The MCA, still the most important Arab nationalist organization at this time, opposed the riots, and some members tried to refute the rumors that fed the violence.[73] The Commission of Inquiry reported that, for the most part, Arab notables played a constructive role in containing the violence and that there was no premeditation or planning on their part.[74]

Once again, the authorities were not adequately prepared, and the commission report reflects the ineptitude of the police, particularly in Jaffa. As an angry crowd gathered outside the immigrants' hostel on May 1st, the police officer in charge "occupied himself with other matters and did not return until the tragedy of the Immigration House was over." He left a second-in-command in charge who "according to his own statement told the crowd to disperse and then went home to lunch."[75] He also took some time to clean the bloodstains from his belt.[76] The actions of particular officers seemed to be determined more by their religious and ethnic affiliations than by their positions. The Haycraft Commission determined that "the police became partisan" and this "rendered them not only ineffective as an instrument for the preservation of security, but resulted in some active participation in violence."[77] The inadequate protection was judged to be a result of "the insufficiency of training, service and traditions," and manpower which did not possess the "quality required to withstand the crush of racial strife."[78] However, the military performed far better than the police and in Petah Tikva,

Rehovot, and Hadera helped drive off Arab attacks involving hundreds and perhaps thousands of men.[79]

The Yishuv was similarly unprepared. The attacks found the Jews in Palestine in a complacent mood, believing that they were now under the protection of a sympathetic British regime with a pro-Zionist commissioner at the helm. The Haganah forces in Tel Aviv were so disorganized at the time that they could not locate the stash of weapons they had hidden in the sands near the city.[80] However, the Haganah showed some improvement since the Nebi Musa riots. Having learned their lesson, members of the Haganah sneaked into the Old City of Jerusalem before the British could prevent their entry.[81]

All told, 48 Arabs had been killed and 73 wounded, while 47 Jews had been killed and 146 wounded in the riots.[82] While most of the Arabs killed had been shot by the British authorities and the Haganah, there were cases of Jews lynching Arabs as well. For example, the commission reports that in Tel Aviv, Jews were found by the police beating a group of Arabs, including a woman and a child.[83] In the long term, the riots had an important demographic legacy, particularly in Jaffa. Thousands of Jews left Jaffa and moved to Tel Aviv, and the authorities increased this trend of separation by drawing new municipal boundaries separating Tel Aviv and Jaffa into separate cities.[84]

1929 Riots

The Jaffa riots were followed by an extended period of quiet. This was at least partially due to the lack of success of that round of violence. While some concessions were given to Arab demands, the British authorities did not put an end to Jewish immigration or revoke the Balfour Declaration. In fact, the ratification of the British Mandate by the League of Nations on July 1922 was a significant blow to Palestinian nationalism. Now, instead of a vague British commitment, Zionism received official recognition from the international community.[85] Furthermore, the military response was harsher than it had been in the Nebi Musa riots, and more Arabs had been killed in the riots than Jews. Thus, in the period following the outbreak, the leadership and most Arab notables supported government measures to suppress violence.[86] Following the Jaffa riots, the British government provided increased security support to Jewish settlements. They integrated the settlements into regional military plans and developed rapid response capabilities. Turning a blind eye to the illegal obtainment of weapons by the Haganah, they provided a certain amount of legal weaponry to the organization as well.[87]

In the meantime, the Arab national movement in Palestine cemented around a clear leader, Haj Amin al-Husayni. He had established his reputation as one of the key activists involved in the Nebi Musa riots. Due to his role in inciting the attacks, he was sentenced, in absentia, to ten years imprisonment with hard labor.[88] This greatly increased his popularity, as politically engaged Palestinians saw him as the first leader who dared to stand up to both the British and the Zionists.[89] However, the future Mufti was considered pro-British in army circles and would continue to tow a pro-British line for over a decade. He had helped recruit volunteers from pro-British forces during the war and served as an official in the headquarters of the British Military Governor of Jerusalem.[90]

Al-Husayni managed, with pressure from the powerful al-Husayni family, to obtain official power by securing the position of Grand Mufti of Jerusalem in May 1921.[91] The British granted greater autonomy for the Muslim population in Palestine and transferred authority on internal religious matters to a British-formed Supreme Muslim Council (SMC), formed in 1922 and placed under the authority of the Mufti. Due to his pro-British credentials, the authorities concentrated all religious bureaucratic power in his hands.[92] The government paid the salaries of council officials in order to assure political loyalty. In return, the SMC was granted wide authority and became a religious "state within a state," enjoying full autonomy on religious issues.[93]

The British policy was a mixed success. On the one hand, the Council became the vanguard of the Palestinian national movement and a rival center of power. Haj Amin cemented his position as the most powerful Palestinian leader of his generation by astutely combining religious patronage and family connections with a clever use of Islamic symbolism. The institutional advantages provided by the British were utilized to hinder the creation of institutions representing wider sectors of society.[94] On the other hand, the British managed to limit the scope of the Mufti's political ambitions. By fostering the dependence of the SMC on the authorities, the focus of its nationalist efforts was steered to opposition to Zionism rather than colonialism.[95]

However, despite having a great deal of influence and power, it would be a mistake to see Haj Amin al-Husayni as the effective orchestrator of Palestinian nationalism in the 1920s. The SMC did not possess or attempt to develop popular mobilization capabilities.[96] Furthermore, the Mufti faced increased opposition in the late 1920s. The power of the Nashashibi family, rivals of the Haj Amin's al-Husayni family, was on the rise.[97] The national movement was prone to fragmentation from below, due to the destabilizing effects of nationalism on traditional patterns of life. Finally, Arabs faced divisions fostered by the intentional and unintentional effects of British colonial policy.[98] If so, Wendy Pearlman put it best when she remarked that Palestinian Arab "politicians had influence as spokesmen, not as governors."[99]

This may be seen as the background for the manner in which the Mufti seized upon the dispute over the installation of a screen to divide between men and women at the Wailing Wall.[100] In September 1928, religious Jews had begun using a collapsible screen in order to separate male from female worshippers at the Wall. The Jews had been forbidden from introducing any items or articles such as benches or partitions to the area in the past.[101] The attempts to make any change to prayer arrangements at the wall were portrayed by the Arab leadership and press as part of a Jewish conspiracy to control all the Islamic holy sites in the city. As evidence, postcards created in local yeshivas showing the Star of David superimposed on the Dome of the Rock were presented.[102]

There is little doubt that the Mufti utilized the religious dispute in an attempt to foster political capital.[103] As Yehoshua Porath observed, the SMC and the Arab Executive (AE) exacerbated the tensions since "the Wall affair enabled them to give the struggle against the Jews a religious dimension and to enlist the support of the urban and rural masses, who until then had not been attracted by the secular nationalist slogans."[104] Haj Amin established "the Committee for the Defense of al-Buraq al-Sharif" (the Wailing Wall in Arabic) with branches in several cities.[105] While the Mufti had a significant role in stirring up tensions, his role in fostering the actual violence remains disputed. Officially, he called for calm, but there is a historiographical dispute regarding his role in managing the violence. There are those who believe that he stirred the pot behind the scenes and tried to utilize the violence to achieve political ends, while another school of thought holds that he lost control of the violence.[106]

Another element that encouraged violence in Palestine was the support given to the SMC position by the British authorities. The authorities noticeably slackened their commitment to defend the Yishuv against Arab attacks. On July, 25, 1929, the British authorities took back all the government-issued arms in southern Galilee and the Jordan Valley.[107] This was coupled with the creation of new Arab military units and the gradual removal of Jews from the security services.[108] There was a sense, in the period leading up to the riots, that the British government supported the claims of the Arab leadership in the buildup to the riots. This increased the confidence of the Arab national leadership and produced a more confrontational policy.[109]

The Colonial Secretary responded to the crisis by stating that the government was "bound to maintain the status quo, which they have regarded as being, in general terms, that the Jewish community has a right of access to the pavement for the purpose of their devotions, but may bring to the Wall only those appurtenances of worship which were permitted under the Turkish regime."[110] The Mufti understood this as complete British support and in attempt to put the issue high on the political agenda, the Mufti announced a holy war over the compound.[111] A muezzin called on Muslims to defend the wall five times a day. He initiated provocations by holding noisy religious ceremonies during Jewish prayer, building a new sharia court over the wall, and opening a busy thoroughfare beside it.[112]

In protest, members of the Revisionist movement marched to the Wailing Wall on August 15th. By waving Zionist flags and singing the Hatikva anthem at the religiously sensitive site, they enflamed an already tense situation.[113] A week later, a large group gathered near the Al-Aqsa mosque to hear speeches by the Mufti and others. Rumors circulated that Jews had attacked the Al Aqsa mosque and were massacring Arabs in Jerusalem, and these seem to have played a part in most if not all of the localized disturbances.[114] Many of the worshippers then burst into the Western Wall area armed with knives and clubs, attacking Jews and defacing Torah scrolls.[115] The Haganah was organized enough to prevent large-scale bloodshed within the old city, and only one fatality occurred in the immediate stages.[116]

The violence spread throughout the city, and Jews began attacking Arab passersby as well. Perhaps because of the increased strength of the Yishuv following the large immigration of the mid-1920s, the Jewish community was far more aggressive throughout the 1929 riots. In fact it is still unclear whether the first casualty of the riots was Jewish or Arab.[117] The next day, violence seemed to be dying down until a Jewish teenager was killed in a dispute over a soccer ball near the entrance to Jerusalem. His funeral procession turned into a demonstration, which was repressed by the authorities.[118]

Mutual violence was encouraged by the lack of adequate police enforcement. Perhaps lulled into complacency by years of relative quiet, the police were undermanned on the day the riots broke out. Much of the top brass and a third of the officers were away on summer vacation, and only 142 non-Arab policemen were present in Palestine when violence broke out. The ethnic identity of the policemen on duty was pivotal, as Arab and Jewish officers tended to help their own communities.[119] In Hebron, were some of the most gruesome violence took place, there was only one British officer present.[120] As a result, the Arab national movement felt that they had some support from the Arab-majority police. The Mufti told his followers on the day the violence began that "the government is not against you, nor the police."[121]

The nationwide scope of the violence allows a comparison of the interaction of different communities throughout Palestine. The results are wildly diverse, highlighting the importance of local grievances and familiarities. The nationalist motive seems to have been far more effective when there were internal Jewish-Arab tensions within the community, thus triggering lynching attacks, which in turn could then have further impact on the national level. In some cases, communities attacked their neighbors to which they had sold land in the past—for example, the attacks of the denizens of Lifta on the Jewish neighborhood of Nahalat Shiva and in other places in Jerusalem and Hebron.[122] In other cases almost no violence occurred. In Tiberias, local notables released an official statement stating that it was crucial to avoid the "results that may arise from false rumors."[123]

Hebron saw the highest death toll, with sixty-seven Jews killed—among them, twelve women and three children under five years old. Five men, including a seventy-year-old rabbi had been castrated. A two-year-old child had his head torn off. Rape and torture had accompanied several of the murders.[124] However, most residents of Hebron did not participate in the attacks, and, according to one report, over two-thirds of the Jewish community in Hebron found refuge in Arab houses.[125] Still, the exceptional ferocity of the violence in Hebron requires explanation, especially since Hebron was an unlikely target for nationalist violence. The Hebron community was highly traditional and had few links to the Zionist establishment. It had also lived in relative peace with the local Arab community, and there were no notable precedents of murderous violence between the groups. Furthermore, financial and social ties between Arabs and Jews in the city were considerable.[126]

However, important changes occurred within the Hebron Jewish community during these years. The establishment of the Knesses Yisrael yeshiva in the city in 1925, with 130 students from outside of Palestine, significantly altered intercommunal relations in the city. Many of the yeshiva students dressed in the Eastern European style, some came from the United States, and all seemed distinctly alien to the Arab community. The violence in Hebron may indicate that Arab communities had come to see any Jewish immigration to Palestine (particularly European immigration) as a political and economic threat.[127] One of the Jewish survivors of the attacks recalled that previous to the attacks Hebron had been

> a kind of paradise surrounded by vineyards, where Sephardic Jews and Arabs lived in idyllic coexistence. The long-time Ashkenazi Jews were also treated well by the Arabs. The only ones who really roused the Arabs' anger were the ones they referred to as the "Ashkenazim"—students of the Lubavitcher Rebbe who came to redeem land in the Holy Land and established a community in Hebron.[128]

The isolated village of Motza, not far from Jerusalem, suffered a similar fate. The residents of the village were slaughtered by their neighbors in Qalunya. Rumors had reached the village that thousands of Arabs had been killed by gangs of Jews while coming out of the Al-Aqsa mosque, and the villagers began cutting power lines and stoning traffic on nearby roads. While many of those in the village were ordered to gather in a house defended by the Haganah, those who did not obey the order were slaughtered systematically.[129] Yochanan Ratner, a notable architect and Haganah member, described how some of the Motza villagers struggled with the repercussions of the events and the new reality that it had imposed. One of the villagers, an owner of the local factory, asked the Haganah members not to shoot any local Arabs, hoping that they would return to work in his factory after the dust had settled. Ratner wrote that he had not internalized the fact that "the paternal relations had disappeared, and he was no longer dealing with Ahmad or Mahmud from Qalunya (and they themselves had changed as well) but with the followers of the Mufti, men from the outside, motivated by honest nationalist sentiment."[130]

The murder of innocent Arabs by Jews was far more common in 1929 than it had been during previous waves of violence. A Jewish policeman, Simcha Hinkis, was found guilty of the murder of several Arab adults, both male and female. Two children were injured in the incident, a five-year-old boy and a two-month-old baby.[131] The defense claimed that just prior to the lynching, Hinkis had come upon victims of Arab attacks and that one of the victims had died in his arms.[132] A significant number of Jewish attacks against Arabs took place in Jerusalem. Once tensions became high, unfortunate individuals who found themselves in the wrong place at the wrong time were attacked by members of the other group. For example, noted academic Gershom Scholem reported that an Arab had been beaten to death right outside his home. A local doctor witnessed that murder and reported that six or seven Jews dragged the man on the floor and repeatedly "hit him on the back and on the head with sticks."[133]

Long-Term Consequences of the 1929 Palestine Riots

The wide geographical scope of the violence and its unprecedented ferocity had a role in institutionalizing the conflict and solidifying the intercommunal divide. Jews living in the Arab areas of Jaffa and Jerusalem, as well as in Gaza and what is today known as the West Bank, left their homes never to return, leaving only four mixed communities in Palestine.[134] Official talks between Palestinian and Zionist leaders ceased. A Palestinian boycott of

Jewish goods led to an increased separation between the Jewish and Arab economies.[135] Due to these developments, future rounds of violence between the communities would be more organized and militarized. Spontaneous violence would take on an increasingly marginal role in the conflict, as opportunities were less plentiful.

Jewish perceptions of their Arab neighbors changed dramatically following the events of 1929. The talk of class fraternity seemed increasingly hollow and the realization that Zionism faced a determined and nationally motivated foe became increasingly commonplace. This led Zionist leaders to question their ability to maintain the safety of the Zionist project.[136] From here on out, the Yishuv internalized Brenner's insight that it had established its political project on a metaphorical volcano. Ben-Gurion believed that the uprising represented a strategic danger to the entire enterprise. "The awareness that Jews were sitting on a volcano is likely to undermine the foundations of the entire Zionist movement."[137]

The exacerbated threat perception laid the roots of Jewish militant extremism and terrorism. The increasing incidence of spontaneous murders of Arabs by Jews has already been discussed. But the aftermath of the riots also saw the establishment of what would become the first Jewish terror organization. In August 1929, Avraham Stern joined the Haganah and patrolled the streets of Jerusalem alongside Haganah volunteers determined to prevent Arab mobs from attacking Jewish neighborhoods. News of the Hebron massacre shocked Stern, and he became convinced that the only way to avoid such massacres and to ensure Jewish independence in the future was to create a Jewish armed force, capable of fighting both the Arabs and the British. When the commander of the Haganah in Jerusalem, Avraham Tehomi, left the organization to form a splinter group, he was joined by Stern and other volunteers harboring a violent hostility toward the Arabs of Palestine. This group would eventually become the Revisionist-dominated terror group, the IZL (Hebrew initials for the National Military Organization in the Land of Israel).[138] Stern would go on to found the even more extreme terror organization, referred to by the British as the "Stern Gang."[139]

Another result of the heightened sense of threat was that non-Zionist Jews increasingly gravitated toward Zionism. Prior to the events, the Zionist movement was mostly associated with secular Ashkenazi Jews.[140] However, the riots contributed greatly to the integration of Jews of Arab origin into the Zionist movement. A eulogy delivered by a Jewish boy from an Arab-speaking family in Safed provides remarkably poignant insight into this process. The words mourn not only his fallen sister, but also a lost way of life: "Meeting day after day, bowing and greetings, words and conversations. And we did not know you.... you killed those whose mother tongue was yours, whose ways of life were yours, separated from you by religion only."[141] After the events there was a significant rise in Sephardic Jewish participation in both the Haganah and the splinter groups that emerged from it.[142] The growing importance of physical protection, which could only be provided by the Zionist organizations, greatly empowered the Zionist parties and institutions and spurred Sephardic Jews into greater participation. Hillel Cohen writes that 1929 "cemented the place of the Arab Jews on the Zionist side, and in that sense their identity passed the point of no-return."[143] Attacks on orthodox Jews in Jerusalem and in Hebron also brought these groups closer to Zionism.[144]

For the Arab side, the riots were initially a political success. The Shaw Commission report upheld the Mufti's claim that Zionist provocations were behind the violence. It recommended that Jewish settlement and immigration be significantly curtailed. These sentiments were converted into official policy on October 20, 1930, when the Passfield White Paper recommended permanent limitations on Jewish immigration.[145] However, after some effective lobbying on the part of Chaim Weizmann, Prime Minister Ramsay MacDonald read a letter in the House of Commons on February 13, 1931, repudiating the policy.[146] The letter facilitated the great demographic changes that occurred in the 1930s in favor of the Yishuv. Weizmann would later write that "it was under MacDonald's letter to me, that the change came about in the Government's attitude and in the attitude of the Palestine Administration which enabled us to make the magnificent gains of the ensuing years."[147]

The 1930s saw an unprecedented wave of Jewish immigration due to the closing of the gates into the United States and rising anti-Semitism in Europe. This development, coupled with the correspondingly rapid economic growth of the Yishuv, brought the threat of Zionism home to a wider cross-section of Palestinian Arab society than ever before.[148] As a result of the growing threat and the increasing lack of trust in the Mandate authorities, new forms of resistance and political expression emerged.[149] This process was accompanied by general improvements in health, literacy, and infrastructure in Palestine, which expanded the ranks of the Arab middle class.[150]

The failure of 1929 also fostered disappointment in the existing Arab nationalist leadership. The Arab Executive's policy of opposition to Zionism through cooperation with the British authorities had not yielded the desired results.[151] Palestinian society was undergoing an incomplete transformation into a politically mobilized one and, as a result, the notable families lost much of their grip over Palestinian politics by the mid-1930s.[152] Popular movements, such as the Hizb al-Istiqlal (The Palestinian Independence Party) and the Congress of the Youth, filled the vacuum.[153] Although not particularly successful, the Istiqlal Party was the first attempt at the creation of a mass political party in Palestine, possessing broad membership that cut across clan identities and possessed a clear and well-formulated ideology.[154] The ideology it espoused emphasized direct opposition to the British Mandate government, rather than a concentration on Zionists. In fact, in their demonstrations and actions, the Hizb al-Istiqlal party went out of its way to avoid harming Jewish passersby.[155] The party proved to be a model for several political parties that popped up in the mid 1930s and supported the termination of the British Mandate in favor of Arab independence.[156]

The era also saw the rise of organized guerilla warfare and terrorism among Palestinian Arabs. Izz al-Din al-Qassam trained young men in guerilla warfare, and his unit engaged in lethal terrorist attacks against the Jewish population.[157] The followers of al-Qassam were mostly of the peasantry or recent migrants to the cities. Members of his group prayed five times a day and were taught the virtues of jihad and of self-sacrifice.[158] If so, in this period we can see the roots of modern streams of Palestinian political consciousness, both secular and religious, emerge. Both streams penetrated deeper into society than before and resonated with divergent classes. In the meantime, the Yishuv continued its ceaseless consolidation and development of national institutions.[159]

Part II. The Historical Evolution of the Lynching Phenomenon between the 1929 Riots and the Second Intercommunal Conflict

Changes in Palestinian society from the early 1930s onward meant that the role of spontaneous violence in achieving political goals took on an increasingly minor role. The Arab revolt of 1936–1939 started with attacks similar to those that had occurred in 1920–1921 and 1929. Rumors were spread that Jews had attacked Arabs in Tel Aviv, and this led to assaults on Jews in Jaffa, where nine were murdered. Jaffa Arabs were hesitant to get involved in the riots, as Tel Aviv had become a big and powerful city, and the locals were outnumbered and outgunned. In fact, many local Arabs saved Jews from the violence. The mob whipped up in Jaffa was made up mostly of foreign Arab workers from Syria and Egypt, many of whom were unemployed due to the end of the citrus fruit harvest season.[160]

However, unlike in previous rounds, the leadership took control of Arab frustration. The Supreme Arab Committee was formed, under the auspices of the Mufti, lending the crisis political direction.[161] The committee voiced coherent and consensus-based political demands to the colonial government: the cessation of Jewish immigration, curtailment of land sales to Jews, and a proportionally representative government.[162] The violence also took on a more deliberate and planned character in the revolt. Initial mob riots were soon joined by a more carefully planned campaign of arson, sabotage, and an attempt to impede transportation through terrorism and ambushes.[163]

In the period between the Arab Revolt and the creation of the State of Israel, lynching occurred sporadically. The war that became known as the 1948 War began with mob violence. The Palestinian political leadership opposed the U.N. resolution to divide Palestine into an Arab state and a Jewish state. On December 2, 1947. an angry mob attacked Jews near the old city area and began looting Jewish-owned stores.[164] However, generally this conflict developed into a competition between organized armed groups. There were fewer mixed communities than there had been in the past, due to previous altercations. Those that did exist were better defended, on both sides, than they had been in the past due to the increasing institutionalization and militarization of both groups.

Part III. The Main Types of Lynching Attacks Identified in the Second Intercommunal Israeli-Palestinian Conflict

The outcome of the 1948 war between Israel and its Arab neighbors further reduced the intercommunal interaction between Arabs and Jews and therefore all but eliminated the lynching phenomenon for decades. The Zionist-Palestinian conflict was submerged in the wider dispute between Israel and the Arab states. Until the June 1967 Israeli occupation of the West Bank and the Gaza Strip, most of the Palestinian population resided under the control of Arab states—Jordan in the West Bank and Egypt in Gaza. The local Arabs who remained inside the newly established State of Israel were placed under military rule and therefore their freedom of movement was restricted. However, lynching attacks reemerged as the intercommunal rivalry between Jews and Arabs in Palestine was renewed with the First Intifada in the late 1980s.[165]

While in the British Mandate period, attacks occurred in waves of violence, in the post-1948 period, the incidents are seemingly isolated and unrelated. Therefore, rather than analyze lynching attacks chronologically, we examine them thematically. In our analysis of the attacks that occurred in the second period of intercommunal conflict, we distinguish between different types of lynching attacks depending on the context in which they occurred, the identity of the participants, and the main motivation. Through a discussion of the six main types of lynching attacks that we identify in the second stage of the conflict, we will shed light on the different causes and ramifications of such attacks.

Lynching of a Disarmed Terrorist

These are cases where the victim of the lynching had just taken part in a lethal terror attack but had been rendered harmless before being assaulted by bystanders. This is a punishment-driven rather than hate-driven lynching attack since it is targeted against the terrorist and not against innocent civilians from their ethnic community. We do not include under this category cases where the assailants' motivation was partially defensive.

There were two notable instances of this type of lynching attack. On May 12, 1992, a twenty-one-year-old Palestinian, Adnan al-Afandi, attempted to stab two Jewish teenagers near the Mahane Yehudah market in Jerusalem. After failing to kill the two teens, the terrorist ran into a parking lot while a Jewish mob chased him. They eventually caught up and assaulted him. At that point, Bella Freund, an Orthodox Jew and a mother of eight, shielded him from an angry crowd and absorbed the blows. Some of the assailants called her an "Arab lover," and immediately after the incident some of those present shouted at her "an eye for an eye." Freund later explained that as a daughter of Holocaust survivors she felt compelled to act.[166] While some Israeli commentators criticized her deed, Ashkenazi Chief Rabbi Avraham Shapira ruled that Freund acted correctly when she shielded the terrorist since he no longer presented any danger.[167]

On August 4, 2005, a deserter from the Israeli army, Eden Natan Zada, got on a bus to the Arab town of Shefa-'Amr intending to kill civilians as protest against the Israeli plan to withdraw from Gaza. The terrorist, wearing his army uniform and skullcap, shot dead four civilians and injured nearly twenty people, before one of the passengers managed to neutralize him. He was disarmed and handcuffed by police officers on the scene and then kept inside the bus, from which all other passengers were vacated. When word got out, a large angry mob arrived and attempted to climb into the police-held bus. The police tried to push the rioters off the vehicle, but they were attacked along with any civilians seen aiding the police. The struggle continued for an hour and a half until the officers were forced to flee the bus as petrol had been thrown into the bus (although it was not ignited). Subsequently, the Arab mob climbed into the bus and killed the (now helpless) Jewish terrorist. A dozen officers were injured by stones, iron rods, and bottles thrown at them by the angry mob as they were trying to protect the handcuffed terrorist.[168] As in the case of Jewish revenge attacks, many in the Arab community supported the acts.[169]

Spontaneous Attacks on Innocent Civilians Following Terrorist Attacks or the Funerals of Terror Victims

This type of lynching attack takes place when the blood of the witnesses or funeral participants is still boiling from the effects of terrorism. The lynching attack may be perpetrated by relatives of the terror attack's victim or in the vicinity of the attack, but could also be perpetrated by sympathizers. Since it is directed against passersby in the immediate aftermath of a traumatic event, these attacks are primarily revenge-driven. The most notable incident of this sort took place immediately after a suicide bombing in Netanya. On March 4, 2002, a Palestinian suicide bomber killed himself and three Israelis in an explosion in the heart of the coastal city. The police rounded up around twenty Palestinians in suspicion of residing illegally in Israel. The group was attacked by an angry mob chanting "Death to the Arabs!" Salah Basam, an Arab worker, was beaten unconscious by thirty Jews before the police arrived in time "to prevent a lynching."[170]

"Wrong Place at the Wrong Time" Lynchings

These are attacks of opportunity when a member of one ethnic group falls into the hands of the members of the opposite group after entering an area rife with nationalist hostility. This usually occurs when a Jewish civilian enters an Arab area aggravated by ongoing Israeli military operation or influenced by trends of radicalization. Here, the attack does not reflect rage toward the individual victim, but rather a sense of communal anger. Often, the local community attempts to prevent the victim from escaping by erecting road barricades, and so forth. In some cases, the victims manage to escape if they or the police act quickly enough or if some members of the perpetrating ethnic community protect them until the police arrives.

There are several cases of Jews unintentionally entering the Arab neighborhoods of East Jerusalem or the city's suburbs, thus becoming easy prey for Palestinian lynching attacks.[171] It is not uncommon for Jewish victims to accidentally enter the Palestinian neighborhoods since the neighborhoods are intertwined and not clearly divided. Notably, the pelting of stones at passing cars that enter Arab neighborhoods does not constitute a lynching attack unless there is a clear desire and attempt by the assailants to drag victims out of the car in order to beat them to death. On most occasions, the young Palestinian boys who pelt passing cars usually do not intend to lynch those inside but merely to express their anti-Zionist feelings. Hence, a spontaneous attempt to erect a barrier to prevent the Jewish victim's car from escaping is a first indication that a lynching attack is perhaps the goal of the perpetrators.

The potential for lynching attacks in East Jerusalem is increased by the sparse deployment of Israeli police in these neighborhoods. Although the area is technically part of sovereign Israel, the police are reluctant to enter many parts of the city, which means that opportunities for lynching attacks present themselves. Furthermore, radicalization of the younger generation in East Jerusalem has increased since the failure of the Oslo peace process. In the past, notables and leaders of the older generation had attempted to prevent violence and cooperate with the police, but their authority has declined. Police officials have lamented that Arab parents evince either indifference or fear of appearing to be "pro-Jewish," and often do nothing to prevent violence.[172]

However, a certain level of cooperation between Israeli authorities and local notables remains. On June 26, 2011, an Israeli moving company employee mistakenly entered Isawiya, a neighborhood in East Jerusalem. Upon being identified as a Jew, the locals pelted his vehicle with stones and then pulled him from his van and brutally beat him. Fortunately, the Mukhtar (village leader), Darwish Darwish, came with his sons to rescue the victim, took him into his home, and shielded him there. Darwish later smuggled him out of the village and handed him over to Israeli Border Police unit waiting outside Isawiya's perimeter.[173]

Another lynching attempt in the same village took place on November 5, 2010. Four Israelis made a wrong turn into the neighborhood. As they were lost, they asked a twelve-year-old boy for guidance, but he directed them into the center of the village, where an ambush was prepared. When the Israelis realized that they were heading in the wrong direction and turned back, they discovered that the road had been blocked and locals began hurling bricks and pipes at their car, smashing the rear window. Only the group's decision to drive the car into the newly erected barrier at 110 kilometers an hour allowed them to escape.[174]

The lynching attacks that occurred in cities of the Palestinian Authority partially reflect the ongoing incitement of that group, which has become especially pronounced following the halt of the peace process since the Likud came to power in 2009.[175] Moreover, lynching attacks in the cities often coincided with major Israeli military campaigns. Most famously, two Israeli reserve soldiers mistakenly entered Ramallah on October 12, 2000, two weeks after the beginning of the Second Intifada. At that time, Palestinians were reeling from the sheer number of casualties sustained in early clashes with Israeli forces. The soldiers were arrested by the Palestinian police, who disarmed them and took them to a local police station. Rumors spread that undercover Israeli agents were in the building, and a violent mob of more than 1,000 Palestinians gathered at the station, calling for the death of the Israelis. Shortly afterward, the agitated mob stormed the station, beat, stabbed, disemboweled, and gouged out the eyes of the victims. At this point, a Palestinian appeared at the police station window, displaying his blood-stained hands to the crowd, which erupted into cheers. Soon after, the mob dragged the two mutilated bodies to Al-Manara Square in the city center as a sort of victory celebration. Palestinian policemen did not prevent, and in some cases took part in, the lynching.[176]

The attacks intensified Israeli distrust of the Palestinian Authority and its Chairman Yasser Arafat, held responsible for the incitement that had continuously aired on Palestinian national television since the Intifada's outbreak.[177] Furthermore, the brutality of the murders negatively altered the Israeli public's image of Palestinian society. The picture of the Palestinian killer raising his bloodstained hands was broadcast repeatedly and took on a morbidly iconic status in Israel. Jews increasingly depicted the Palestinians as "monsters," "two-legged beasts of prey," subhuman, and so forth. One Israeli press article commented, "We are confronting a crazed, appallingly hate-filled enemy that is mobilizing en masse for a war of liberation against which the Israeli public must unite in a battle of survival."[178] The lynching was a turning point not only because it further reduced the possibility of dialogue and de-escalation but also because it contributed to widespread mistrust toward the peace process.[179]

The Israeli public called for a harsh reaction, but Prime Minister Ehud Barak's reprisals were relatively restrained due to his interest in promptly returning to the negotiation table.[180] Israeli helicopters attacked the Ramallah police station in which the lynching took place alongside other targets. Yet, three hours before these retaliatory strikes took place, the Palestinians were told to evacuate the targeted buildings. These measures did not satisfy the public desire for revenge.[181]

Notably, there are no Israeli neighborhoods inside Israel proper (within its 1967 borders) that may be considered no-go zones for Arabs. Furthermore, there is a limited record of lynching of innocent Palestinian civilians who happen to accidentally enter Israeli settlements. Indeed, many Palestinians work daily in construction in the settlements.[182] It is also likely that Palestinians generally keep away from more extreme settlements where lynching may occur, for example, in Yitzhar. Finally, it is possible that such lynching attacks were attempted in the more extreme right-wing settlements like Yitzhar but were quickly foiled due to the swift action by the law enforcement authorities since it is well known that the SHABAK (Israel's internal counterterror security agency) has informants in the most radical settlements.[183]

Lynching by Palestinians against Jewish Settler Attempts to Perpetrate "Price Tag" Attacks

In recent years, settlers have vandalized Arab targets through a series of nonlethal attacks referred to as "price tag attacks." The "price" is exacted for government acts that the settlers regard as undesirable, such as the evacuation of isolated settlement outposts. Most of the attacks involve forms of vandalism, such as scattering spikes along traffic routes used by Palestinian vehicles, setting fire to fields and orchards, spraying slanderous racist graffiti, and desecrating mosques. This is how the extremists make it clear to the government of Israel and the IDF—the latter being the sovereign in the West Bank—that there is a cost for acting against the settlers.[184]

Occasionally, Palestinians have caught perpetrators and attempted to lynch them. Lynching here serves the combined purposes of deterring against future potential operations and delivering justice. For example, on January 7, 2014, settlers from the illegal settlement of Esh Kodesh in the Jordan Valley entered the vicinity of the Palestinian village Kusra and began cutting down olive trees there in retaliation for the government's uprooting of two olive groves that the settlers had illegally planted. Local Palestinian farmers chased the settlers, who fled to a house under construction. They were cornered there, and some of the locals beat them and threw stones at them. While some of the locals wanted to continue beating them and lynch them to death, village dignitaries intervened and held them off until the Israeli military arrived at the scene and rescued the settlers. Ziad Odeh, deputy mayor of Kusra, stated, "Today we sent a message to the settlers that next time they storm the village we will beat them in defense of our lands and people."[185]

Lynching by Bored, Uneducated Youth

In this type of lynching attack, there is no major action on the part of the victim or his community triggering or provoking the lynching mob. In some cases, a group of young individuals may just be looking for something to do, which is why many of these attacks occur during summer vacation. In most cases, due to their youth—and often, lack of education—they are easy to incite. Therefore, a comment by the victim, a claim by a Jewish girl that she was molested by an Arab, or a call for action on social media can trigger violence. The attacks may also be triggered by minor brawls or arguments. In other cases, the combination of group dynamics and racist views push the perpetrators into mob violence, which can easily deteriorate into a lynching attack. For example, the notably racist fans of the Betar Jerusalem soccer team routinely attack Arab workers in the mall adjacent to the stadium following matches.[186]

Since these attacks are not triggered by a specific action and are not motivated by feelings of revenge, often the perpetrators are not consciously seeking to kill the victim. In most of the recorded cases, the perpetrators were Jewish youth (often from Jerusalem). However, in two cases, the assailants were Arab citizens of Israel attacking Jewish passersby: the lynching on the Tel Baruch beach in Tel Aviv in August 2009 and near Rambam Hospital in Haifa in February 2012.[187]

Two lynching attacks perpetrated by young Jews against innocent Arabs in the Western part of the city are typical. In May 2008, dozens of Jewish teens carried out a brutal attack on two Arab youths in Pisgat Ze'ev, a Jewish neighborhood in East Jerusalem. The boys responded to a message on the ICQ instant messaging program calling to "put an end to Arabs running around the Pisga." They gathered outside the local shopping center armed with knives, sticks, and bats, and once they spotted two Arab teens they attacked them. One of the victims managed to escape, but the other was rendered unconscious.[188] Similarly, in July 2008, two Palestinians narrowly escaped a lynching attempt in Jerusalem after they were assaulted by dozens of ultra-Orthodox Jews. The victims had a financial dispute with an Orthodox store owner, and once the young people from the nearby yeshiva heard the argument they attacked the Arabs. The two Arabs were wounded, while a Jewish resident who protected them with his body was stabbed as he was being insulted by the lynchers for "saving Arabs." The Rabbi who headed the perpetrators' yeshiva would later harshly condemn the attackers.[189]

Most attacks of this sort occurred in Jerusalem. However, since the Jewish neighborhoods of West Jerusalem are the center of economic and governmental activity in the city, the Palestinian residents of Jerusalem often enter these neighborhoods. Given that Palestinians from East Jerusalem frequent the more affluent Jewish-dominated areas on a regular basis, these attacks are rare, and generally speaking, West Jerusalem does not constitute a "no-go" zone for Arabs.

Intercommunal Tensions in the Mixed Cities Spiraling into Riots and Lynching Attacks

Riots in tense mixed communities may be triggered by a variety of factors, such as small provocative acts committed by a member of one of the communities. The lynching attack could occur either in the earliest stages of a riot or at its culmination. For example, in October 2008, an Arab resident outraged a group of Jews by driving to relatives in a predominantly Jewish neighborhood and disturbing the quiet of the Jewish holiday of Yom Kippur. He and his teenage son were initially pelted with stones and then chased after by a Jewish mob. The potential victim was eventually rescued by a Jewish construction site guard who hid him from the mob. The attack triggered riots between Arabs and Jews of the city, lasting for several days. The violence seems to have been driven by the growing resentment of the Jewish population toward Arabs residing in predominantly Jewish areas. Hence, they reflected larger intercommunal racial tensions, rather than rage over a single incident. Indeed, during the riots, Jewish gangs roamed Acre's streets and torched several Arab homes, forcing dozens of Arab families living in Jewish-dominated areas to flee.[190]

Conclusion

A comparison between the first and second stages of the intercommunal conflict allows us to analyze how the causes and consequences of lynching attacks have changed over time. In terms of their causes, we see that the proximate causes or triggers for lynching attacks are not altogether different between the two periods, but the underlying motivations or rationales have changed significantly.

The Proximate Causes and the Main Motivations

The proximate causes or the circumstances conducive for the occurrence of lynching attacks in both periods are the following. First, lynching attacks have been a largely urban phenomenon. Lynching requires a community that constitutes the majority in a specific place and time in order to overpower the victims. Therefore, lynching attacks are likely to occur in mixed towns where there is a large community of potential perpetrators as well as a significant pool of potential victims. Hence, the paucity of lynching attacks previous to the Nebi Musa riots stems from the fact that Arab-Jewish violence in Palestine had centered mostly on the rural area, where coexistence was fragile in comparison to the mixed urban communities. The delay in the development of violence in urban areas is due to the existence of urban Jewish communities predating Zionism, while agricultural settlements were almost all a product of the Zionist movement and therefore politically significant and more disruptive.[191]

Second, rumors served as an important trigger, even though the content of the rumors varies wildly. In the Mandate years the common rumor was that Jews murdered Arabs, whereas in the statehood years, victims were accused of being undercover SHABAK agents. A libel that Jews were threatening Muslim holy places or mosques served as a trigger in both periods. Our argument regarding the importance of police presence proved to be relevant in both periods. The 1929 riots occurred partially because Jews were disarmed by the British in 1928 and were not properly protected by the British police. Similarly, multiple attacks were averted in West Jerusalem, thanks to heavy police presence, and many took place in its eastern neighborhoods due to its absence.

The Jews' high level of faith in the ruling institutions' intention to bring perpetrators to justice and sustain law and order was a major factor in discouraging Jews from lynching Arabs in most periods. This is particularly true in the early years of British rule in Palestine.[192] The sharp rise in Jewish lynching activity following the Al-Aqsa Intifada seems therefore surprising since, during that confrontation, the state proved capable of catching terrorists, bringing them to justice, and militarily avenging the victims' deaths. The explanation is rooted in the rise of racist tendencies in Jewish society. These trends were partly triggered by the African illegal immigration since 2005. The rise of racist forces had been delegitimized by Israeli authorities in the past, as in the case of the outlawing of the racist party led by Meir Kahana. However, in recent years, the Israeli government has turned a blind eye to an increase in racism toward Arabs.[193] This was part of an overall shift to the right in Israeli politics, beginning with the outbreak of the Second Intifada and deepening with Hamas's takeover of the Gaza Strip in 2007. It not only led to the weakening of the Israeli left but also generated political incentives for Prime Minister Netanyahu to avoid condemning jingoistic elements lest others outbid him from the right.

For the Arab residents of Israel, their lack of faith in the Israeli justice system increased their tendency to resort to the lynching of Jewish terrorists. The Palestinians' tendency to resort to lynching attacks was more a function of their assessment of whether they would be punished by the government authorities—the British and later the Palestinian Authority—than by their trust in the authorities' intention to protect them. This attitude is predictable since the Palestinian public was dissatisfied with the status quo, which seemed to be in the Jews' favor, in both periods.

Finally, incitement and other cues from the governing authorities greatly influenced the onset of mob violence. Notably, Arafat and al-Husayni used incitement, albeit for different reasons—Arafat, whose incitement led to the

Ramallah lynchings, did not want to be held responsible for the anti-Israeli violence and therefore sought to benefit from the appearance of having no control over the spontaneous events, whereas al-Husayni lacked political institutions and military resources and therefore had to indirectly mobilize the masses.[194]

For the Palestinians, the basic rationales for employing lynching attacks were partially similar in both periods. During the pre-statehood years, lynching was used as a strategic tool by the Palestinian leadership in order to pressure the British authorities to stop Jewish immigration and in order to intimidate Jews from settling in certain places. In the statehood years, mob violence was used in order to undermine Israeli sovereignty in East Jerusalem and to deter the Israeli army and settlers from entering their towns and villages. In both periods, developments that endangered the Palestinians' ethnic security and territorial goals—Jewish immigration and, later, Israeli settlement activity and occupation—served as important factors.

Nevertheless, religion had a completely different causal importance for generating Palestinian attacks in the two periods. Until 1929, mobilization was often religious due to a lack of separation between church and state in Islamic tradition and the strength of religious sentiment vis-à-vis the weakness of Palestinian Arab nationalist sentiment. In stark contrast, in the Israeli statehood years the political institutionalization of religious movements, such as Hamas and the Islamic movement in Israel, meant that religious actors were acting to promote their agendas either through nonviolent political advocacy or through terrorism. Religion played a minor role in the onset of mob violence among the more nationally cohesive and motivated Jewish population. Jewish religious motives at times provided the spark, as in the Acre riots of 2008, but seldom provided the deeper cause.

For both Jewish and Arab citizens of the state of Israel, lynching reflects both a form of mob justice against terrorists and underlying societal hatred and racism toward the other group. It is a testament to the intercommunal gulf due to the radicalization of the youth on both sides and the deterioration in the authority of notables, such as mayors, teachers, and the older generation—who often have a greater stake in peaceful coexistence. The lynchings that were perpetrated in mixed cities by Jews are most alarming since they reflect a purer desire to exclude Arabs racially rather than an expression of nationalist goals or security fears.

Significantly, the local relationships between the two communities serve as an important mediating variable, which can either mitigate or exacerbate the impact of events at the countrywide level. While in Hebron the 1929 riots led to the most brutal lynching attacks due to the preexisting tensions there, the Jewish community in the mixed city of Tiberias was largely spared from such attacks because the Jewish and Arab notables enjoyed good relations. Similarly, Palestinian suicide attacks during the Al-Aqsa Intifada triggered anti-Arab riots and lynching in Jerusalem and Netanya but not in Haifa, since preexisting Jewish-Arab relations in Haifa were robust.

Diverse Impacts on the Severity of the Conflict

Lynching attacks have had a hand in shaping both the demographic dispersion of the two communities as well as their mutual perceptions. Lynching attacks were more significant in separating the two communities during the British Mandate years. The Jewish presence in places like Hebron or East Jerusalem disappeared almost overnight. Moreover, the 1921 and especially the 1929 riots occupy a prominent place in the Israeli collective memory. Therefore, they have a role in shaping the prospect of cohabitation in the future. For instance, eighty years after the riots, the Israeli senior minister Naftali Bennett rejected the idea of having Jewish settlements remain in a future Palestinian state due to bitter past experience. Bennett argued that "Everyone knows that if an Arab wanders into Herzliya he will leave safely, but that if a Jew gets lost and ends up in Jenin he will be killed."[195]

Interestingly, lynching attacks have had diverging effects on Arab tendencies to enter Jewish-populated areas. Acre's Arab residents did not leave the more affluent Jewish neighborhoods despite the riots. Similarly, Arab residents of East Jerusalem continue to frequent the Western part of the city. The problem is that while the Jewish and Arab residents of the city mingle freely in the parks and shopping malls of West Jerusalem, there is less meaningful interaction between the two populations (except for some workplaces like the Hadassah hospitals), since mutual perceptions have changed for the worse.[196]

Indeed, in both periods lynching attacks have had a detrimental impact on mutual perceptions, both regarding the nature of the other community and regarding the intentions of its leaders. This is hardly surprising since lynching attacks, unlike terror attacks that are planned and performed by a few select individuals, are undertaken by a large group of people, and—since they are performed in broad daylight—often involve the acquiescence of even larger groups. Moreover, the mob often reacts to inflammatory messages sent by the government, and therefore the victim's public can see the direct result of the policy of the rival ethnic community's leadership. Counterterror efforts, which inevitably involve a secret intelligence component, are harder to observe and measure for the public than efforts to prevent lynching attacks. Finally, lynching attacks are perceived as more brutal since they involve not only killing but also humiliation of the victim.

Interestingly, among those personally affected by the lynching attacks of 1929 were Israeli political and military leaders. Generally speaking, this experience fostered dogged militancy toward the Palestinians. For example, Mordechai Maklef, the third Chief of Staff of the IDF, survived the attack on Motza in which his parents were killed in 1929. Rehavam Ze'evi, Commander of the Central Military District and later Minister of Tourism in the Israeli government, was a three-year-old child when his neighborhood in Jerusalem was attacked. He later advocated the complete transfer of all Arabs from Palestine as the solution to the conflict. Yisrael Tal, a child in Safed during the slaughter of the Jewish community there, became commander of the Armored Corps and the developer of the Merkava tank.[197] Finally, the legendary chief of Staff and Minister of Defense Moshe Dayan, who was also the guiding hand behind the initiation of Israeli occupation in the territories, saw the attacks of 1929 as a local version of the pogroms that Jews experienced in Russia.[198] In this manner, Arab lynching attacks played a significant role in cementing militarism and militancy in the Zionist community and the State of Israel.

In sum, the fact that lynching attacks continue to occur in both communities demonstrates not only an absence of peace-oriented education, on both sides, but also highlights the danger of Israel's current policy of maintaining the status quo of settlement construction and occupation. Grassroots hatreds and racism permeate both societies and not only lock them into a cycle of violence but also pose danger to Israel's democratic character. Indeed, while lynching was a strategic tool employed mainly by Palestinians in the past when the community still lacked proper institutions, its employment by Jews inside sovereign Israel, which has its own army, police, and legal system, is deeply reflective of racial views and nationalist ideologies and shows deep disdain for Israel's democratic principles.

Notes

1. Such attacks included both the 1941 Farhud in Iraq, and the post-1948 defeat pogroms in most Arab states, except Algeria. Martin Gilbert, *In Ishmael's House* (Cornwall: Yale University Press, 2010), chapters, 12, 15–17.

2. Joel Beinin, "Mixing, Separation, and Violence in Urban Spaces and the Rural Frontier in Palestine," *Arab Studies Journal* 21, No. 1 (2013): 15–18.

3. Salim Tamari, "Jerusalem's Ottoman Minority: the Times and Lives of Wasif Jawhariyyeh," *Jerusalem Quarterly* 9 (2000): 12.

4. For a good overview of this period, see David Fromkin, *A Peace to End All Peace: The Fall of the Ottoman Empire and the Creation of the Modern Middle East* (New York: Henry Holt, 1989).

5. Ilan Pappe, *The Rise and Fall of a Palestinian Dynasty: The Husaynis, 1700–1948* (Berkeley: University of California Press, 2011), 188.

6. Rashid Khalidi, *Palestinian Identity: The Construction of Modern National Consciousness* (New York: Columbia University Press, 1997), 157.

7. Tom Segev, *One Palestine, Complete: Jews and Arabs under the British Mandate* (New York: Henry Holt, 2000), 87–101; Christopher Sykes, *Crossroads to Israel* (London: Collins, 1965), 37–57.

8. Yehoshua Porath, *The Emergence of the Palestinian-Arab National Movement, 1918–1929, Volume 1* (Ann Arbor: University of Michigan, 1974), 78–100; Pappe, *Rise and Fall of a Palestinian Dynasty*, 176–177, 184.

9. Porath, *Emergence of the Palestinian-Arab National Movement*, 81–82.

10. Khalidi, *Palestinian Identity*, 172.

11. Mohammed Derweesh to Lord Allenby, April 1920, quoted in Isaiah Friedman (ed.), *Riots in Jerusalem—San Remo Conference* (New York: Garland, 1987), 53.

12. Herbert Samuel, "An Interim Report on the Civil Administration of Palestine, During the Period 1st July, 1920–30th June, 1921," August 1921, http://unispal.un.org/UNISPAL.NSF/0/349B02280A930813052565E90048ED1C (accessed August 21, 2014).

13. Yehoshua Porath, *The Palestinian Arab National Movement, 1929–1939: From Riots to Rebellion, Vol. 2* (London: Frank Cass, 1977), 90.

14. Porath, *Emergence of the Palestinian-Arab National Movement*, 34–35.

15. Baruch Kimmerling and Joel Migdal, *The Palestinian People: A History* (Cambridge: Harvard University Press, 2003), 95.

16. Helena Lindholm Schulz, *The Reconstruction of Palestinian Nationalism: Between Revolution and Statehood* (Manchester, U.K.: Manchester University Press, 1999), 26–27.

17. Porath, *Emergence of the Palestinian-Arab National Movement*, 52–53.

18. Segev, *One Palestine, Complete*, 127.

19. Shaul Avigur et al., *The History of the Haganah*, 1:B (Tel Aviv: Ma'arachot, 1960), 609.

20. Segev, *One Palestine, Complete*, 128.

21. "Report of the Court of Inquiry," July 1, 1920, quoted in Friedman, *Riots in Jerusalem*, 134–135.

22. Ibid.

23. Ibid., 136.

24. Ibid.

25. Ibid., 122–124.

26. Avigur, *History of the Haganah*, 1 (B), 611.

27. Ibid., 620–621.

28. Ibid., 124–125.

29. Zionist Executive, "Memoranda circulated by the Zionist Executive to members of Parliament," in Friedman, *Riots in Jerusalem*, 154.

30. "Report of the Court of Inquiry," 117.

31. Ibid., 113.

32. Pappe, *Rise and Fall of a Palestinian Dynasty*, 195–196.

33. Zionist Commission, "Correspondence between the Zionist Commission and General Bols," April 1920, quoted in Friedman, *Riots in Jerusalem*, 146.

34. For an overview of the roots of Zionist defense forces and their heritage as a force for the security of agricultural settlements, see Yaacov Goldstein, *From Fighters to Soldiers: How the Israeli Defense Forces Began* (Brighton: Sussex University Press, 1998), 16–71.

35. Segev, *One Palestine, Complete*, 132–133.
36. Ibid., 135.
37. Anita Shapira, *Land and Power: The Zionist Resort to Force, 1881–1948* (Stanford: Stanford University Press, 1999), 113–114.
38. Segev, *One Palestine, Complete*, 137–138.
39. Shapira, *Land and Power*, 112.
40. Segev, *One Palestine, Complete*, 135.
41. Hillel Cohen, *1929: Year Zero of the Jewish-Arab Conflict* (Jerusalem: Keter, 2013), 83.
42. Shapira, *Land and Power*, 112.
43. Ibid., 115–117; Baruch Kimmerling, *Zionism and Territory: the Socio-Territorial Dimensions of Zionist Politics* (Berkeley: University of California, 1983), 187–188.
44. Kimmerling, *Zionism and Territory*, 188.
45. Ibid., 187–188.
46. Richard Meinertzhagen, "Colonel Richard Meinertzhagen to Lord Curzon," March 31, 1920. In Friedman, *Riots in Jerusalem*, 5.
47. "Report of the Court of Inquiry," 67.
48. Ibid., 70.
49. Ibid., 88–90.
50. Khalidi, *Palestinian Identity*, 150–151.
51. Ibid., 158.
52. Porath, *Emergence of the Palestinian-Arab National Movement*, 100–122.
53. Wendy Pearlman, *Violence, Nonviolence, and the Palestinian National Movement* (Cambridge: Cambridge University Press, 2011), 29–32.
54. Segev, *One Palestine, Complete*, 143.
55. Sahar Huneidi, *A Broken Trust: Herbert Samuel, Zionism and the Palestinians, 1920–1925* (London: I. B. Tauris, 2001), 114–116.
56. Ibid., 127.
57. Commission of Inquiry, *Palestine, Disturbances in May, 1921 and Correspondence Relating Hereto* (London: His Majesty's Stationary Office, 1921), 23–25.
58. Ibid., 6, 12–13.
59. Ibid., 12–13.
60. Ibid., 53.
61. Ibid., 32, 44.
62. Segev, *One Palestine, Complete*, 176–178.
63. Huneidi, *Broken Trust*, 129.
64. Segev, *One Palestine, Complete*, 188.
65. Martin Van Creveld, *The Sword and the Olive: A Critical History of the Israeli Defense Force* (New York: Public Affairs, 1998), 23.
66. Commission of Inquiry, *Palestine, Disturbances*, 44.
67. Ibid., 50.
68. Segev, *One Palestine, Complete*, 175.
69. Anita Shapira, *Brenner: a Life* (Tel Aviv: Am Oved, 2008), 246–247, 335–337.
70. Segev, *One Palestine, Complete*, 182.
71. Porath, *Emergence of the Palestinian-Arab National Movement*, 131.
72. Pearlman, *Violence, Nonviolence*, 33.

73. Porath, *Emergence of the Palestinian-Arab National Movement*, 131.
74. Commission of Inquiry, *Palestine, Disturbances*, 45.
75. Ibid., 26–27.
76. Ibid., 49.
77. Ibid., 49.
78. Ibid., 47.
79. Yehuda Slutsky, *The History of the Haganah*, 2 (A) (Tel-Aviv: Ma'arachot, 1964), 87–88. Commission of Inquiry, *Palestine, Disturbances*, 10–11.
80. Slutsky, *History of the Haganah*, 2 (A), 95–96.
81. Ibid., 137–138; Van Creveld, *Sword and the Olive*, 23.
82. Commission of Inquiry, *Palestine, Disturbances*, 60.
83. Ibid., 29.
84. Segev, *One Palestine, Complete*, 184.
85. Porath, *Emergence of the Palestinian-Arab National Movement*, 305.
86. Ibid., 133–134.
87. Slutsky, *History of the Haganah*, 2 (A), 313.
88. Pappe, *Rise and Fall of a Palestinian Dynasty*, 201.
89. Zvi Elpeleg, *The Grand Mufti: Haj Amin al-Hussaini, Founder of the Palestinian National Movement* (London: Cass, 1993), 6–7.
90. Porath, *Emergence of the Palestinian-Arab National Movement*, 76.
91. Elpeleg, *Grand Mufti*, 7–10.
92. Ibid., 12.
93. Rashid Khalidi, *The Iron Cage: the Story of the Palestinian Struggle for Statehood* (Boston: Beacon Press, 2006), 54–59.
94. Kimmerling, *Palestinian People*, 96.
95. Khalidi, *Iron Cage*, 62–63.
96. Pearlman, *Violence, Nonviolence*, 38.
97. Slutsky, *History of the Haganah*, 2 (A), 180–182.
98. Pearlman, *Violence, Nonviolence*, 33–34.
99. Ibid., 32.
100. Avraham Sela, "The 'Wailing Wall' Riots (1929) as a Watershed in the Palestine Conflict," *The Muslim World* 84 (1994): 69.
101. Segev, *One Palestine, Complete*, 295–298.
102. Elpeleg, *Grand Mufti*, 18.
103. Segev, *One Palestine, Complete*, 304.
104. Ibid.
105. Porath, *Emergence of the Palestinian-Arab National Movement*, 266.
106. See Pappe, *Rise and Fall of a Palestinian Dynasty*, 243–245, for the case that restraint was attempted. Christopher Sykes says there is strong evidence that the Mufti organized and incited the riots. See Sykes, *Crossroads to Israel*, 142–144. For an overview of the controversy, see Cohen, *1929*, 152–159.
107. Slutsky, *History of the Haganah*, 2 (A), 313.
108. Ibid., 207–213.
109. Sykes, *Crossroads to Israel*, 128.
110. Porath, *Emergence of the Palestinian Arab National Movement*, 267.

111. Ibid., 268–269.
112. Pappe, *Rise and Fall of a Palestinian Dynasty*, 238.
113. Elpeleg, *Grand Mufti*, 21; Cohen, *1929*, 125–126.
114. Slutsky, *History of the Haganah*, 2 (A), 309, 321, 326, 328, 332.
115. Elpeleg, *Grand Mufti*, 21–22; Segev, *One Palestine, Complete*, 310.
116. Cohen, *1929*, 173–174.
117. Ibid., 192–196.
118. Segev, *One Palestine, Complete*, 310.
119. Ibid., 329.
120. Slutsky, *History of the Haganah*, 2 (A), 313.
121. Pappe, *Rise and Fall of a Palestinian Dynasty*, 244.
122. Cohen, *1929*, 163.
123. Slutsky, *History of the Haganah*, 2 (A), 333–334.
124. Segev, *One Palestine, Complete*, 324.
125. Ibid., 325–326.
126. Ibid., 318.
127. Cohen, *1929*, 215–216.
128. Beinin, "Mixing, Separation, and Violence," 25.
129. Ibid., 276–279.
130. Ibid., 286.
131. Ibid., 62–63, 70.
132. Ibid., 70–71.
133. Ibid., 181.
134. Ibid., 82; Dan Rabinowitz and Daniel Monterescu, "Reconfiguring the Mixed Town: Urban Transformations of Ethnonational Relations in Palestine and Israel," *International Journal of Middle East Studies* 40 (2008): 207.
135. Sela, "'Wailing Wall' Riots," 85.
136. Shapira, *Land and Power*, 174.
137. Ibid., 175.
138. Ibid., 580.
139. Eran Kaplan, *Jewish Radical Right: Revisionist Zionism and Its Ideological Legacy* (Madison: University of Wisconsin Press, 2005), 164.
140. For a critical analysis of the Ashkenazi-dominated nature of Zionism, see Ella Shohat, "Sephardim in Israel: Zionism from the Standpoint of its Jewish Victims," in Anne McClintock et al., *Dangerous Liaisons: Gender, Nation and Postcolonial Perspectives* (Minneapolis: University of Minnesota Press, 1997), 39–68.
141. Cohen, *1929*, 298–299.
142. Ibid., 99–100.
143. Ibid., 100.
144. Ibid., 184–188.
145. Segev, *One Palestine, Complete*, 335.
146. Sykes, *Crossroads to Israel*, 148.
147. Ibid., 148.
148. Porath, *Palestinian Arab National Movement*, 44–45.
149. Pappe, *Rise and Fall of a Palestinian Dynasty*, 265–267.

150. Pearlman, *Violence, Nonviolence*, 39–40.
151. Porath, *Palestinian Arab National Movement*, 34–35.
152. Kimmerling and Migdal, *Palestinian People*, 97.
153. Elpeleg, *Grand Mufti*, 33–34.
154. Khalidi, *Iron Cage*, 83–84.
155. Slutsky, *History of the Haganah*, 2 (A), 458–459.
156. Pappe, *Rise and Fall of a Palestinian Dynasty*, 267–268.
157. Ibid., 265.
158. Porath, *Palestinian Arab National Movement*, 133–137.
159. For a concise overview of the idea of the Yishuv as a state in the making, see Baruch Kimmerling, "State Building, State Autonomy and the Identity of Society: The Case of the Israeli State," *Journal of Historical Sociology* 6 (1993): 402–404.
160. Slutsky, *History of the Haganah*, 2 (A), 633–634.
161. Van Creveld, *Sword and the Olive*, 37.
162. Slutsky, *History of the Haganah*, 2 (B), 638.
163. Ibid., 643–646.
164. Yehuda Slutsky, *History of the Haganah*, 3 (B) (Tel Aviv: Zionist Library, 1972), 1372.
165. For an analysis of the difference between the intercommunal Zionist-Palestinian conflict and the interstate Arab-Israeli conflict and its importance, see Oren Barak, "The Failure of the Israeli-Palestinian Peace Process, 1993–2000," *Journal of Peace Research* 42 (2005): 719–736.
166. Abraham Rabinovich, "Israeli Woman Protects Arab from Lynching," *Sun-Sentinel*, May 16, 1992.
167. Washington Report on Middle East Affairs, July 1992, http://www.wrmea.org/archives/141-washington-report-archives-1988-1993/july-1992/10042-issues-in-the-news.html (accessed August 23, 2014).
168. Ahiye Raved, "We Tried to Prevent Lynch," *Ynetnews*, August 5, 2005, http://www.ynetnews.com/articles/0,7340,L-3122870,00.html (accessed August 21, 2014).
169. Editorial, "A Lynching Is a Lynching," *Haaretz*, August 9, 2005.
170. David Pratt, *Intifada: The Long Day of Rage* (Philadelphia: Casemate, 2006), 108–109.
171. The Arab neighborhoods that are part of metropolitan Jerusalem—to the east, north, and south—were absorbed into the capital's boundaries after the 1967 war, and its Arab residents were offered citizenship. Yet, while the Arab residents work for Jews and receive health and social benefits from Israel, they maintain a strong Palestinian identity. Culturally and politically, they are inseparable from the Palestinian cities surrounding them. Indeed, most of them chose not to be Israeli citizens but to only carry Jerusalem residency cards.
172. Ryan Jones, "Israeli Man Nearly lynched in Jerusalem," *Israel Today*, June 27, 2011.
173. Yair Altman, "Israeli Man Narrowly Escapes Lynch in Issawiya," *Ynetnews*, June 27, 2011, http://www.ynetnews.com/articles/0,7340,L-4087521,00.html (accessed August 19, 2014).
174. Yair Altman, "Israelis Attacked on Way to Jerusalem Pub," *Ynetnews*, November 5, 2010, http://www.ynetnews.com/articles/0,7340,L-3980165,00.html (accessed August 23, 2014).

175. Yosef Kuperwasser and Asher Fredman, "The Incitement and Culture of Peace Index: Methodology and Trends," in Alan Baker (ed.), *The Changing Forms of Incitement to Terror and Violence* (Jerusalem: Jerusalem Center for Public Affairs and the Konrad-Adenauer-Stiftung, 2012), 55–60.

176. Shai Feldman, "The October Violence: An Interim Assessment," *Strategic Assessment*, November 2000, http://d26e8pvoto2x3r.cloudfront.net/uploadImages/systemFiles/The%20 October%20Violence%20An%20Interim%20Assessment.pdf (accessed August 5, 2014).

177. Ibid.

178. Ron Mieberg, "We Won't Forget, We Won't Forgive," *Maariv*, October 13, 2000.

179. Uri Ben-Eliezer, *Old Conflict, New War: Israel's Politics toward the Palestinians* (New York: Palgrave Macmillan, 2012), 86–87.

180. Gilead Sher, *Israeli-Palestinian Peace Negotiations, 1999–2001: Within Reach* (Abdington: Routledge, 2006), 166.

181. Yoav Limor et al., "The Missiles on Gaza and Ramallah Are Just a Signal," *Maariv*, October, 13, 2000.

182. The belief in the Jews' entitlement to Eretz Israel does not preclude the continued presence of Arab residents as long as they do not have political aspirations.

183. A Major in the IDF who had served in the West Bank, but preferred to remain unnamed, claimed so in an interview with the author, August 5, 2014. It is a strategic interest of the Israeli authorities to prevent any lynching attack by settlers since this could play into the hands of the Palestinian Authority; this would then call the international community to send U.N. peacekeepers to defend the local Palestinians from the settlers, thus depriving the IDF of their authority and control over the occupied territories. Hence, it is not inconceivable that, if such attempts did occur and were foiled, there was a gag order to prevent the story from getting publicized.

184. For an analysis of the "price tag" attacks, see Daniel Byman and Natan Sachs, "The Rise of Settler Terrorism: The West Bank's Other Violent Extremists," *Foreign Affairs*, August 14, 2012.

185. Tovah Lazaroff and Khaled Abu Toameh, "Elder Palestinians Protect Settlers from Lynching in West Bank Village," *Jerusalem Post*, January 7, 2014.

186. Oz Rosenberg, "Hundreds of Beitar Jerusalem Fans Beat Up Arab Workers in Mall; No Arrests," *Haaretz*, March 23, 2012.

187. Seth Frantzman, "Terra Incognita: Is Israel's Justice System Broken?" *Jerusalem Post*, May 3, 2011. Maor Buchnik, "Soldiers Nearly Lynched by Arabs in Haifa," *Ynetnews*, February 25, 2012.

188. Ofer Neuman, "Be Careful: Racist Violence Percolates," *Ynet*, July 7, 2008.

189. Roi Mandel, "2 Arabs Narrowly Escape Lynching in Jerusalem," *Ynetnews*, July 22, 2008.

190. Jonathan Cook, "Death to Arabs! The Acre Riots," *Counterpunch*, October 16, 2008, http://www.counterpunch.org/2008/10/16/the-acre-riots/ (accessed August 20, 2014).

191. Beinin, "Mixing, Separation, and Violence," 15. For an analysis of the disruptive nature of Zionist agricultural settlement, see Gershon Shafir, *Land, Labor and the Origins of the Israeli-Palestinian Conflict* (Cambridge: Cambridge University Press, 1989).

192. Shapira, *Land and Power*, 132–133.

193. Jodi Rudoren and Isabel Kershner, "Israeli Schools Confront Hate after Youths' Attacks," *New York Times*, August 28, 2012; Ami Pedahzur, *The Israeli Response to Jewish*

Extremism and Violence: Defending Democracy (Manchester: Manchester University Press, 2002), 82–83.

194. Pearlman, *Violence, Nonviolence*, 32; Kuperwasser and Fredman, "Incitement and Culture of Peace," 55–60.

195. Herb Keinon, "Bennett: Jews Living under PA Rule Would Be Killed," *Jerusalem Post*, January 28, 2014.

196. Isabel Kershner, "Young Israelis Held in Attack on Arabs," *New York Times*, August 20, 2012.

197. Cohen, *1929*, 312–314.

198. Moshe Dayan, *Avnei Derech* (Tel-Aviv: Dvir, 1976), 39.

Contributors

LAURENS BAKKER is assistant professor of anthropology at the University of Amsterdam in the Netherlands. Bakker specializes in sociolegal research, notably in Southeast Asia. He works on militias in Jakarta, Kalimantan, and North Sulawesi as part of the "State of Anxiety" Project, a comparative ethnography of militias in four Indonesian areas.

SHAIEL BEN-EPHRAIM is currently a PhD candidate at the Centre for Military and Strategic Studies at the University of Calgary and is a recipient of the Israel Studies Fellowship from the Kahanoff Israel Studies Program at the University of Calgary. His dissertation deals with the role of settlements in the occupied territories on bilateral U.S.-Israeli relations. His work has been published in the *Journal of Settler Colonial Studies*, the *International Policy Digest*, and the *Jerusalem Post*. He previously worked as a journalist, policy analyst, and political advisor.

NANDANA DUTTA is professor of English at Gauhati University in India. Her areas of teaching and research include American Studies, Postcolonial Literature and Theory, Women's Studies, and Narratology. Her other research interests include issues of identity, violence, and memory (especially in India), disciplines, and representations. Among her publications are the book *Questions of Identity: Location, Migration, Hybridity* (Sage, 2012) and essays on "Massacres and Media Representations: Viewing North-East Violence," "Narrative Agency and Thinking about Conflicts," and "The Face of the Other: Terror and the Return of Binarism."

WEITING GUO, an instructor at Simon Fraser University, is finishing his doctoral dissertation in Asian Studies at the University of British Columbia on the history of summary execution in modern China. His research focuses on late imperial and modern Chinese history, Taiwanese history, law and society, violence, and local politics. His recent publications include "Living with Disputes: Zhang Gang Diary (1888—1942) and the Life of a Community Mediator in Late Qing and Republican China," *Journal of the Canadian Historical Association* (2013); and "Social Practice and Judicial Politics in 'Grave Destruction' Cases in Qing Taiwan, 1683—1895," in *Chinese Law: Knowledge, Practice, and Transformation, 1530s to 1950s*, eds. Li Chen and Madeleine Zelin (Brill, 2015).

OR HONIG is assistant professor of political science at Tel Aviv University. He earned his PhD at UCLA, focusing his dissertation on the dynamics of violence in intrastate conflicts. His research focuses mainly in two areas: strategic studies with a particular focus on the issues of coercion and intelligence studies and problems of threat perception; and the dynamics of violence in intrastate ethnic conflict with a particular emphasis on the strategies of the occupying or controlling governments to address different strategic challenges emanating from within the ethnic community. Empirically, he focuses on the Middle East and especially on the interactions between the State of Israel and its regional rivals and on U.S. foreign policy in the region. He has published articles in journals such as *Security Studies*, *International Relations*, *Studies in Conflict and Terrorism*, and the *Journal of Strategic Studies*.

FRANK JACOB is assistant professor of world history at the City University of New York (QCC). He received his MA in Modern History, Ancient History, and Japanese Studies from Würzburg University (2010) and his PhD in Japanese Studies from Erlangen University (2012). His research involves Modern Japanese History, Modern German History, and Global History. He is the editor of the interdisciplinary journal *Global Humanities* (Neofelis Press), and one of his recent books is *Japanism, Pan-Asianism, Terrorism* (Academica Press, 2014).

MICHAEL J. PFEIFER is professor of history at John Jay College of Criminal Justice and the Graduate Center, City University of New York. His books include *Rough Justice: Lynching and American Society, 1874—1947* (University of Illinois Press, 2004), *The Roots of Rough Justice: Origins of American Lynching* (University of Illinois Press, 2011) and, as editor, *Lynching Beyond Dixie: American Mob Violence Outside the South* (University of Illinois Press, 2013). He has published numerous articles in journals, including the *Journal of American History*, *Louisiana History*, and *American Nineteenth Century History*.

YOGESH RAJ is Chautari Fellow of Public Life and Public Knowledge, Martin Chautari, Nepal. He has published several books on Nepalese history and articles in, among other journals, *Studies in Nepali History and Society*, *Journal of Nepalese Studies*, and *Contributions to Nepalese Studies*. He holds a PhD from Imperial College, London.

NICHOLAS RUSH SMITH is an assistant professor of political science at the City University of New York—City College. His main research interests are on the politics of crime, policing, and vigilantism in democratic states, with a particular focus on postapartheid South Africa. He is currently working on a book project, tentatively titled "Resisting Rights: Vigilantism and the Contradictions of Democratic State Formation in Post-Apartheid South Africa." He has received grant and fellowship support from, among other organizations, the Social Science Research Council and Fulbright-Hays. He holds a PhD from the University of Chicago.

Index

Ahmadis (Ahmadiyyah): violence against in Indonesia, 17–21, 24, 29
al-Husayni, Haj Amin: and the Nebi Musa Riots, 195–198
Arendt, Hannah, 88

Bates, Miner Searle, 85
Berg, Manfred, 137–138
British colonial rule: and perceptions of legal order in India, 128, 140–145
British Mandate period in Palestine, 7, 186–204, 211, 213
Bryjak, George, 137–138

Cebongan Prison, Indonesia: vigilantism in, 21–25
Chang, Iris, 78, 80, 82–83
Chinese Cultural Revolution, 5, 36
Colombjin, Freek, 14–15
Comaroff, Jean and John, 177n1

Darul Islam (Islamic State) movement, 132

East Timor: annexation of, 12
Evans-Pritchard, E. E., 177n1

First Intifada (Palestinian Uprising), 7

Gandhi, Mahatma: and nonviolence, 136; and swaraj (self rule), 6, 128, 145–146

Haar, Barend ter, 37

Higashinakano, Shudo, 81–82
Huang, Philip, 42

Indonesian independence, 12
Internet: and violence in Indonesia, 25–28

Jaffa Riots, 192–195

Katsuichi, Honda, 81
Katz, Paul, 71n24
Kolsky, Elizabeth, 141
Kuhn, Philip, 37

Lary, Diana, 37
Lewis, Mark, 37
lynching: in China, 5–6, 34–68; definition, 1, 10, 128; and global cultures, 1–2, 4, 7–8; in India, 6, 127–151; in Indonesia, 4–5, 10–33; in Latin America, 158–159; and media representation in India, 129–136, 147–149; in Nepal, 6, 103–118; in Palestine/Israel, 7, 185–215; in South Africa, 6–7, 156–157; and the state, 1, 4, 7–8, 10, 28–29; in the United States, 2–4

Mandela, Winnie: response to necklacing, 170
McCallum, Reverend James: and the Rape of Nanking, 86–87
Memorial Hall of the Victims in Nanking, 79

men of force: in Late-Qing China, 34–68, 72–73, 75

Nebi Musa Riots, 186–192, 195, 211
necklacing: in South Africa, 6–7, 156–177
Newari medieval historiography, 107–118
1929 Palestinian Riots, 195–203
Ningbo Riot of 1911, 62–68

Pfeifer, Michael J., 91, 136–137
PRRI/Permesta Rebellion, 12

Rabe, John: and the Rape of Nanking, 87
Rape of Nanking, 5–6, 78–102
roaming braves: in Late-Qing China, 34–68, 72–73, 75
Robinson, David, 70n22
Rowe, William, 37

Second Intifada (Palestinian Uprising), 207–208, 214
Senechal de la Roche, Roberta, 8n2, 137
Skhosana, Maki, 7, 161, 166–169, 171–173, 182n73, 182n78
Soweto Uprising, 162
Suharto: abdication, 13; and New Order government, 11–12
summary execution: in China, 5, 34–70

Tagore, Rabindranath: on swaraj (self rule), 146
Taiping Civil War, 5, 35, 37, 40–41, 45, 50, 57–58
Tambo, Oliver: response to necklacing, 170
Tanaka, Masaaki, 81
Tilly, Charles, 104–107
Timperley, Harold J., 82
Tsao, Ruby, 79–80
Tutu, Desmond: response to necklacing, 169–170

Vautrin, Minnie: and the Rape of Nanking, 86–87
violence and war: theory of, 88–91

Wakabayashi, Bob Tadashi, 95–96n29
Wang, David Der-wei, 37
Weber, Max, 1, 8n2, 10
Welsh, Bridget, 15
Wendt, Simon, 137–138
Wilson, Dr. Robert O.: and the Rape of Nanking, 87
Wood, Amy Louise, 139, 149–150

Xianfeng, Emperor, 5, 34–35, 40